# CURRENTS OF THOUGHT
# IN AFRICAN SOCIOLOGY AND THE
# GLOBAL COMMUNITY

# CURRENTS OF THOUGHT IN AFRICAN SOCIOLOGY AND THE GLOBAL COMMUNITY

## How to Understand Research Findings in the Context of Sociological Perspectives

Joshua Adekunle Awosan

University of Massachusetts Dartmouth

Universal Publishers
Boca Raton, Florida

*Currents of Thought in African Sociology and the Global Community:*
*How to Understand Research Findings in the Context of Sociological Perspectives*

Universal Publishers
Boca Raton, Florida • USA
2009

ISBN-10: 1-59942-999-3 (*paperback*)
ISBN-13: 978-1-59942-999-1 (*paperback*)

ISBN-10: 1-59942-939-X (*ebook*)
ISBN-13: 978-1-59942-939-7 (*ebook*)

www.universal-publishers.com

Library of Congress Cataloging-in-Publication Data

Awosan, Joshua.
  Currents of thought in African sociology and the global community : how to
understand research findings in the context of sociological perspectives / Joshua
Adekunle Awosan.
    p. cm.
  Includes bibliographical references and index.
  ISBN-13: 978-1-59942-999-1 (pbk. : alk. paper)
  ISBN-10: 1-59942-999-3 (pbk. : alk. paper)
  1. Sociology--Research--Nigeria. 2. Sociology--Research--Africa. I. Title.
  HM578.N6A96 2008
  301.096--dc22

                            2008048472

*Dedicated to my mother,*
Madam Victoria Foyeke Awosan

"…as home of research, universities [and other institutions of higher learning] explore…As communities of scholars, they are committed to probe through the appearances of things, whether in the human or in the natural order, and to discover the laws and the realities which explain them."

-L. Fulton


"That Amilcar Cabral came up with…theory in spite of being an agronomist tends to underscore the encyclopedic nature of sociology."

-The author


"The fascination of sociology lies in the fact that its perspective makes us see in a new light the very world which we have lived all our lives."

-Peter L. Berger

# CONTENTS

CONTENTS

# PREFACE

One of the purposes of this book is to provide, in one compact and convenient form, information on sociological research studies undertaken by the undergraduates and postgraduates of Ahmadu Bello University (ABU), Zaria, Nigeria, as well as by scholars whose works are widely acknowledged.

Another purpose is to focus on the transition of sociology at ABU. The transition itself basically tends to blossom within the context of theoretical and methodological orientations, culminating in the development of an indigenous African sociology. Thus, this piece of work serves as a typical example of sociological enterprise in Africa. If these purposes have been achieved, then a landmark would have been made not only in what has globally come to be a burgeoning and vital discipline, but also in local research endeavors, which are intertwined with sociological perspectives and which appear to be rather complex and equally burgeoning.

Yet another purpose is to focus on the various subdisciplines of sociology, with each chapter serving as a unique, introductory tool as to what the subdiscipline it contains is really all about.

Since the inception of the Department of Sociology at ABU in 1967, theses and dissertations produced have grown from a mere trickle of three titles in 1970 to a floodtide of titles. The large number of the theses and dissertations directly reflects the large number of courses constantly offered in the department. Indeed, what has continued to be a veritable and pleasantly surprising source of attraction to many a visitor (including external examiners from Africa and outside of Africa) to this department is the rich and diverse spectrum of courses embracing a corresponding, diverse spectrum of the subdisciplines of sociology. When I was commissioned at one of the departmental meetings to classify the theses and dissertations in the department's "archives" by subject-matter, it did not in the least occur to me that, that special assignment would subsequently expand beyond the frontier of classification to that of research findings, further enriched by currents of thought within the emergent, wider context of an indigenous African Sociology. The original classification of the theses and dissertations constitutes a handbook.

Having embarked on the classification by subject-matter with an avid and penetrating eye, I almost unconsciously became familiar with most of the contents of the theses and dissertations. It then occurred to us that I should commit some of these to writing, in order that I might not keep them exclusively to myself. Hence, the expansion of the exercise to the frontier of research findings. No sooner had I embarked on the expansion than I realized that it was not as easy as I had earlier envisaged. Happily, the expansion and indeed the entire exercise, which, more often than not, left me groaning under the weight of what appeared an infinite bibliography, were eventually accomplished.

This book is devoted by subject-matter to the findings of a good number of the various empirical studies undertaken. Thus, the reader will be given an insight into the results emanating from these vital studies. Where the methodology used in any of the studies appears, to some extent, to be a rarity or is reflective of the peculiarity of a given subdiscipline, attempt is made to spell out this in as succinct a manner as possible. Moreover, currents of thought among highly-reputed scholars, whose works are not among the empirical sociological studies at ABU, but are duly acknowledged, are, where appropriate, articulated and discussed. This book takes cognizance of research objectives, the historical context, if any, of what is being studied and, in addition to research findings, the accompanying suggestions or recommendations, where appropriate.

In this book, the theoretical and methodological orientations which are intimately connected with the accompanying research findings are figured out. Thus, the real kernel of meaning surfaces. And theories which otherwise would have been extremely difficult to understand are readily simplified. The theoretical coverage straddles a wide variety of paradigms—from structural-functional theory and conflict theory to symbolic interactionism, ethnomethodology, dramaturgy, phenomenology, exchange theory, etc.

Research is very important not only to the reader, but also to the socio-economic development of the society itself. This clearly explains why research is one leg of the tripod on which a university or an academy stands. The remaining two legs are teaching and dialogue. Interestingly, research readily provides the requisite springboard for maximal and effective participation in the remaining two legs. And research, teaching, and dialogue constitute a solid foundation for gown and town to meet. In other words, this paves the way for the academic citadel to get involved with the community. This book constitutes an experiential celebration of gown-town paradigm, understandably devoid of ivory-towerism. The landmark stance of gown-town paradigm consists in what I call **deivory-towerism.**

This book has enormous potential to serve as a guide to study and, more important, to further research. Readers can also have their understanding regarding any of the topics or subject-matters enhanced. This is all the more so as each chapter, as indicated above, contains a subdiscipline of sociology and starts off with an introductory explanation of what that subdiscipline is really all about. Besides, the research findings and analyses within a given subdiscipline or in two subdisciplines are synthesized and correlated, particularly where they are of outstanding national, global, or academic significance. Fundamental to this is the fact that the topics involved are of an interdisciplinary nature. This should not be a surprise package: sociology, by its encyclopedic nature, is an extremely wide discipline, straddling as many human endeavors as there are. Herein lies a wealth of resources not only for students of sociology, but also for students of such other disciplines as political science, economics, history, mass communications, international relations, public administration, education, psychology, etc. The advantage in this connection is not only for research endeavors, but generally for the acquisition of knowledge by interested people anywhere in the world.

Within the discipline of sociology, this book can be used in such courses as introduction to sociology, research methods, social theory, anthropology, Third World societies, rural sociology, sociology of development, global human issues, social stratification, social problems, deviant behavior, African and African American studies, medical sociology/anthropology, women's studies, and criminal justice.

Provided at the end of this book is a glossary of words, which has potential to add luster to the book as well as to the understanding of the reader.

J.A.A.

# ACKNOWLEDGMENTS

Before all else, I give profound honor and effervescent adoration to the Almighty God for seeing me through this book project that at times made me feel I was totally lost in the forest of research, intertwined insightfully with theories. Glory be to Him for sustaining me so solidly that I was, all along, blessed with an abundance of wisdom, knowledge, insight, and, most of all, good health.

I would like to express gratitude to 'Femi Odekunle, Paul Omaji, Steven Nkom, Karim Aliyu, Joseph Hellandendu, and other intellectuals in Nigeria and the United States for their encouragement.

My wholehearted gratitude is accorded Robert J. Durel of Christopher Newport University, Newport News, Virginia, for his encouragement when he was a Fulbright Scholar at Ahmadu Bello University, Zaria, Nigeria, in 1989-90 academic year and for his extremely helpful suggestions in the U.S., having thoroughly read through the whole manuscript. I am deeply indebted to Michael E. Brown and Maurain Kelleher of Northeastern University, Boston, as well as Felix Pandella of Yale University for their unstinted efforts in reading through the manuscript and for encouraging me to make sure that this book is prompted to see the light of the day. I am also indebted to Carol Owen, Judith Parolle, Ron Bailey, and LeRoy Johnson of Northeastern University, Kwasi Sarkodie-Mensah of Boston College, and my friend, Mwangi Ireri, for their kind support. My gratitude goes to Larry Miller, Thom Ranuga, Colleen Avedikian, Penn Reave, John Fobanjong, and Chidi Nwaubani of the University of Massachusetts Dartmouth for their kind support which indirectly relieved me of tension that might have prevented me from working on this book so successfully.

The untiring efforts of T.A. Ameh, Mary Onyemah, Agnes Ude, John Oduh, Babatope Ojo, Bola Toye, Helen Nwachukwu (all of Ahmadu Bello University, Zaria, Nigeria) in putting the manuscript into an admirable, typed shape are most gratefully acknowledged. Abel Agada and I. Babati deserve my sincere gratitude for making it possible for me to have an easy access to our "archives." Also, Betsy Monday deserves my sincere gratitude for contributing in the U.S. to making the manuscript assume an admirable, typed shape.

I would like to thank Kehinde Oluhaiyero and Samson Adeyemi for assisting with preliminary proof-reading as well as with the initial compilation of the glossary of words and references. Similar gratitude goes to Bob Williams for drawing the figure, to Stella Ojeme for diligently working on the manuscript at the initial stage, to Lester Naing for scanning the images, to my brother, Olawuyi Orimogunje, and to my son, Sola (Samuel), for assisting in the process of preliminary name-indexing. My daughters, Rachel (Lawumi), Eunice (Yemisi), Christiana (Lola), and my son, Samson (Akin), deserve my heartfelt thanks for supportively bearing with me during the long period that this book was being worked upon. And I hereby accord them the thanks from the bottom of my heart. My sincere gratitude goes to my daughter, Felicia (Sade), for taking the trouble to scan the manuscript and, together with my son, Simeon (Sayo), for readily finding solutions to complicated, computer-related problems.

I am much beholden to Rebekah Galy, the acquisition editor of Universal Publishers, and her successor, Jeff Young, for the unparalleled promptness with which they worked. Jeff Young's unparalleled dedication to working meticulously on this book is most gratefully acknowledged. Many thanks to Christie Mayer for working so closely with me that she did whatever it took to make this book a masterpiece. An expert of no mean measure in publishing, she left no stone unturned. I am thankful to those in the production department for their indefatigable efforts in making this book a reality. My gratitude goes to Shereen Siddiqui together with her highly-talented crew for coming up with such a fitting, beautiful cover.

It now remains for me to express profound gratitude to my dear wife, Dorcas (Morolake), for typing part of, and proof-reading the whole, manuscript at a time she was singlehandedly taking care of other family matters. Her unflinching support is thankfully noted.

While a good number of people have contributed to the publication of this book, I alone am responsible for the views expressed by me.

# ·I·

# AN OVERVIEW OF THE DOMINANT THEORETICAL AND METHODOLOGICAL PERSPECTIVES

S ociology is not confined exclusively to one perspective, since it is not by its nature imbued with a monolithic and uniform orientation or approach. Hence, to be able to present a genuinely less ambiguous picture, one needs to demonstrably focus on *sociological perspectives* and not on a single perspective. If anything, a monolithic and uniform outlook could not only lead to ambiguity, but also to distorted and misleading facts.

The various perspectives in sociology are simply different ways of trying to understand the social world (Cuff *et al.*, 1979). Sociologists, themselves, differ in their individual preferences for these perspectives in terms of their academic orientations and ideological leanings. Clearly, this explains why—aside from its being an encyclopedic discipline—sociology is itself not a unified discipline. This very nature of sociology opens the floodgate to a wide variety of theoretical and methodological orientations. Thus, sociological perspectives are not aimed at coming up with the final truth about the social world. They are representative of different ways of attempting to understand the social world in its various nuances. This no doubt demonstrates the maturity and the scientific nature of sociology as a discipline.

A theory is a generalization about social phenomena, and it is scientifically established to serve as a logical basis for sociological explanation or interpretation. Typically, a theory is organically related to methodology which is the means by which a piece of scientific work or study is being effected. It is instructive to note that inherent in these two concepts—theory and methodology—are ideological underpinnings which tend to easily escape attention. This will be clear from the research undertakings highlighted in this book.

Sociological perspectives at Ahmadu Bello University (ABU) have undergone appreciable changes at both the macro- and micro-levels. At the macro-level, changes in the 1960s through 1970s led to changes in the discipline of sociology as well as changes in the Third World, particularly Nigeria. Indeed, there had been a spectacular shift in the 1950s and early 1960s, particularly under the way the subject was accepted in sociological community (Eisenstadt *et al.*, 1985). Before 1968, there had emerged scholars who were clearly sympathetic to Marxism in a non-emasculated sense, though one unrelated to contemporary politics (Therborn, 1985).

At the micro-level, the Department of Sociology at ABU, founded in 1967, experienced shift in its academic programs and personnel, with newer, mainly indigenous, academic staff being most open to Marxism and neo-Marxist perspective and more African in the 1970s (see Table 1), just as it was the case with other sister Departments of Sociology in Africa. There was, for example, a similarity in terms of the experience being shared by the Departments of Sociology in the University of Kumasi, Ghana, University of Sierra Leone, University of Nairobi, Kenya, University of Dar-as-Salem, Tanzania, Makerere University, Uganda, University of Malawi, and University of Zambia. In the same way, the production of docile and obedient civil servants—the high watermark of the success of the Department of Sociology at ABU so far—gave way to that of graduates of a critical, scholarly orientation. No sooner had the structural-functional perspective been introduced from the inception of the department in 1967 than Marxist thought spread from the macro-level in the 1970s to the department, and continued to flourish thereafter. This was attributable to the historical and intellectual environment of the period which was an extension of the pre-1960s (i.e., pre-independence period). Class consciousness was triggered not only by the Western capitalist mode of production, but also by colonial conquest as well as the resultant predatory and parasitic character of the domineering, Western capitalism being experienced in Africa. What, however, is responsible for the continual existence of all these is the protean form of colonialism since independence, namely, neo-colonialism.

From a purely intellectual point of view, the wind of independence that blew across the continent in the 1960s was connected with the pedagogic orientation of the departments of sociology on the continent. This was in sharp contrast to the original structural-functional orientation of these departments which were no more than a prototype academic outpost of their Western European parentage of the 1950s.

The same explanation can be given in respect of neo-Marxist perspective in the Nigerian or African intellectual environment and social reality. This neo-Marxist perspective emerged around the mid-1970s to, *inter alia,* grapple with the *neo-colonial concomitants,* prominent among them the psychological, sociocultural, and political subjugation as well as the technological pre-eminence of the Western world.

It is true then that the state of the sociological art in Nigeria, or in Africa for that matter, is not static but dynamic (Akiwowo, 1983). That the changes at the micro-levels are highlighted in the manner they are in the preceding paragraphs is a testimony to the dynamic nature of sociology in Africa. The emergence of an African tradition fits in well with this dynamic nature, developing, as it is, within an internal history of its own. Table 1 on page 20 sheds more light on all of these.

Our sociological knowledge of the contemporary Nigeria or Africa within global, epochal, theoretical, and methodological contexts has potential to strike the right chords toward some revolutionary possibilities. Given the dynamism of sociology and the changes within it, a liberating impact cannot be ruled out (Akiwowo, 1983). In this way, consensus and bizarre legitimation of the *status quo* and the entrenchment of the culture of silence—all of which are out of context with societal needs and peculiar circumstances—will tend to be subjected to a critique.

The historical character of the Nigerian or African Sociology in general and that of the Department of Sociology at ABU in particular dictate the order of the arrangement and the nature of the theoretical and methodological positions or orientations articulated in this book. To illustrate, anthropology courses were, at the initial stage, largely offered and later in the 1970s there was a change to sociology courses in the actual sense of the term. Correspondingly, structural-functional and largely survey method orientations pervaded the intellectual air up to that period, from which Marxist or conflict orientation and largely historical materialism or Marxism-Leninism began to gain popularity. The post-1969 theoretical and methodological orientations can be seen to have emerged as a result of dissatisfaction with the original ones. Typical examples of the former are modernization theory and survey method, while those of the latter are political economy and archival or library source method. So a radically viable alternative has been found. In spite of this, the use of empirical evidence is still discernible within a given study. This is not a contradiction of the high premium being placed on radical approach *vis-a-vis* the original structural-functional conceptualization and the accompanying positivist tool. Hence, a radical approach is still being embraced.

Indeed, this statement underlines the fact that in a given study a combination of two or more methods might be used. Where, for instance, the methods utilized are both interview/questionnaire method and archival/library source, which approximates historical source to which the materialist approach is suited, the latter can serve as a basic cross-checking device against the former. The complementary use of both approaches tends to pave the way for the demerits or weaknesses of the interview/questionnaire method to be outweighed by the merits and strengths of archival/library source. If only the first method were used in each of the studies concerned, then weaknesses inherent in it might render it to be nothing more than positivist-empiricist research endeavor. Consequently, the possibility of probing beneath the mere appearance of the social reality at work would be precluded.

It is interesting that the development of African sociology, since the period covered by Table 1, is further enhanced by another shift. The shift is largely connected with applied sociology. In this connection, graduates of sociology take up appointments as clinical sociologists, specialists in human resources, counselors, etc. And the tempo of the shift is in part expedited by economic downturn —one that has dealt a staggering blow on graduate employment.

**Table 1- Toward an Indigenous African Sociology: The Case of Sociology at ABU**

| Description Relating to Phases | Phase I (1960–1974)* | Phase II (1975-1984) | Phase III (1985-date ) |
|---|---|---|---|
| Major Focuses of Sociological Analysis: | Neo-Colonial | Cultural Indigenous | Structural Indigenous |
| Dominant Theoretical Perspectives: | Structural-Functionalism+ | Structural-Functionalism; Marxist Political Economy and Neo-Marxism | Marxist Political Economy and Neo-Marxism |
| Research Problems Defined by: | Neo-Colonial and Anglo-European Interests | European and American Interests; Nigerian/African Interests | Nigerian/African Interests |
| Topics: | Ethnographic Studies of different cultures and communities | Problems of social order and obstacles to modernization | Problems of social order, underdevelopment, and self-determination |
| Academic Staff: | Expatriates only + | Expatriates/foreign-trained indigenes | Foreign-trained and Locally-trained Indigenes (or *vice-versa*) |
| Relations with International Sociological Communities: | Ideological Dependent/Material Dependent | Ideological Dependent/Material Dependent | Ideological Dialectic/Material Dependent |

\* Departments of sociology in Africa (including that at ABU), which are located in countries that attained independence from colonial authorities, regardless of their respective dates of inception (most African countries attained independence in the 1960s). This Table 1 summarizes the trajectory of indigenous African sociological enterprise.

+ A shift to Marxist Political Economy and Neo-Marxism emerged in the 1970s in Phase I, continued and became more embraced and popular in Phase II. However, Structural-Functionalism was not discarded. Similarly, academic staff ceased to be "Expatriates only" in the 1970s.

The shift can be justifiably regarded as a stepping-stone to another strand of professionalism. For a good number of sociology graduates do undertake post-graduate studies in industrial relations, which is part of industrial sociology, individually earning a Master of Industrial Relations (MIR), as typified by that at the University of Ibadan, Nigeria. They then go on, if they desire, to take the examination of the Nigerian Institute of Personnel Management, the Institute of Personnel Management in Ghana, or the Institute of Personnel Management in Kenya. This shift takes a unique, spatial dimension in Uganda, where the Department of Human Resource Management is one of the departments at the Uganda Management Institute. Another professional area in which the shift is easily identified has to do with graduate studies in Master of Business Administration (MBA), albeit not purely sociological. A good number of sociology graduates, who do or do not earn this degree, successfully strive to become members of the institutes of personnel management. Their training in statistics, research methods, industrial relations, social work, and sociology of work and occupation, among others, comes in handy at this juncture. In other words, they activate a practical and creative *extension* of the knowledge, perspectives, and skills they have acquired in sociological practice *to* human resources and other careers.

The application of the sociological imagination of C. Wright Mills (1959) to marketing research constitutes a sharp focus that has turned out to be a shift of marketing significance in that sociologists, armed with sociological imagination, are researchers in the field of marketing and decision science. Marketing scholars or researchers do, via training, "inherit" this sociological imagination.

Another shift is in terms of the appointment of sociologists to governmental positions as special advisers or commissioners. Yet another shift is that which is medically-based. In the field of medicine, colleges of medicine, colleges of pharmacy, and schools of nursing are becoming increasingly aware of the indispensable, sociocultural components of medicine. Thus, the appointment (or at times joint appointment) of sociologists or their interdepartmental transfer from sociology departments to the medical complex as full-time academic staff is necessitated.

Under the following sub-headings, based on the various subdisciplines of sociology, the dominant theoretical and methodological perspectives which are connected with the various research undertakings are articulated:

## Criminology

A substantial number of research undertakings tend to be characterized by structural-functional approach. This orientation is fostered by the use of positivist-empiricist approach. Take, for example, the studies by Obafemi (p. 35) and Salawu (p. 36). Relying heavily on empirical data, these studies demonstrate how prisoners, particularly those charged for theft, find it difficult to adjust to their erstwhile congenial social milieu after release from the prison. Thus, the urge to recidivate becomes difficult to resist. However, one could convincingly discern some radical/Marxist stance. For instance, Marxist orientation tends to underpin the awareness of the researcher that the private means of production is the hallmark of social relations in Nigeria. Hence, there is the incidence of privately-owned property crime in the first instance.

Radical/Marxist stance is discernible in the study on the indigenous criminal law of substance and procedure by Alubo (p. 36) on account of its being imbued with historically-concrete understanding of the paraphernalia of indigenous legal system in Nigeria. For the study reveals that this indigenous device makes it possible for convicted offenders to be treated in the society rather than within the four walls of a prison—no doubt a qualitatively-derived indictment of "colonially-inherited legal system" (Odekunle, 1985). The same multidimensionally-oriented remark can be made about the studies on police-public relations by Mamman (p. 37) and the evaluation of Nigeria Police Force performance by Bogunjoko (p. 37), having been obviously dominated by positivist approach. Nonetheless, they are not implicitly devoid of political economy approach. This explains the arrival at the conclusion by the latter that "... the police are just members of society encapsulated in bribery and corruption... within the prevailing pattern of behavior."

The research into patterns of Nigerian lower courts by Owomero (p. 37) combines both positivist-empiricist method and Marxist-cum-political economy approach. Hence, the finding regarding the awareness on the part of the judges that the Nigerian socioeconomic order is crime-generating and that these judges do not take into consideration the social background of the accused, but rather that their responses reflect a retributive and deterrent, instead of corrective, philosophy. The use of criminal record books of the courts, as distinct from pure empirico-statistical approach, pave the way for situating the study in a philosophical setting of fundamental importance.

The findings of the studies on *yan-iska* (deviant or wayward children) in Zaria (Gyam, p. 39), on juvenile delinquency in Benin City (Agbontaen, p. 39), and on delinquents and non-delinquents in Zaria and Kaduna (Saror, p. 40) are marked by empiricist stance. However, by exposing the socioeconomic deprivation of the children both at home and in the larger society, these empiricist studies are blended with Marxist consideration. For the underlying production relations are not ignored.

The study on Juvenile justice and corrections in Nigeria (Ahire, p. 40) is a clear example of praxis. Its practical evaluation of the Nigerian juvenile justice system against theoretical purpose, using the Children and Young Persons' Laws, testifies to this within the Marxist tradition of readily upholding practice rather than empiricist-positivist theory-testing *per se*. The fact that direct observation was utilized and questionnaire administered does not disorientate the study from this Marxist tradition. Hence, the recommendation that interventions must take cognizance of the constraints inherent in the prevailing social, structural arrangement favoring the wealthy.

## Demography

A weak association revealed by the study in Ilorin (Are, p. 47) between education and fertility is one of positivist-empiricist value. An examination of the empiricist nature of the study would prove that the methodology employed is still useful. This is verifiable from the explanation offered by the study that, since Ilorin is an urban commercial center, it can be expected that some characteristics of urban centers such as a high cost of living, upward social mobility, inadequate housing, etc., together act as inducement to having smaller families, regardless of one's education. The use of similar methodology in the study on labor circulation among the Bassas (Zhizhi, p. 47) which focuses attention on rural-urban migration strikes an empirical balance in exposing both the positive and negative consequences of labor circulation, with the latter having potential for planning rural development. This can be safely applied to the entire Nigerian rural areas. All this is in spite of structural-functionalism exhibited by the afore-mentioned study, as exemplified by the finding regarding the existence of cooperation and interdependence between migrants and nonmigrants, with the former taking care of the farms of the latter, who give them gifts on their return. A more penetrating investigation with a different theoretical orientation (e.g., political economy or class analysis) might remove the façade of gift-giving, providing a down-to-earth insight into what might turn out to be no more than doling out mere pittances.

## Development Studies, Economy and Society, and Ethnomusicology

The studies on the problem and prospects of settlement scheme due to the establishment of irrigation in Kano State (Iliyasu, p. 49), on the impact of the Oyo State Cocoa Development Unit on the participating farmers in Ejigbo Local Government Area (Adekunle, p. 50) and on the impact of the oil industry on Nigerian agriculture in Ogoni area of Rivers State (Okoli, p. 50) are typical of positivist-empiricist configuration.

However, by using non-numerate, evaluative approach in the Kano State study, by tracing, in the Oyo State study, the historical growth of cocoa production in Nigeria and, in the Rivers State study, by utilizing such records as those containing the Mineral Ordinance of 1948 and others, these studies have been equipped to project the appalling social realities at work in the three study areas concerned within the context of the class character of the subjects under investigation.

The empirico-historical orientation of the study on the extended family and economic change at Farman village (Labesa, p. 55) made the discovery of the individualistic mentality of the prevailing capitalist system in the study area possible.

The use of dialectical as well as materialist approach (in combination with other sources) by the study on economic crisis (Fulata, p. 56) and, in particular, the use of the Marxist theory of economic crisis culminated in the confirmation of its hypothetical postulation that the Nigerian economic crisis is triggered by international finance capital in collaboration with the national bourgeoisie.

The study on ethnomusicology by Igoil (p. 58) comes up with findings which are direct outgrowth of the dialectical texture of the theoretical and methodological orientations underpinning it. For, apart from unfolding the psychologistic stance of the view of Keil (1967) on Tiv's music, the study argues that the musical activity of the Tiv people does not merely typify their very human nature, but that it responds to society's needs as well. The authenticity of historical materialism in this context is best illustrated by the fact that, amongst the Tiv, a musical activity is treated and performed, only because there is a condition to be highlighted. Interestingly, an examination of the whole phenomena within symbolic interactionism would throw more light on the definition of the situation (on the part of the Tiv) that tends to belly their tenacity of purpose in their meaningful, dogged response to the onslaught of the British colonial power.

Among other things, music serves an integrative function which smacks of the non-conflict/harmonious stance of structural-functional approach. It is, nonetheless, a unifying force in response to the peculiar needs of a given epoch in the Tiv history, against the onslaught of, and liberation from, the British colonial authority's political subjugation. Herein lies the theoretical and methodological significance of historical materialism. It is untenable to say that this significance is debased by Popper's opinion, as contained in the work of Naletov (1984), that, since dialectical statements are not analytical like those of logic or mathematics, their 'fallacy' is inherent and can neither be circumvented nor neutralized. After all, the concrete reality concerned is unfolded by the study in a qualitative manner.

## Medical Sociology, Political Sociology, and Rural Development/Rural Sociology

The findings of the research into drug abuse in Sokoto by Garba (p. 66) is implicitly blended with dependency theory. For it portrays a situation in which poisonous drugs are possessed and increasingly used by people. This is possible because Nigeria is a dependent capitalist society into which dangerous and expired drugs are being dumped by multinational corporations. The role of advertising in cajoling Nigerians, like other people in the peripheral economy, into seeing the drugs as most effective and ones that would give them good value for money, is a potent factor in the dependency syndrome.

Primary Health Care delivery service being researched into by Yahaya (p. 67) is a topic involving the use of only library source together with informal interviews. This methodological approach enhances our identifying the basic medical care services with modernization theory, by which the rural-urban imbalance revealed in this study can be readily understood. This is because the borrowing of the values and structures of the developed countries in terms of grandiose hospital buildings, highly trained medical doctors, and sophisticated equipment—all in an effort to tread the Western capitalist path of socioeconomic development through culture contact—has given rise to the dearth of health care services in rural areas, compared to urban centers. This is in spite of the fact that people tend to attend medical units closest to their homes, as in the case of Jema'a village (p. 66). There is also the simultaneous existence of traditional medicine, the efficacy of which is acknowledged by the majority of the people, as exemplified by Hellandendu's study amongst the Kilba (p. 71).

Doctor-patient relationship in University College Hospital (UCH), Ibadan (Aboderin, p. 68) becomes clear within the context of class analysis. For the relationship is not cordial, to the disadvantage of the patients on account of their differing sociocultural backgrounds. The situation becomes worse if both of them are not in the same social class. This is in sharp contrast to the traditional birth attendants (TBA's) who are homophilous with their clients (Alti-Mu'azu, p. 77), that is, who have the same attributes as their clients. The implication of the prevailing class character is that constraints to health education are given rise to, since the doctor cannot descend to the level of persuading the patients out of their mistaken or anti-health beliefs regarding the etiology of disease, though it is also revealed that poor treatment and non-cooperation are attributed to some patients' failure to follow the doctor's advice on drug-taking. Hence, the time-honored theoretical model—the activity-passivity model—tested by this study turns out to produce a contrary result to the position of Zasz and Hollender, portraying doctors to be active and patients passive.

Similarly, anchored on the class model is the finding by the study at the Kaduna Psychiatric Unit of Ahmadu Bello University Teaching Hospital, Kaduna (Tuggarlergo, p. 72) that higher educational achievement is protective of stressful lifestyle. The same class character can be linked to the identification by another study of maternal education and child mortality, with a moderate positive association between education and use of protein foods for weaned children (Sanyu, p. 72). The class character can also be linked to the high incidence rate of malnutrition among children whose parents are in low socioeconomic status and who live with their parents in rural areas (Ujiri, p. 76). All this will no doubt strengthen the maintenance of hierarchical *status quo* in Nigeria, with grave consequences for the health status of the children later in life.

Psychosocial consequences of urological diseases (Kyom, p. 79) constitute a research whose findings readily mirror Erving Goffman's dramaturgical theory. For patients in this connection utilized presentation of self or impression management as a strategy to conceal their urethra stricture—a urological condition, which, by its nature, is easily identifiable.

Of great conceptual significance is the study on reform and power in the Nigerian local government with the Habe ruling dynasty, 1900-1976, as a case study (Bawa, p. 86). For this study utilizes social network concept as an analytical tool in addition to utilizing mainly archival and oral sources, supplemented by intensive interviews. Hence, in spite of the merger in 1966 of the Native Authority Police Force and the Native Authority Courts (hitherto within the jurisdiction of emirs), the traditional political authority in the study area used social connection to maintain its status, power, and influence. This resultant, practical phenomenon between the ruler and the ruled has its root in exchange theory, characteristically anchored on the principle of reciprocity.

The studies on the Chad Basin Development Authority (Abba, p. 93) on the socioeconomic impact of the Green Revolution (Othman, p. 94) and on rural proletarianization, with the lake region in Mali as a case study (Balobo, p. 94) are all crystallized within the theory of imperialism. Concerning Mali, in particular, the dualist nature of the dependency paradigm, that characterizes Mali and its metropolis, France, is portrayed, the former being a mere satellite. This, of course, is to the chagrin of the toiling masses, confronted with disrespect for human dignity.

The research into agro-industrialism in the Greater Zaria (Agbonifo, p. 96) comes up with findings readily understood within the class theory, for the far- mers and the existing rural traditional rulers (with some local leaders) stand in a particular relation to the means of production, with the latter exploiting the for- mer. It can be safely surmised that the participant observation method utilized is eloquent testimony to the on-the-spot, esoteric act of capturing the objective aspects of the concept of class on the part of the researcher himself. The seem- ing confusion on the entire rural scene, engendered by the dissatisfaction of the change-agents with the role of the local leadership and the dissatisfaction of the farmers with the role of the change-agents, goes to explain the prevailing ideo- logical superstructure. Devoid of class analytical framework, such a situation as this would tend to obscure the objective aspects of the concept of class. Thus, the actual social forces at work would remain obscured. And this is unjustifiable, since it is to the advantage of those dominating the existing socioeconomic ar- rangements.

The Lafia Agricultural Development Project (Tukura p. 97) is cast within dependency theory—dependence of food production on Western technology. Being effected via local exploiters under the auspices of the Lafia Agricultural Development Project, the connection of the farmers' operation with class theory becomes clear. The study on the effects of the Funtua Agricultural Development Project by Kungwai (p. 98) is situated in the Marxist-Leninist theoretical political economy framework. Hence, this study is devoid of the essentially static mode of analysis typical of the organic intellectuals of imperialism, viewing underdeve- lopment as normal and emphasizing the spread of capitalism. With the use of archival records and downright Marxian approach, social relations of production relations in peasant commodity production in Kaura Namoda Area of Sokoto State (Abdullahi, p. 99), a radical approach—as distinct from, say, structural- functional approach—comes to the fore, with, among other things, the basic findings that the existing nature of labor and property relations in peasant agri- culture best facilitates the maximization of the exploitation of the peasants. This is not because peasant agriculture is 'traditional', but rather as a result of its being subordinated to exploitative relationships with foreign or domestic capital. The rejection of structural-functionalism, together with its conceptual affinity with the existing structural and institutional set-up, is clearly evident in the recom- mendation by this study of a progressive social change, namely, the elimination of those structures of domination and institutions of exploitation.

The political economy of farmers' cooperatives in the Jema'a area of Kaduna State (Nkom, p. 100) aptly utilizes political economy approach—a methodology that derives from Karl Marx's Method of "successive approximation" by which social phenomena are empirically verified from the abstract to the concrete. Al- though sources other than library source are used, yet logico-deductive and arc- hival/historical methods are simultaneously used. This explains why rather than be trivialized, phenomena, as they relate to the farmers, are concretized. Consequently, it is revealed that cooperatives are conditioned by the historical and structural character of the overall national economy. Mistaking the effect for the cause does not, therefore, come in. More important, historicity and holisticism—the hallmarks of the political economy approach—are methodologically discernible.

## Sociology of Education

Focusing on a comparison of urban and rural primary schools performance in National Common Entrance Examination, and the migration of school leavers in Borno State, Alkali's study (p. 134) finds practical expression in the dependency theory. Urban schools perform better than their rural counterparts, for example, due to lesser facilities in the latter—a center-periphery problem reflecting at the domestic level in the context of global Western (colonial) education with its attendant class relations. Further, just as the urban schools are being developed at the expense of their rural counterparts, so there exists the tendency, as revealed by the study on home influence on school performance in Igbiraland (Yesufu, p. 135), to develop Western education at the expense of indigenous societal values.

## Sociology of Industry

Social organization of pottery among the Attakar of Jema'a area of Kaduna State (Dandien, p, 140) is representative of neo-functionalism. For, being a study focusing on how the processes of pottery are dependent upon a 'convenient social patterning' of the people in a society composed of interacting, harmonious parts, this patterning paves the way for differentiating the system from its environment. More important, the majority of the potters (86%) engaged in this craft depend entirely on it for their economic needs, regardless of other occupations derived from Western education. Hence, even though rapid educational development is anticipated, abandoning the craft completely is unlikely.

The study at Nigerian Fertilizer Company limited, Kaduna, constituting an empirical verification of Frederick Herzberg's theory of motivation (Opaluwa, p. 144) reveals that it is such a financial factor as salary and societal evaluation rather than intrinsic value in work itself (as maintained by Herzberg) that determines job satisfaction or motivation. This finding is better understood within the context of dependency theory. For monetary incentive, as a great motivator is informed by the low standard of living of workers in such a neo-colonial society as Nigeria with a relatively low salary. Moreover, that a similar study at Nigerian Tobacco Company, Zaria (Ingbiankyaa, p. 144) comes up with a finding that highlights working conditions—another factor regarded by Herzberg as a dissatisfier—exposes the class-related vacuum or loophole inherent in dependency theory. This is so since the workers, aided by class consciousness in the face of the inflationary market economy, are inclined to come to the realization that what matter are not purely financial factors, but rather power-dependency relationships, otherwise known as class relationships. In this way, the applicability of

Herzberg's theory of motivation to the Nigerian situation is sharply out of touch with the prevailing realities in the industrial terrain.

Of great and illuminating significance is the methodology used in the study mainly on efficiency and productivity in labor turnover and management techniques at Nigerian Tobacco Company in the northern states of Nigeria (Koripamo, p. 150). For the use mostly of the information contained in the personnel records on who had left, for what reasons, etc., clearly brings to the surface the ideological superstructure within the set-up of the company. For instance, one comes to see that an individual's efficiency is not determined or maximized by his salary level *per se*, but rather by the way he attains promotion or increment, which way, of course, is symbolically representative of the company's ideology. The use by the company of a formula, which ignores the reason for separation/turnover and the categories of workers, tends to give credence to an identifiable ideological mystification. Theoretically, the class character of the entire industrial set-up is identifiable in the context of the relationship between the management and the toiling workers.

## Sociology of Law, Sociology of Marriage and the Family, Sociology of Mass Communications, and Sociology of Religion

"The Nigeria Criminal Law: A sociological examination of the form, content and operation" (Omaji, p. 156) undertaken within the Marxist perspective, and holding the view, among other things, that an examination of law should be done through concrete historical and sociological methods of inquiry, makes instructive reading. Concerning this study's findings on the incoherent manner in which the legal norms are organized, the act of lumping incompatible offences together and separating compatible ones would seem to more readily lend itself to eclecticism than to dialectics which, within the Marxist tradition, tends to unfold concrete, living objective contradictions. This is all the more salient since the arbitrary combination of any opposites and identities is the preoccupation of eclecticism. This study, therefore, analytically exposes the incoherent manner in which the legal norms are systematized.

Moreover, the dualist character of dependency orientation finds practical expression in the fact that the linguistic and structural nature of the Nigeria criminal law is a reflection of its English legal parentage. Little wonder, then, that a close affinity between the content or orientation of the Nigeria criminal law and the enduring nineteenth century bourgeois socioeconomic formation in England is further revealed by this study.

As its title implies, the study on the impact of modernization on marriage custom among the Igala (Opaluwa, p. 159) is typical of modernization theory. However, the very dual nature of the institution of the family—its universality and variability—makes it not to be wholly immersed in modernization theory. It, therefore, cannot be expected to be so 'modernized', as to exhibit the exact characteristics and configuration of the marriage/family institution in the developed countries of the world. After all, the basic needs of human beings, irrespective of their geographical locations, cultures, etc., are identical since those needs are bio-logically based. However, the means by which those needs are met are not identical, since they are socially determined. Modernization theory is better understood in this context from eclectic perspective. This is all the more glaring since marriage scene among the Igala today has changed through modification within the context of modernization, even though it still retains some of its customs.

The extremely clear insight into the print media, made possible through research on the influence of the 'gatekeepers' in mass communication (Lawal-Osula, p. 160), is better understood within the context of Marxist theory. For the government has, through enormous pressures put to bear on the news editor, turned the newspaper house into nothing more than the 'megaphone' or mouth-piece of the ruling class rather than the public watchdog it is supposed to be. Clearly, then, the state is itself no more than an instrument of exploiting the ruled.

Modernization theory predominates in the study on radio audience (Atirba-biri, p. 161), since, based on the findings of this study, the magnitude of radio stations and receiving sets being highly cherished should not be seen as indices of development. This is justified by the findings that programs capable of gene-rating feed-back from the audience are not run, in spite of the large number of radio stations and receiving sets—an unproductive attempt at copying the tech-nologically-advanced countries without an educative/enlightenment role on the part of the radio stations.

A somewhat different situation viewed from neo-Marxist perspective obtains with regard to the T.V. industry (Ayam, p. 161): the sociocultural values of the foreign producing countries are found to have been reflected in the foreign pro-grams.

The study on the imperialistic nature of television broadcasting (Joshua, p. 162) utilizes the Marxian political economy approach. Hence, the television in Nigeria is found to reflect the interest of the dominant class, the bourgeoisie, while the television has been used as a tool by the multinational corporations to cajole people into buying their products. The focus on the multinational corpo-rations, normally characterized by monopoly capitalism, is one purely on the economic domain. In this way, neo-Marxist approach, unlike in the case of the T.V. industry (Ayam) on account of sociocultural values referred to in the pre-ceding paragraph, is non-existent. It must be made quite clear that the neo-Marxists do not just ignore the economic realm, but rather avoid focusing exces-sively on it to the absurd extent of becoming, or being given the appellation, *eco-nomic determinists*.

Cultural images in children television programs (Baba, p. 163)—a study uti-lizing content analysis within the context of Marxist-Leninist political economy tradition—comes up with a down-to-earth x-ray of a number of children's pro-grams produced by N.T.A., Kaduna. Consequently, the roots of the structur-al-functional stance of the programs are laid bare. The concealment of reality by *cooperation*, the portrayal of lopsided relationship as natural and good, the avoidance of *social conflict* by stressing *cooperation* and the unilateral condemnation of children mostly of poor family background, etc., are eloquent testimony to this stance. Hence, it is revealed by this study that the rationale for carrying out the various T.V. programs is to maintain the establishment and existence of the system of private ownership of production and the 'promise' of a better tomorrow, with the attendant killing of children's initiatives.

Even though the maintenance of the establishment and existence of the system of private ownership of production suggests or presupposes a focus on the economic realm, the transmission of the cultural traits of the ruling class—dictated by those of their foreign allies—constitutes cultural values in which neo-Marxists are particularly interested. In this connection, the dominant theoretical orientation of this study is the neo-Marxist perspective. A similar situation obtains with regard to the research into cinema in Ibadan (Solanke, p. 163), highlighting Western film as a medium of cultural imperialism. This is so since Western films are found to have constituted a drain not only on our foreign currency, but also on our culture.

The study on the impact of agricultural broadcasting on farmers in Jos and its environs (Orewere, p. 164) tends to be true to the neo-Marxist concern for cultural values. Even though interviewing method was used, cultural factors lay at the root of the sampling technique. For the peculiar rocky and hilly topography of the study area, which affects the reception and clarity of television messages, was taken into consideration, with a view to ensuring that the samples involved had a nearly equal media reception. Besides, this study reveals that interpersonal communications—as a source of farm information—are more effective than mass communications. And this situation is due to the fact that the farmers tend to prefer interpersonal communications on account of their being situated in a social network of corresponding interpersonal relationships and within patterns of sociocultural life, governed by the values and norms of their society. This study, again, is inclined toward a new sociological perspective, and a neo-Marxist orientation at that. It is instructive to note that, since the farmers are to make their choices on cost-benefit grounds, preference for interpersonal communications is most likely.

The theoretical orientation of the study on the bori spirit mediumship cult in Malumfashi (Matankari, p. 170) is reflected in the class character of this indigenous religion, imbued with healing power *vis-a-vis* Western medicine. The class character finds practical expression in the competition between both sources of healing.

Oral tradition and archival source as well as structural functionalism permeates the methodological and theoretical fabrics of the study on the continuity of the *Sango* Cult in Koso-Oyo (present-day Oyo) despite change (Bamidele, p. 172). As is usual with structural-functionalism, this study reveals the teleological relationship between religion and the wider society of which it is an integral part. For religion meets certain social needs which include divination at the coronation of a new *Alafin* (traditional ruler) as to what the future holds in stock for him. Avoidance of future re-occurrence of fire-outbreak for victims on becoming a member of the cult and initiation of its worshipers' male children are few among such social needs. Likewise, the functions of the Itapo festival in the Ososo Community of the Akoko-Edo area of Bendel State (Ladipo, p. 171) include initiation of young men into adulthood (i.e., rite of passage) and solidification of the matrilineal kinship ties. Since rite of passage involves a passage of individuals from one stage of life to another, it occupies a distinct position in the community.

The study on the Aladura Church (Ahimie, p. 173) utilizes interview method, archival source and participant observation. The finding of this study that the Aladura participated in the founding of African Churches, as distinct from churches modeled on the missionary type, is indicative of unique values. And the unique values find practical expression in the introduction of new forms of worship blended with indigenous culture, doxology, and African heritage. Theoretically, this 'culture consciousness' constitutes a guide to the characteristic of class theory, namely, class consciousness, from which this study can be viewed.

## Urban Sociology and Women in Society/Women's Studies

Class structure and housing problems in Zaria (Adamu, p. 185) epitomizes the class context of urban housing in Nigeria in particular and Africa in general. Given the findings that class relations are reflected in housing arrangements and housing policies of governments, stratification theory becomes juxtaposed with class theory. This tends to culminate in an adequate understanding of how class situation can and does reflect in the life chances of members of society. In this study, class situation does reflect in the life chances of acquiring housing. Indeed, class situation has to do with class inequality. Hence, the recommendation by this study borders not only on housing needs, but also on other areas of human needs.

Even in a situation where certain members of society belong to the same voluntary association, as in the case of the study in Dekina (Yunusa, p. 185), those with highest level of education tend to participate more than others, most probably due to their competence. This tends to fit in with the Weberian theory (or functionalist theory) of social stratification. Social stratification can, *ipso facto,* be justified as a factor which necessarily leaves room for benefiting from the competence of skilled members of a given society by others, if things are to get done in that society. However, the finding of this study that the high socioeconomic group dominates the other groups, with the tendency that members of the former use the association to personal advantages in their career, is an empirical expression within the context of the Marxist theory of stratification.

The economic role of women in Mangu, an expanding market town (Drew, p. 189), is a study whose basic thrust has to do with gender inequality. An analysis of the productive relation of women ensued, and the analysis owes much to the use of verbally-administered questionnaire with heavy reliance on informal discussions. This methodological reliance, which borders on the history of Mangu, the traditional economic role of women, etc., paves the way for analytically identifying the subordination of women and their dependency on their husbands. More fundamentally, the historical growth of male-owned private property, according to Engels, is the factor responsible for this domineering relationship. Interestingly, this relationship was aboriginally free and equal.

The entire study readily lends itself to 'role-cluster' model within the wider paradigmatic context of role theory. This is clearly evidenced by the fact that *no one single system* of stratification is applicable to *all women* in the study area. Two roles, for instance, have affinity for each other and, simultaneously, are somewhat mutually exclusive in terms of religion, ethnicity, and socioeconomic status of husbands.

## Concluding Remarks

As is evident in the overview made so far, the nature of sociology as a scientific discipline in its own right is such that it is characterized by a wide variety of theoretical and methodological perspectives. Each of these perspectives has some ideological underpinnings that might escape attention, if care were not taken.

Like that of any other part of the world, Nigerian or African sociology is characterized by the afore-mentioned intellectual tradition. Its emergence at the time that Africa was herself just evolving—albeit in the name of passive, non-revolutionary independence—from the shackles of colonialism informs its structural-functional orientation in Africa. The structural-functional stance was the strategy that the colonial overlords had been using to enhance continuing political and economic domination in a congenial atmosphere of harmony, consensus, peace, and tranquility to the chagrin of the overwhelming African populace. This situation, needless to say, indirectly continues to this day within the context of the neocolonialist configuration of the prevailing socioeconomic order.

The emergence on the scene of Marxism and neo-Marxist approach around the late 1960s and the early 1970s to date has marked a watershed in the evolution of sociological thought. This watershed is in terms of the fact that the structural-functional, bourgeois approach has begun to be pictured merely as being ahistorical. Contrarily, with the aid of dialectical and historical materialism, it has been possible to focus on the subjects under investigation not merely as discrete units, but concretely as a mass of people in a given situation of material conditions. A sharper focus on the relations of the people to the means of production is emerging.

In the course of responding to the works of some of the researchers, readers could be encouraged to develop new perspectives, thereby broadening their theoretical, as well as their methodological, outlook with deliberate immediacy. The various sociological perspectives form the basis, in a real-world situation, for a balanced curriculum, since they span the gamut of social nuances. Thus, the criticism often leveled at researchers or intellectuals of exhibiting ivory-towerism and, therefore, negativism is rendered untenable.

Just as the theoretical framework constitutes a means to the potential goal represented by the methodological framework employed, so both of these theoretical and methodological frames of reference in this book serve as a means to an end in a wide array of research studies, enriched by currents of thought among eminent scholars in their various spheres of intellectual endeavor. In this way, the various research findings articulated in this book become crystal clear, not only in the peculiar context of African sociology, but also in the wider context of a global character.

## DISCUSSION QUESTIONS/EXERCISES AND ESSAYS

1. Why is sociology not confined exclusively to one perspective?

2. "A unified discipline!" Is this an apt description of sociology?

3. Examine changes at the micro- and macro-levels in the Third World, particularly in Nigeria or Africa as a whole.

4. Discuss the relationship of the wind of independence that blew across the African continent to theory and methodology, and to the attendant ideological underpinnings.

5. Using your knowledge of structural-functional theory and conflict theory, what methodological orientations are applicable to each of these theoretical orientations?

6. Compare and contrast the conditions or circumstances under which theoretical and methodological orientations are brought to light in the various subdisciplines of sociology.

7. Discuss the shifts that have occurred in sociology on the African continent as a substantive discipline in its own right.

# ·II·

# CRIMINOLOGY

C riminology is concerned with criminal behavior in society. Hence, it studies crime. The word 'criminology' is said to have been first used by the French anthropologist, P. Topinard (Transler, 1977).

Research undertakings at ABU in the substantive field of criminology appear to be captivating in terms of their being in large numbers. Research studies in the field of criminology undertaken at ABU are categorized into two major areas. These are (a) sociology of crime, punishment, and correction (with particular reference to adults) and (b) sociology of crime, punishment, and correction (with particular reference to juvenile delinquents). The latter is not as much popular, in terms of researcher population, as the former. Rather than being triggered by sheer scholastic aridity, the lesser popularity of the latter is the result of relative scholastic development: it is comparatively at its infancy.

Adequately typical of unequivocal concern with criminal behavior in society is the research study by Obafemi (1977) on social stigma of imprisonment and its socioeconomic effects on exconvicts. This is a case study in Ilorin. The problem of social stigma of imprisonment is looked at from three dimensions, namely, the prison, the employers, and the public.

This study demonstrates some degree of resourcefulness by substituting recidivists (i.e., people who have been imprisoned more than once and are currently serving a prison term) for exconvicts, who are actually out of prison. The desire to obtain results whose quality is not adversely affected makes this possible. For, due to suspicion arising from an attempt to avoid social stigma on their part, exconvicts might not feel disposed to respond as freely as might recidivists, not yet 'released' into the outside society. Interestingly enough, exconvict-related results are obtained: the recidivists are exconvicts too.

Analysis of the social relationships of exconvicts with their friends on release from last imprisonment shows that 65% of them reported negative changes. This was due to their previous imprisonment(s). It also reveals lack of skill-training and education as well as non-receipt of visits or letters from people outside prison. All of these factors may lead to recidivism. Additionally, exconvicts are prone to feel unwanted in society, and thus the urge to recidivate becomes more difficult to resist.

Whether or not exconvicts are eligible to be made chiefs is another social aspect investigated, with 63% of the respondent indicating ineligibility of exconvicts. This sort of 'social rejection' is also revealed by the findings of the Kaduna case study on property criminal victimization and public attitudes toward crime and crime-prevention (Salawu, 1979). Here, friendship with ex-prisoners is the focus of attention. And 70.7% of the respondents interviewed indicated their intention not to have exprisoners who served a jail term for stealing as friends. This was to avoid being regarded as thieves like the latter—a strategy for avoiding any aspersion on their own reputation. The same negative response obtains in the case of marrying, and co-living with, people imprisoned for theft. However, the response regarding people imprisoned for assault was in the positive.

The negative effects of all this on exconvicts are duly taken into consideration by the recommendations put forward by both studies (i.e., those by Obafemi, 1977; and Salawu, 1979). The former makes a number of recommendations for post-prison adjustments of exconvicts. This is imperative particularly as employers, too, are empirically found to have exhibited negative attitude toward employing exconvicts. The latter recommends measures for combating property crime and also for mitigating the effects of criminal victimization.

The study on criminal law of substance and procedure among the Idoma (Alubo, 1977) is of classical significance in terms of its concretely demonstrating that criminology is, *inter alia,* rooted in law. This is all the more so as both indigenous and alien courts are focused upon.

This study is mainly concerned with the role of law in society and the influence of society on law. It stresses that society and law are not static and that law is influenced by socio-legal systems.

Like any systems of customary law and procedures, the system of customary law and procedures of Oglewu community (the study area) made it possible for convicted offenders to be treated within the society, rather than within the four walls of a prison. This system, understandably, entailed little stigma, thus encouraging adjustment. The advent of alien courts, as shown by this study, marked the beginning of the end of Oglewu customary law and procedures for trial.

It can be safely surmised that, if such alien court as those at Oglewu were not imposed on the indigenous courts in Nigeria as a whole, the crimogenic nature of the contemporary Nigerian society might not have assumed such staggering proportions with which it is now saddled. Worse still, this imposition of alien legal system is not in the interest of the overwhelming majority of Nigerians. As Odekunle (1985) succinctly puts it:

> ...Our colonially-inherited legal system and its substantive criminal, penal and procedural laws should be "socialized" to remove inherent and obvious prejudices and obvious contradictions that make it a "loaded dice" against majority of the citizens, among other crime-aggravating insufficiencies.

The study by Mamman (1977) on police-public relations (with Funtua as a case study) is typical of the areas to which research endeavors have been directed. This study puts police-public relations in Nigeria in historical perspective, backing up these relations with the fundamentals of group relations generally.

According to this study, policemen were originally used for the pursuit and eventual achievement of colonial objectives. The "winner-take-all" type of Nigerian politics on attainment of independence made ruling political leaders use the police in guarding themselves during campaigns and in beating up political opponents.

Most of police respondents (43.82%) said they joined the force for 'job security', and would stay in the service for the next twenty years or so. Other factors that motivated them to join the force were, according to 37.5% of them, "relatives' influence" and, according to 12.1% of them, "uniforms and authority". The public respondents have negative attitudes toward the police. Hence, this study comes up with the recommendation that the police and the public should not regard each other as 'outsiders'.

The study on the evaluation of Nigeria Police Force performance, with Okene as a case study (Bogunjoko, 1978), is basically concerned with a sociologically objective evaluation of the Nigeria Police Force regarding some of their assigned functions.

This study utilizes questionnaire method for both the police and the public, informal interviews with some of the police and direct observation of policemen at work in the police station.

The findings of this study reveal that in terms of "protection of life and property", the police are ineffective, as regards their crime clearance rate.

Other findings are that the police lack adequate material resources in terms of manpower and machinery, and that even available resources are not equitably distributed, e.g., police patrol is confined mainly to Government Reservation Area (G.R.A.) and government offices. There is gross differential treatment of different socioeconomic groups, with bribery and corruption reigning supreme; that unwillingness on the part of the police to render "community function" and consequent lack of confidence on the part of the public in the police are easily noticed.

This study concludes that both the police and the public are to blame, and that the police are just members of a society encapsulated in bribery and corruption and whose social pressures, values, and constraints they, like members of any other social group, commonly share.

The research into patterns of Nigerian lower courts (Owomero, 1980)[1] examines the modes of dispositions generally employed by Nigerian lower courts, viz., magistrate, area, and customary courts. Precisely, five types of offense—assault, theft, burglary, embezzlement, and traffic—are examined.

Methodologically, the magistrate court, which, operationally, is uniform throughout the country, was chosen from Zaria, while the area and customary courts were chosen from Zaria (Kaduna State) and Oyo (Oyo State), since both are somewhat similar in terms of being traditional towns and seats of defunct traditional governments as well as having both urban and rural characteristics. Mode of data-collection involves reading through the adjudicated cases for the five offenses in the criminal record books of the courts for the years 1971-77 and filling in the questionnaire by judges, not only those in the sampled courts, but also other judges in Kaduna and Oyo states.

This study comes up with the findings that the judges lack coherent and consistent orientation about crime causation and criminals as well as methods for their corrections. Even though the majority of the judges hold that the Nigerian socioeconomic order is crime-generating, yet it is revealed that they recommend heavier penalties than the existing ones. Further, the judges do not consider the social background of the accused as an important determinant of the type and severity of a given sentence. More basically, the responses of these judges, particularly area court judges, reflect a retributive and deterrent philosophy, thus implying the likelihood of their passing retributive and deterrent, rather than corrective, sentences most of the time.

It is also revealed that the three courts (i.e., magistrate, area, and customary courts) are oriented toward imprisonment sentences for property offenses (e.g., stealing, burglary, embezzlement, etc.), since these offenses account for 82% of the total imprisonment sentences passed. This is confirmed by the findings of a study by Adeyemi (1972), with 80% of the total imprisonment sentences in an adult court being for property offenses. On the other hand, often disposed of by sentences or fine with the alternative of imprisonment are person and traffic offenses.

Other findings are that the magistrate court and the customary court make frequent use of fine with the alternative of imprisonment, while area courts make more use of imprisonment. Intra-court disparities in sentences are revealed due to discernible significant relationship between legal representation and the outcome of a case, especially in the customary court. For example, judges may be inclined to sympathize with their lawyer colleagues, whose services are engaged by accused persons, and so dispose their cases favorably, to avoid jeopardizing the 'daily-bread' of their colleagues. Therefore, two offenders charged for a similar offense are likely to receive different sentences (or similar amount of the same sentences), depending on whether one or the other of them has the ability (measured by educational and occupational status) to hire a lawyer.

Still on the findings, the courts rarely ask for information about the accused: only 9% of the cases on which information is sought are from the magistrate court and 38% from the customary court. As high as 53% are from the area courts, which, ironically, are the most 'punitive', accounting for 63% of all the imprisonment sentences passed by all the three courts.

This study suggests the need to decriminalize certain offenses bordering on minor deviance, which Nigerians are now willing to tolerate, e.g., minor assaults, noise-making, idleness, wandering, etc. It also suggests that traffic rule violations such as failure to insure a vehicle, driving without license, exceeding speed limit be removed from the ambit of the criminal law, and the police empowered to handle them. Other suggestions are placing of emphasis on individualization of punishment rather than the present standardized sanctions of fine and/or punishment; punishment according to severity of offense; university-sponsored courses and conferences in social and behavioral sciences for judges; inclusion of stenographers in the court staff to take down court proceedings, in order to enhance the quality of what is recorded, more so as the magistrate or judge takes notes only in longhand; and seeing of the sentence as an instrument of crime correction, prevention, and control rather than as a punitive instrument, thus making for a successful rehabilitation of the offender and eventual protection of the society from criminality.

## Sociology of Crime, Punishment, and Correction
## (With Particular Reference to Juvenile Delinquents)

On the question of sociology of crime, punishment, and correction, with particular reference to juvenile delinquents, the research studies undertaken are quite revealing of the problems with which juvenile delinquents are confronted mostly through no faults of theirs.

The research in Zaria by Gyam (1976) into the presence of *yan iska* (i.e., undesirable elements, deviants or wayward children) shows that, even though some children are labeled *yan iska,* this appellation can best be regarded as being relativistic. Thus, *iskanci* (i.e., a Hausa word meaning deviance and anti-social conduct) can best be regarded as a relative term. For what is deviant in one society may not necessarily be regarded as deviant in another. The findings of this study shows that socioeconomic deprivation both at home and in the larger society compels these children to exhibit various forms of anti-social conduct, namely, stealing, pickpocketing, etc. Begging and fighting are other forms of conduct exhibited by them.

Juvenile delinquency in Benin City (Agbontaen, 1973) is a study reflective of the characteristic of an emergent society. The definition of juvenile delinquency given by an educator respondent in Benin City is not different from that obtaining in other societies, namely, that juvenile delinquency is an "anti-social behavior, outside of the patterns of normal behavior, which is so extreme as to endanger society and the delinquent." Anti-social behavior, which is a characteristic of juvenile delinquents in Benin City, is synonymous with that of *yan iska* in Zaria, referred to above. This is irrespective of difference in the choice of terminology.

While, according to the study by Agbontaen (1973), changing fashion (in terms of dereliction of parental duties of guidance, discipline, and affection) and economic changes (ones not equally affecting both the 'top' and 'bottom' of the society, i.e., changes making some to be very poor and others to be rich) are factors causing juvenile delinquency, the findings of the study in Gboko by Ahire (1977) reveals the prevailing capitalist social order, characterized by inequality, as the factor causing juvenile delinquency. Labeling some juveniles as delinquents is, therefore, in the interests of the ruling class.

The study on the comparison of delinquents and non-delinquents in Zaria and Kaduna (Saror, 1978) focuses upon the inmates of the Bostal Institution, Kaduna, and the school boys of Kufena College, Zaria. The responses of the latter are self-reports—a self-confession of any deviant acts on their part.

This study comes up with one finding that 92.6% of delinquents are children whose mothers are civil servants, skilled, and semi-skilled professionals, while only 4.2% and 3.2% are children of petty traders/businesswomen and farmers/housewives respectively. This is perhaps because most parents of the delinquents live in urban centers, while the majority of non-delinquents' parents live in rural areas. Furthermore, uncovered by this study is the superficiality of wage-earners' apparently better status vis-a-vis the farmers who could feed their children better. Indeed, the fact that a significant number of parents in the Nigerian cities go to work and entrust their children to the care of others shows that it is expected that many of such children are likely to become delinquents.

This study further reveals that the school boys confessed to a wide range of delinquent acts, with many confessing to more than one act. However, property offenses were almost non-existent among these schools, while 68.4% of the inmates (as opposed to only 10% of the school boys) committed property offenses, especially stealing. Hence, the inmates were incarcerated.

It is, therefore, observed that a juvenile is labeled delinquent, not only because of the intrinsic quality of the acts he commits, but also because of some sociocultural factors and, generally speaking, because he is so labeled by the law-enforcement agents. This question of labeling is corroborated by the statement by Gyams (1976) on page 39 that deviance (iskanci) can best be regarded as being relativistic.

The study on juvenile justice and corrections in Nigeria (Ahire, 1981)[2] attempts to critically evaluate the practical operation of the Nigerian juvenile justice system against theoretical purpose, as contained in the Children and Young Persons Laws, with juvenile institutions in Lagos, Enugu, Kaduna, and Gboko as a case study.

The modes of data-collection utilized were official records (the Children and Young Persons Laws, records of incarcerated juveniles, and the 1979 constitution of the Federal Republic of Nigeria), direct observation, questionnaire (administered only to judges' sample, due to inability to grant audience to the investigator, in spite of their paucity) and interviews (with the police, social welfare officers, and inmates).

This study comes up with the findings that only 17.1% of the inmates admit to having friends who smoke cigarette, while only 12.6% of them do admit to smoking cigarettes themselves and only 18% of them admit to being members of such youth organizations as the Boys' Brigade, the Boys' Scout, the Girls' Guide and others like debating clubs, etc. Further, 30.6% engage mostly in loitering and performing odd jobs, while 69.4% engage in such social activities as hawking, farming, playing games, hunting, and wrestling. And 82.9% enjoy playing with their brothers, sisters, and peers.

This study also shows that the average offender is a male young person, aged between 12 and 15 years, with some primary schooling and a desire to continue schooling. His pre-incarceration residence is either completely outside his family of origin or with only one parent. Furthermore, it is shown that the average inmate is non-recidivist and that delinquency is not yet gang-oriented nor is the juvenile offender as hardened and sophisticated as he is often thought to be. Rather, the average juvenile offender is a victim of circumstances: a child of parents of unfortunate socioeconomic circumstances who runs into trouble with official agencies in the process of trying to make ends meet.

The foregoing findings portray the average offender as an adolescent. And adolescence for all youngsters, even the most normal, is a period of profound change and conflict and also a period during which youngsters develop their sex role and try to assert their maturity and independence from parental authority. Consequently, care and caution are required on the part of parents and other adults in their dealings with adolescents.

On social control mechanisms, it is revealed that negative sanctions are used by both Remand Homes and Approved Schools, the most commonly used being corporal punishment. Worse still, this sort of punishment is used as a *rite de passage* (or 'welcoming' punishment) for new arrivals. Also, Remand Homes are entirely custody-oriented, without exposure of inmates to the outside world and with regulated and restricted movement within the institutional walls. The Approved Schools, by contrast, though similarly walled, are institutions where inmates enjoy greater freedom both within and outside the walls. Moreover, most personnel of the Nigerian juvenile justice system are found to be ill-trained and so ill-suited to handling youths' behavioral problems. The criminal court judges and magistrates are harsh in their disposition of Juvenile cases, always applying Penal Code provisions, instead of those of the Children and Young Persons Laws, to juveniles. Worse still, the flamboyant language of the Children and Young Persons Laws apart, very little attempt has been made at translating the idea of diversion[3] into reality.

The recommendations made by this study are that a body (to be called National Institute of Criminology) to spearhead a reorganization of the juvenile system and to generate necessary data for planning be set up; that an interdisciplinary panel to review the Children and Young Persons Laws be set up; that status offenders be removed from the jurisdiction of the juvenile courts; that welfare boards be established in every Local Government Area; that special schools for problem children like the slow learners and the emotionally unstable be established in every state; that recreational facilities be provided for local communities within the context of rural development; and that the existing juvenile courts be modified, since delinquency is multicausal and, consequently, the juvenile courts cannot always serve as an effective correctional measure, and since brutality and dehumanization merely strengthen the offenders' hostility against the society. More fundamentally, it is recommended that efforts to control any of Nigerian social problems and/or their effect must be cognizant of the constraints inherent in the present sociostructural arrangement favoring the wealthy few.

## Endnotes

[1] This is a Master's thesis.

[2] This is a Master's thesis.

[3] Ordinarily, diversion always conveys the notion of a change in direction or course, with the element of side-tracking being implied. With a touch of legality, diversion is a structured, informal intervention in the criminal justice process, making it possible for the individual offender to be referred equally informally to a community agency for treatment or supervision, usually outside the conventional criminal justice system.

## DISCUSSION QUESTIONS/EXERCISES AND ESSAYS

1. What is criminology?

2. Explain the degree of resourcefulness demonstrated in the study by Obafemi.

3. Discuss the factors that might contribute to recidivism.

4. Examine the factors that are contributory to 'social rejection' experienced by exconvicts. Relate these to the situation in the U.S. or any other country.

5. What are your views regarding the recommendations on post-prison adjustments and measures for combating criminal behavior and phenomena.

6. Evaluate the system of customary law and procedures in Oglewu community. Relate this to the advent of alien (Western) court and its attendant modern problems.

7. Discuss the roles of police in Nigerian society. Relate these to the U.S.

8. Discuss the merits and demerits of decriminalizing certain offenses bordering on minor deviance in Nigeria and other countries (e.g., U.S.A., Canada, and Britain). If some of your classmates rule out the possibility of merits while others do not, then break into two groups for cross-fertilization of ideas in form of a debate!

9. What is the role of sociocultural and socioeconomic factors as causative agents as far as juvenile delinquency is concerned?

10. The average offenders have been portrayed as adolescents. Compare them with adolescents or teenagers in America or any other country.

11. Compare and contrast Remand Homes and Approved Schools.

12. With a touch of legality, how would you evaluate diversion? How applicable is this within the juvenile justice system of any country or state of any country that you know of?

# ·III·

# DEMOGRAPHY AND DEVELOPMENT STUDIES

## Demography

Demography is a Greek word, derived from 'demos', meaning people or populace, and from 'graphy', meaning writing of/about. The word 'demography', according to Grebenik (1977), was first used by the Frenchman A. Guillard in his textbook, *Elements de Statistique Humaine.*

Demography is the scientific study of population, including changes in the structure, size, and spatial distribution of the population either at a given time or over time. The definition given by the United Nations (1958) is about the same as this one. It states that demography is "the scientific study of human populations primarily with respect to their size, their structure and their development."

Demography is also concerned with such factors as migration, fertility, and mortality which influence population growth.

It should be pointed out that "Developments in census-taking and vital registration in Europe, during the nineteenth century, led to a considerable improvement in the quality of basic data available to demographers, and stimulated the study of changes in population structure and of productivity (Grebenik, 1977)". The situation in Nigeria and most tropical African societies leaves much to be desired. This is no doubt a challenge, in particular to Nigeria, where the question of census is so controversial that it has remained unresolved. And so long as this situation persists, that long will, to our chagrin, wide-spread unavailability of basic demographic data continue to live with us. In view of the fact that census-taking in Nigeria is characteristically politicized, a viable alternative to census-taking is census sample survey, which is a useful kind of survey.

The study by Tawiah (1984) on determinants of cumulative fertility in Ghana, based on data drawn from a census sample survey in 1971, provides us with a most illuminating example of the usefulness of census sample survey. This is all the more so with respect to the improvement of the quality of vital basic data available to demographers on the African continent in general and in Nigerian society in particular.

The findings of the study on seasonal labor migration from Igalaland to the Western State of Nigeria (Adaji, 1971) reveal that the first migrants from Ife district of Igalaland were generally believed to be people who in one respect or another behaved aberrantly in society.

This study also comes up with the findings that on his return to his village, the recurrent migrant is immediately absorbed into the existing system. He returns home in November/December to take advantage of adequate rains for his cultivation, but mainly in a bid to evade tax payment in western state, since similar tax payment in his own district is a 'must'.

This type of migration, being a rural-rural migration, has not resulted in any major economic change (for the better) in the Ife district of Igalaland. A rural-urban migration, in which the urban center normally has better opportunities than the rural area concerned, has the potential to bring about economic change in the latter.

The study on migration to Gboko rice mills settlement (situated in a socioeconomic perspective) by Zasha (1977) examines the various theories of migration and proves that these theories have often not been successful, let alone enjoy universal applicability.

This study comes up with the findings that the reasons given by 15.8% of people who migrated more than twice before coming to 'Injin', i.e., the location of the rice mills settlement, were varied. However, the majority of the entire respondents constituting 62.1% gave economic factor, in terms of rice-milling, trading, and farming, as the overriding factor that motivated them to migrate to 'Injin'. It is further revealed that 59.2% of the migrants are mere retail traders in rice, and not owners or managers of the mills.

The impact of the migration on the rural source areas is likely to be a readjustment of the residual population in relation to the utilization of land resources. The impact on Gboko—which is about just 1.4 kilometers to 'Injin'—is the increase in the population of the town.

Sociological and comparative study on the acceptors and non-acceptors of family planning methods, with Maiduguri as the focal point (Bah, 1979), comes up with the findings that educated working-class mothers desire fewer number of children than non-working mothers.

Other findings show that discussion by wives with husbands increases with level of education which, in effect, facilitates the use and practice of contraceptives among acceptors: only 50% of women with no formal schooling or with Koranic education freely discuss with their husbands, while 82.3% of those with post-secondary and secondary education have free discussion with their husbands. This finding tallies with that of a study in Ghana by Tawiah (1984) that "... increasing level of education is associated with a steady fall in fertility. Illiterate women have 1.3 more children than their counterparts with post-middle education." (This is one of the findings of the study by Tawiah, referred to in the fifth paragraph of this chapter regarding census.)

It is also found by Bah's study that early marriage of females is a blockade to discussion with husbands: 36.6% of those whose ages are between 11 and 14 years and 13.1% whose age are between 15 and 19 years do not have discussion with their husbands, while all of those between 20 and 24 years do have discussion with their husbands.

The study on labor circulation among the Bassa in Bassa District of Benue State (Zhizhi, 1981) is a study on rural-rural migration, involving the Bassa in the Otukpo Local Government Area of Benue State, who first migrated to rural areas in the Yorubaland.

On the findings, the largest proportion of all the migrants working on cocoa farms in the Western State are between the ages of 20 and 29. There is a labor shortage in rural Bassa: those who constitute the labor force have moved out on labor circulation.

The positive consequences of labor circulation are cooperation and interdependence between migrants and non-migrants (since the former take care of the farms of the latter, who give the former gifts on their return home); introduction of artifacts like corrugated iron sheet and modern mode of dressing (as a result of visits to Yoruba urban centers); and accumulation of wealth. The negative consequences are food shortage in Bassa District; inadequate remuneration for migrants by the "Aga-Badu" (an individual who recruits subordinate migrants for labor circulation and keeps the money earned on the farm); and divorce due to the absence of male migrants. There is also the effect of culture-contact, resulting in giving Yoruba names (names of their hosts) like Iyabo, Bamidele, etc., by the migrants to their children, though this is better than bearing non-indigenous or non-African names.

It should be noted, at this juncture, that the findings of studies on migration are useful for planning rural development projects in our villages, where those Olatunbosun (1975) refers to as 'Nigeria's neglected rural majority' live. The usefulness of such studies as the ones discussed above is amply demonstrated by Makinwa (1981) with the village-to-Benin study, thus:

> In sum, what we know from our study of Bendel State about migrants' characteristics, their motivations, adjustment mechanisms and their impact on source areas and destinations are useful inputs for planning rural development projects in Nigeria.

The study in Ilorin on socioeconomic status and fertility differentials among married women (Are, 1980) is quite revealing of some variables influencing fertility and which easily escape attention. The finding shows that there is a weak association between education and fertility. One factor that might explain why the relationship between these two variables is not strong consists in the fact that Ilorin is an urban and commercial center, with some characteristics of urban centers such as high cost of living, upward social mobility, and inadequate housing, together serving as an inducement to having smaller families, regardless of one's education. Similarly, there is a negligible relationship between age at marriage and fertility, presumably because of a weak relationship between education and fertility. Moreover, there is no relationship between fertility and birth control, presumably because women use birth control mainly to space births rather than to reduce fertility, or use birth control only after having had many children.

The study on the influence of age at marriage, type of marriage and socioeconomic status on fertility, with Gyellesu (a residential area in Zaria) as a case study (Osatuyi, 1980) comes up with the findings that a low age is associated with a high mean number of children born, and that the relationship between age at marriage and fertility is statistically significant and quite strong. However, the relationship between husband's age at marriage and fertility is not statistically significant, presumably because a man's age at marriage does not necessarily determine the number of children his wife would have and also because an old man does not necessarily marry an equally old woman.

It is also found that polygynously-married women have more children than their monogamously-married counterparts. The relationship between socioeconomic status and fertility is such that women in high socioeconomic status have fewer children than those in low socioeconomic status. That is, those having resources do not give birth to many babies.

## Development Studies

Development Studies have to do, in the main, with the dynamics of development and underdevelopment.

In Africa, like in any other community in the world, development and underdevelopment are no more than two sides of the same historical coin. The two-fold explanation, offered by Walter Rodney (1972) and stated below, sheds light on this:

> Development in the past has always meant the increase in the ability to guard the independence of the social group and indeed to infringe upon the freedom of others something that often came about irrespective of the will of the persons within the societies involved.
>
> ...underdevelopment... expresses a particular relationship of exploitation, namely, the exploitation of one country by another. All of the countries named as 'underdeveloped' in the world are exploited by others; and the underdevelopment with which the world is now preoccupied is a product of capitalist, imperialist and colonialist exploitation.

These two sides of the same historical process are epitomized in the following writings of Ademola Adebo (1985) and Fasina (1985), with Nigeria as the focal point, the former reflecting on the past and the latter illuminating the relatively modern techniques of underdevelopment in its various exploitative ramifications:

> What actually emerged in Nigeria was a dependent state which, lacking any "relative autonomy," functioned according to the need and requirements of British capitalism that subjected it to exploitation. (Ademola Adebo, 1985)

... the attempt to work out reformist promises could not be carried out without a further deepening of the exploitation of the Nigerian workers and peasants by international capital.

To fulfill reformist aspirations, Standard, Mobil, Gulf, Texaco, etc., had to lead oil exploration and distribution, Julius Berger, road construction, Volkswagen, the transport drive, etc., etc. Consumer durables, capital equipment, industrial supplies—all came to be supplied by multinational capitalist agencies. (Fasina, 1985)

However, Nigerians, or, on a continental plane, Africans, cannot be exonerated from being accused of having a dubious stake in the continuing sustenance of underdevelopment within their own geopolitical boundary. A cursory examination of Nigeria or Africa within the context of her class character, fostered by capitalist socioeconomic formations, would reveal eloquent testimony to this. The Nigerian or the African elite perpetuate underdevelopment with a selfish purpose. For, echoing Wilmot (1983), "To protect themselves from the wrath of the exploited indigenous population the MNCs [Multinational Corporations] have created a parasitic native class of compradors and commission agents who serve as a buffer and transmission line between the exploiter and the exploited".

Having criticized the black people for romanticizing the past without making sincere effort to develop their society, Oyebola (1976) urges them to change for the better, optimistically asserting that "The black man can make it. But we need the hurricane of change... And ours is a race against time. Time is running out."

On the question of the findings of the empirical studies contained in this book, one evaluative study regarding the problems and prospects of resettlement scheme is that on the Kadawa Irrigation Scheme in Kano State, Nigeria (Iliyasu, 1978).

The findings of this study reveal that, with the establishment of the Kadawa Irrigation Scheme, farmers lose control over their land. Worse still, the location of the irrigation scheme there makes the area swampy, with water consequently accumulating in the compounds throughout the wet season. The villagers are exposed to cold and mosquito bites. Pipe-borne water is not available, thus compelling them to wash inside, and drink from, the same canal.

Regarding compensation paid by the government, the only compensation received by the farmers covers only loss of houses, while that for economic trees has merely been promised, but not paid. The scheme, however, encourages people more than before to practice farming, solely as their occupation. Also, feeder roads, to facilitate transportation of farm products to the markets, are built.

The socioeconomic impact of the Oyo State Cocoa Development Unit's Cocoa project on the participating farmers in Ejigbo Local Government Area (Adekunle, 1981) depicts the somewhat vitiating role of development project in yet another part of Nigeria.

This study traces the history and growth of cocoa production in Nigeria to its introduction around 1840 from Fernando Po and the establishment in the late nineteenth century of the earliest cocoa farms in the former Western Nigeria by

Lagos farmers and traders, due to low returns to commercial activities, with a few Ijeshas and Ondos planting farms near their trading communities.

The introduction of the project of the Cocoa Development Unit (CDU), according to the findings of this study, seems to be affecting the traditional form of land-tenancy in Ejigbo Area. Besides, the project (i.e., cocoa program) also has the potential to entrench inequality with respect to land, labor, and capital in the study area. For example, even though most of the respondents inherit land, 30% cultivate over 20 acres of land, while 26% have between 10 and 19 acres. Consequently, the former resort to employing the labor of the latter. Worse still, 44% of them are granted cash loan, while 56% are, unfortunately, not granted cash loan due to unavailability of adequate funds.

Devastating as it turns to be, the impact of the oil industry on Nigerian agriculture, with Ogoni area of Rivers State as a case study (Okoli, 1981), is of classical significance.

On a general plane and situating this study within the context of 'the statement of the problems', the investigator observed that the oil industry which may be divided into four main operational sectors, namely, exploration for crude oil and its commercial production, refining, transportation and marketing has far-reaching effects on the producing areas in Nigeria.

The findings of this study reveal that the glare and excessive heat from the flames, in particular, create great bodily discomfort to the people.

Infrastructural facilities are provided by the oil industry, notably Shell Company. Nevertheless, they are all geared primarily toward more efficient exploitation and oil marketing. The overall effects include a reduction in arable land, disastrous oil spillages and blow-outs, and the havoc caused by the gas flare, all of which adversely affect human life, farmland, fishing grounds, food and cash crops, and economic trees. Those affected by all of these are not compensated, the Mineral Ordinance of 1948 (re-enacted in 1969)[1] notwithstanding.

The study on river basin development projects as a strategy for national development, with the impact of Goronyo Dam project in Sokoto State on surrounding communities as a case study (Noma, 1984) serves as a key to the understanding of the negative and positive effects of the so-called development projects in rural Africa.

The positive effects of the Goronyo Dam project under investigation are location of a bank in the area and provision of job opportunities for people to work on the dam itself.

The negative effects of the dam are destruction of land and properties, danger posed by flood and non-payment of compensation to the people. Non-payment of compensation tends to lead to migration on a large scale. These negative effects invalidate the positive effects of the dam.

As is evident from the Kadawa Irrigation Scheme in Kano (Iliyasu, 1978), cocoa project of Oyo State Cocoa Development Unit (Adekunle, 1981), and the oil industry in Ogoni area of Rivers State (Okoli, 1981), referred to above, the effects of our so-called development projects are devastating. These devastating

*Ugly scenery of devastated farmland, crops, and trees*

effects are country-wide: in the southern part of the country, rural dwellers and their properties, including the means of earning their livelihood, are bombarded with oil spillages and blowouts, they experience loss of control over their land, the presence of potential to entrench inequality, due to the establishment of cocoa development project, and non-payment of compensation; in the northern part of the country, farmers are exposed to cold and mosquito bites, non-payment of compensation and consequent migration and, with respect to the Bakolori episode[2] (Usman, 1982), are killed.

### Endnotes

[1] The Mineral Ordinance of 1948 (re-enacted in 1969) was designed to protect the interests of the local people. It stipulates that a fair and reasonable compensation be paid to the victims of oil exploration and extraction. However, the companies concerned, contrary to expectation, resort to doling out mere pittances to these victims.

[2] The Bakolori episode is not included among the studies here. It is, by way of positive digression, included, in order to complete the country-wide picture of the so called development projects in their true gruesome perspective. The Bakolori episode is one of violent repression unleashed on the peasants of Bakolori in Sokoto State on Saturday, April 26, 1980. This obnoxious repression found dastardly, practical expression in the terrible massacre of peasants in their hundreds, simply because they fought against non-payment of compensation for their own land unilaterally taken over from them by the government. The land was used for irrigation project by the Sokoto-Rima Basin Development Authority. Generally speaking, through this Authority, "plan-

ning for agricultural development in this part of Nigeria became intimately linked with the desire of industrial firms in Western Europe, North America and Japan to find export markets for industrial products that go as inputs into agriculture" (Oculi, 1982).

## DISCUSSION QUESTIONS/EXERCISES AND ESSAYS

### Demography

1. Etymologically, what is demography?

2. How would you define demography?

3. What is the relationship between migration, fertility, and mortality on one the hand and population growth on the other?

4. Explain the usefulness of developments in census-taking and vital registration in Europe during the nineteenth century.

5. Explain the rationale underlying tax evasion by the migrant. Relate this to tax evasion in such a society as America.

6. Discuss the main reason for migration and the impact of migration to Gboko, the destination of migrants.

7. Enumerate the positive and negative consequences of labor circulation.

8. What are the characteristics serving as an inducement to having smaller families in urban centers?

9. Explain the role of education in women's willingness to be receptive to family planning methods and the role of education in free discussion between wives and husbands generally.

10. What is the relationship between socioeconomic status and fertility?

### Development Studies

11. Given the statements by Walter Rodney and Ademola Adebo, together with that by Fasina, is it correct to say that the statement by the latter is an embodiment of concrete, country-specific examples of how development and underdevelopment are no more than two sides of the same coin? Expatiate on your answer.

12. Regarding the multinational corporations, explain what Patrick Wilmot has described as "a parasitic native class of compradors and commission agents who serve as a buffer and transmission line between the exploiter and the exploited."

13. Discuss the impact of the Kadawa Irrigation Scheme on farmers.

14. Discuss how the introduction of cocoa project has the potential to entrench inequality.

15. Enumerate the four main operational sectors into which the oil industry may be divided.

16. Discuss the effect of devastation by the oil industry on agriculture and human life.

17. How do the multinational corporations (companies) comply with the Mineral Ordinance of 1948 (re-enacted in 1969)?

18. Justify the statement that the devastating effects of the so-called development projects are country-wide.

# ·IV·

# ECONOMY AND SOCIETY, ETHNOMUSICOLOGY, AND GROUP AND INTERGROUP RELATIONS

## Economy and Society

This area of study seeks to focus on the relationship between the economy of a given society and that society. Attempts are made here to ascertain the effects of the economy on the society, and *vice versa*.

Economy and society is better understood within the context of social economy. Social economy means the study of the structure of the actual and desirable means of organizing, conserving, and utilizing social resources (inanimate, animate, and superorganic). The criteria involved here are organic community welfare and normal personal and family standards of living. Put alternatively, social economy is the actual organization and utilization of social resources of material and energy in any given economic habitat area, nation or culture pattern (Eliot, 1977).

One of the advantages inherent in focusing on economy and society within the context of social economy has to do with the abstract nature of the term 'society'. Social economy, indeed, strips society of the ambiguity, arising from its apparently being no more than an abstraction. Hence, a clear understanding is made possible by the term 'social economy' in terms of the utilization of human and material resources in "any given habitat area, nation or culture pattern" by the inhabitants of that social grouping or area (Eliot, 1977).

Economy and society has not been heavily studied as are sociology of industry, criminology, and sociology of marriage and the family, for example. Perhaps this is due to the obvious fact that economy and society, as an area of study, impinges on so large and common an aspect of our lives that other areas of studies tend to directly or indirectly overlap with it.

The study on the extended family and economic change at Farman village (Labesa, 1977) examines the impact of economic change on a rural society (Farman) in Southern Zaria, Kaduna State.

This study utilizes direct observation, formal and informal interview method, and questionnaire method. Another source of data collection is National Archives in Kaduna.

It is revealed by this study that social and economic change in Farman has had little impact on the extended family, as is evidenced by the relationship between education and support for extended family system: 73% of the respondents (who are illiterates) signify this support. However, support for the extended family varies, with educational attainment being highest among the literates. Interestingly, the former cherish the extended family system since joint assistance from family members in time of need is assured, and so they see people trying to be individualistic as selfish creatures, lacking human feelings. Other finding are that 82% of farmers, 67% of traders, 64% of artisans and 60% of professional support the extended family, while the highest percentage of disapproval (40%) is among the professionals, with 36% of artisan, 33% of traders and only 18% of farmers disapproving. Understandably, the farmers, unlike the professionals, need many hands on the farm and the extended family constitutes the reservoir, from which these hands could be drawn. The traders and artisans indicate their desire to live a luxurious life, which, they argue, will not be possible with large family.

The insignificant impact of socioeconomic (educational and professional) change on the extended family notwithstanding, this study concludes that, with the introduction of the Universal Primary Education (UPE) launched in September 1976 across the country, coupled with rapid industrial development, the survival of the extended family system seems unlikely in future generations.

"The genesis of the Nigerian economic crisis" (Fulata, 1985) constitutes a study focusing on the root-cause of Nigerian economic crisis and on the contradictions that are inherent in the capitalist mode of production, and which ultimately exert a negative effect on the economy, thereby culminating in jeopardy and potential, final collapse of the economy.

This study utilizes largely primary data-collection and dialectical as well as materialistic approach. It casts the genesis of the Nigerian economic crisis within the basic and global context of the capitalist economic crisis.

Using the Marxist theory of economic crisis, this study reveals findings which confirm the hypothetical postulation that the Nigerian economic crisis is a handiwork of international finance capital in collaboration with the national bourgeoisie operating the dependent capitalist economy in Nigeria. Hence, this study recommends a development-oriented and crisis-free solution to the Nigerian economic crisis—the overthrow of the capitalist economy. Interestingly enough and not unexpectedly, this study falls under, and is even fundamentally relevant to, the field of political sociology.

## Ethnomusicology

Ethnomusicology is the cross-cultural study of music. The beginnings of ethnomusicology are usually traced back to the 1880s and 1890s, when studies were initiated primarily in Germany and in the United States (Marriam, 1968).

According to Marriam, two polar positions on a definition of ethnomusicology are frequently enunciated, namely, (1) the total study of non-Western music, and (2) the study of music in culture.

The first definition is, needless to say, confined exclusively to a particular geographical area. And a cursory examination of the prefix 'ethno' would reveal the implicit tendency of this geographical exclusiveness toward ethnocentrism. This is evident in such other words with the prefix 'ethno' as ethnohistory, meaning the study of primitive or folk historical beliefs; ethnolaw, meaning the study of primitive law in its social context; ethnophilosophy, meaning the study of primitive philosophical ideas; and ethnopsychiatry, meaning the study of mental disorders in primitive societies (Reading, 1977).

The second definition (i.e., the study of music in culture) does not carry any ethnocentric connotation. Hence, it is on an opposing pole. These polar positions seem to be reflective of the meeting-point between ethnomusicology and anthropology, itself an embodiment of similar polar positions.

Anthropology, which, of all the social sciences, is the closest to sociology, is "a comprehensive study of man the animal and man the social being through time and space. Thus, anthropology has been called the holistic social science "(Garbarino, 1977). The origin of anthropology dates back to the 1850s, and social anthropology, which is the study of human cultures or ways of life, later broke out of anthropology.

The early social anthropologists like Lewis Henry Morgan (1818-1881), Edward Burnett Tylor (1832-1917) and James Frazer (1854-1941) were interested in studying simple or primitive societies, i.e., societies characterized by simple technology and low-level division of labor, with a view to having the knowledge they possessed of their own societies—which were characterized by complex or sophisticated technology—enhanced. But a deep-seated ethnocentrism was readily discernible. For they looked upon their own technologically advanced societies as being superior to other societies (e.g., those in Africa, Asia, Latin America, etc.) that are not technologically developed.

Moreover, since the early European travelers, explorers, missionaries and colonial administrative officers undertook some social anthropological studies which turned out to be useful in facilitating or even making possible colonial rule, anthropology was branded "a child of imperialism" (or, alternatively, "a child of colonialism"). This was the standpoint of Gough (1968). A front-line Nigerian sociologist, Onigu Otite (1971), has, however, argued, and, quite rightly so, that "...rather than being *a child* of imperialism (Gough, 1968), social anthropology was *a tool* of imperialism." (Emphasis added.) For social anthropology was used and misused as an aid to the colonial system.

As is the case with the study of music in culture (i.e., the second definition of ethnomusicology, as opposed to the first, which is "the total study of non-Western music"), modern social anthropology is no longer interested in the study of simple or primitive societies as such, but in the study of culture, which study may utilize a comparative tool of analysis. Herein, then, lies the meeting-point between ethnomusicology and anthropology.

It has been observed that ethnomusicologists have begun to turn to problem of general aesthetics within the illuminating context of cross-cultural perspective of comparative music, with a strong suggestion that, for most peoples outside the Western and Eastern civilizations, music may be a functional rather than an aesthetic complex (Marriam, 1968). This observation is made regarding the relationship of ethnomusicology to the arts as a whole.

Regarding the relationship of ethnomusicology to the social sciences, approaches adopted include the study of music as symbolic behavior (Marriam, 1968). Marriam further notes that political, social, legal, economic, and religious contents can all be symbolized in musical sound and behavior, and that reference is made not only to 'use' but to integrative function as well. All these can be summarized in the words of Lateef (1983) that:

> ...music is used as a language (message system) and...this system is capable of reflecting people's thoughts, feelings, and actions and in turn shape the way people think, feel, and act.

Of paramount significance to research endeavors is the point well made by Marriam that:

> It is well known that songs can serve functions of social control, as well as *educational and historiographical functions*. The relevance of music studies to social science is indeed great, and both disciplines might derive considerable benefit from organizing this fact. (Emphasis added.)

Interestingly enough, one of the postgraduate thesis discussed in this book utilizes a praise-song in tracing the origin, the political status, and the founder of the study area (Satiru community), which happens to be a historic settlement and which has since its historic collapse been rendered absolutely desolate—an approach constituting an indispensable basis for the entire study (see p. 89). And the fact that praise compositions are delivered much faster, and in a higher tone than ordinary prose utterances, that they can be in verse or prose forms and that they can be chanted as musical compositions or recited with a melodious voice (Surakat, 1986) is eloquent testimony to the fact that songs have the potential to serve a useful purpose in a given sociocultural grouping.

The research into "The cultural aspects of Tiv music: A perspective of the musical activity as ritual behavior" (Igoil, 1985)[1] focuses on Tiv music as a ritual behavior which, in essence, is unequivocally symbolic of some social phenomena and processes, invariably bound up with the survival of people.

This study took place in Gboko, Gwer, Makurdi, Katsina-Ala, Kwande and Vandelikya local government areas of Benue State. Also, some of the most important concentrations of the Tiv people in Gongola and Plateau States were covered. Library sources in Zaria, Kaduna, Jos, and Makurdi were utilized.

Moreover, conducted were formal and informal interviews with both musicians and non-musicians, with a view to reconstructing the profile of the Tiv musical activity as far back in time as was possible. Observation was utilized. Musical performances were tape-recorded and analyzed.

This study first starts arguing with Keil (1967), whose view on Tiv music smacks of a tendency toward psychologism (i.e., the attempt to explain social phenomena in terms of facts and theories about the make-up of individuals). For Keil's attempt to answer some questions (*viz.*, Why is dancing so important to the Tiv? Why half a dozen new dances every year? What motivates the Tiv to spend so much time and energy dancing?) is based on the following psychological and psychiatric premises:

> ...culture universal...(dance as a life force);...to diminue the thick layer of paranoia of disease and death so as to reinforce and expand the core of Tiv optimism and surface cheerfulness (*ibid.*, p.33).

These premises of Keil suggest that the musical activity of the Tiv people is no more than an outgrowth of their very human nature. Contrarily, it is argued by this study that such an activity is in response to societal needs and the conditions giving rise to them within a given epoch, since, to echo Karl Marx as does Ollman (1976) "each stage in history creates its own distinctive needs in men and with the passing to the next stage these needs disappear, along with their owners, to be replaced by new people and new needs."

It is revealed that there are two major categories of music, namely, sacred and profane (or secular). The sacred category concerns all the music and dance embedded in the tradition or indigenous religion of the people.

The profane category has to do with topical songs and dances outside the realm of the sacred. Generally, there is no clear-cut distinction between the sacred and profane categories, since both possess qualities that overlap. Instructive it is to know that, among the Tiv, a musical activity is treated and performed, only because there is a condition to be highlighted. (This gives credence to the periodized changing needs of man referred to in the penultimate paragraph.) And modification of a given condition is outside the power or control of the composer, but from some authority or force more powerful than him. Hence, the bestowal of ritual qualities upon the Tiv musical activity. The modification of a given condition over which the composer has no power or control is best understood within the context of symbolic interaction, since a thorough understanding and an interpretation of the musical activity, together with its ritual qualities, must be focused on relationship with an outside authority or force, albeit, in this context, a transcendental one.

Further, it is revealed that intercultural relations of the Tiv people with non-Tivs, notably the British colonial authority, were violent, culminating in correspondingly violent and even stressful political evolution of the former, whose musical activity, which served as a vital means of communication, stood them in good stead toward their liberation from political subjugation. Symbolic interactionism looms on the horizon at this juncture. The behavior of Tivs was no doubt a meaningful response to a social reality, corporately shared by them within the political culture into which they had been socialized. It was like moving from theory to reality, the brunt of which was felt by them in the wake of an onslaught from British colonial authorities. It was, indeed, a matter of life and death, one that threatened their political culture, juxtaposed with external political subjugation. Our appreciation of the definition of the situation would render their plight readily appreciable. Phenomenology (the relationship between the states of human consciousness and the social world) coupled with Max Weber's *verstehen* (an approach by which the subjective meanings people have of their behavior and others' behavior are examined and understood) will throw more light on this. A consideration of the relationship between the states of human consciousness and the social world alongside the subjective meanings, i.e., personal beliefs, feelings, motive, and perceptions that guide the actions of the Tiv, just as they guide the action of any other human beings, would give us a deeper and a more informed understanding of the violence between the Tiv and the British colonial authority, and not merely an understanding of intercultural relations between them.

This study notes that their costumes together with the symbolisms of the costumes have proved to be a very difficult area to study on account, among other things, of the fast-spreading effects of social change in the Tiv area that make it look as though the costumes for their music and dance are either dead or dying. It is, therefore, opined that further investigations are still necessary and required, to be able to throw more light on the people's costumes, no doubt an important aspect of their music and dance.

## Group and Intergroup Relations

Group and Intergroup Relations constitute a study of relationships within a social group and between two or more social groups.

The research studies which constitute the theses discussed in this book relate to groups either at the national or international level or both.

The research study on the traditional gift exchange in Wudil, Kano State, by Ibrahim (1971) is typical of research into relationships among people within a given social group. The purpose of this study is to ascertain how the establishment of social relations through gift exchange integrates human community.

This study comes up with the finding that the kind of symbiotic relationship existing between hunters and blacksmiths in the town owes its origin to the past. It was even more crucial then than now. All this was, and still is, possible due to the prevailing interdependence. Moreover, the pattern of exchange is seasonal—flow of farm implements at the beginning of the rainy season from blacksmiths to hunters/farmers and old implements resharpened free-of-charge; and at harvest, flow of foodstuff from hunters/farmers to blacksmiths.

Trade by barter was originally practiced at Wudil. Monetization of the economy pushed this pattern of trade out of existence. Reciprocal exchange, which is not a fixed pattern but effected at will when one can afford, nonetheless supersedes trade by barter.

A joking relationship is revealed by this study. As is usual with this sort of relationship, emotional outburst is not a rarity. Gift-giving between the parties concerned is strategically used to release tension, however.

The overall significance of exchange, as is portrayed by this study, is that exchange integrates the social network within a given community.

Cultural festival, as an integrating factor, is being focused upon by the research conducted by Mohammed (1974) into the famous Argungu fishing festival in Sokoto State.

The twofold purpose of this research is (a) to describe the Argungu fishing festival in its historical context and (b) to examine the way in which the richness of this cultural institution is used (1) to promote unity and continuity of Kebbi society, (2) to reconcile Argungu and Sokoto, and (3) to promote the much desired unity within the context of one Nigeria. Integration is the theme around which all this revolves.

At the local level, the fishing festival has been fostering understanding and peaceful co-existence among the Kebbi people.

Concerning Kebbi-Sokoto relation, the gracing of the fishing festival with their presence by Sokoto people (led by their Sultan) has over the years resulted in the amicable settlement of petty quarrels between these two groups.

Agricultural and cultural exhibition is one of the highlights of the festival. An opportunity is thus provided for showing the potentialities of the vast resources—both agricultural and cultural—of the people.

On the question of national unity within Nigeria, the festival attracts Nigerians from the length and breadth of the country. With the loss of individuality, these people tend to be interested in the gestures and harmonic rhythms of musical instruments. They also tend to appreciate the similarity of their cultural traits to the cultural traits of their hosts. This, then, tends to cement a common sense of belonging.

Regarding international relations, far from being marred by the Anglo-French Imperial Treaty of 1898, which gave two-thirds of the old Kebbi Empire to Niger, the Kebbi-Niger relation is enhanced by the presence of the president of the Republic of Niger and the participation of his people at the festival.

The dynamics of group and intergroup relations are clearly exemplified by the research into the readjustment of Nigerian returnees from Ghana. The investigator, Ayinla (1975), focused on Igbetti as a case study.

This study reveals that the estimated population of Igbetti migrants in Ghana at the time expulsion order was issued in 1969 was approximately 800-1,000. This constituted the greatest concentration of Igbetti migrants anywhere. The people were well received on their return to Igbetti. This was due to the earlier, continuing contact they maintained while in Ghana, with their people back home in Nigeria.

Cooperative thrift and credit societies emerged with the return of migrants. Notable among these societies was one named *Balelayo* (literally meaning 'meet home happily', i.e., 'we arrive home happily'). The purpose of these cooperative thrift and credit societies was to keep them going. However, this Balelayo Society was dominated by fairly wealthy migrants. Later, the then Western State Government loaned 3,600 naira (Nigerian currency) to this society, with each member receiving 60 naira.

Perhaps the highlight of the findings of this study is that, while the migrants were, though not fully, integrated into the Ghanian culture, they were not uprooted from the culture of their homeland. They thus admirably did strike a balance between their group and intergroup relations.

**Endnote**
[1] This is a Master's thesis.

## DISCUSSION QUESTIONS/EXERCISES AND ESSAYS

### Economy and Society

1. What is social economy?

2. Give an explanation of how the advantage of *economy and society* eliminates the disadvantage of the term society in terms of the ambiguity arising from its apparently being no more than an abstraction.

3. To what extent is it correct to assert that *economy and society* impinges on our lives?

4. (a) One of the findings in this chapter is that socioeconomic change in Farman has little impact on the extended family. To what extent is this explained by the relationship between education and support for the extended family system?

   (b) Can you or any of your relatives or friends relate to this phenomenon?

5. Justify why the findings that the Nigerian economic crisis is caused by the international finance capital in collaboration with the national bourgeoisie is best explained by the Marxist theory.

### Ethnomusicology

6. What does the prefix 'ethno' mean?

7. Define ethnopsychiatry.

8. Define anthropology.

9. Critically examine the statement that anthropology was branded a "child of imperialism" and the more comparatively recent statement that anthropology is a "tool of imperialism".

10. Explain why songs have the potential to serve a useful purpose in a given society. Additionally, consider the role of music as a language (message system).

11. Explain the relevance of the methodology used in the research on the cultural aspects of Tiv music to ritual activity.

12. Does psychologism have a place in the discipline of sociology?

13. Regarding human nature on the one hand and societal needs and the conditions that give rise to them on the other, which of these two factors is realistic as far as the musical activity of the Tiv people is concerned? Explain and relate this to your own life experience.

14. How would you explain that symbolic interactionism is applicable, even when it comes to the question of transcendental authority or power?

15. What is the role played by Tiv musical activity that was instrumental in their liberation from British political subjugation?

## Group and Intergroup Relations

16. Discuss exchange theory within the context of the study on the traditional gift exchange in Wudil.

17. What is the economic and political significance of Argungun fishing festival?

18. How did the migrants from Ghana strike a balance between their group and intergroup relations?

# ·V·

# MEDICAL SOCIOLOGY

Medical Sociology is concerned with the problems associated with physical and mental health from the social perspective, in which case the main sociological theories relating to health and illness behavior come in handy and are put to practical test.

Rather than focus narrowly on the clinical aspects of illness, one is, with the knowledge of medical sociology, better able to focus on the sociocultural basis of the etiology of a given disease, for example. Thus, the interplay of clinical and sociocultural factors will, it is expected, ameliorate physical and mental problems. This is all the more so in the context of the meaning which, according to Lewis (1976), medicine has come to have now, that is, that medicine is the study of the diagnosis, treatment and prevention of disease rather than just the traditional English meaning of the art of healing. Moreover, this is not out of place, especially regarding the etiology of disease itself. As Ojanuga (1979) succinctly puts it:

> ...many reported diseases are closely linked to poor environmental, social or economic conditions.

The development of medical sociology is a comparatively recent one. For instance, the first journal devoted primarily to medical sociology appeared only in 1960, later to become an official organ of ASA, i.e., the American Sociological Association.

Still on the youthful or adolescent status of medical sociology within its parent discipline of sociology, itself having emerged as a discipline in its own right only in the nineteenth century, the observation by Badgley and Bloom (1973) would seem to be instructive:

> Sociology did not assume a recognized position *vis-a-vis* medicine until after World War II, when the first collaboration with psychiatry occurred.

The methodology used by medical sociology, is the social science methodology. This abundantly explains why it is not the same as clinical medicine *per se.*

The study on the factors underlying concern on indifference to medical care among the Hausa in Zaria (Zamani, 1975) examines a number of factors responsible for positive or negative attitude to the help-seeking behavior of the Hausa in Tudun Jukun and Jema'a village in Zaria.

It is revealed by the findings of this study that there is a tendency for people to attend medical units that are closest to their homes. Only 20% in Tudun Jukun and 2.5% in Jema'a attend medical units. The simultaneous existence of traditional medicine, however, constitutes an alternative treatment source.

This study predicts that in the near future traditional medicine will gain universal recognition, while, comparatively, modern medical treatment will probably experience some dislocating set-backs, especially if the latter is not given free-of-charge.

In spite of the prohibition of taking or being in possession of poisonous drugs under section 15 of the pharmacy law of 1966, the research into drug use in Sokoto township by Garba (1976) discovers that not only have these poisonous drugs been possessed and used, they are on the increase.

Further findings revealed are that 37.5% of the respondents use drugs, notably marijuana (*wiwi*), through "influence of friends", 25% "for purpose of action, i.e., bravery, hard work, etc.", 25% "to feel good or 'feel high', i.e., for pleasure, etc.", and 12.5% "to set user 'free', e.g. from anxiety or shyness."

It is also revealed that drug use is a characteristic of the youth and that the more unrewarding the occupation, the greater the chance of drug use.

The study by Tuggarlergo (1977) focuses on mental disorder, specifically examining sociodemographic characteristics of inpatient admissions. The study, with the Psychiatric Unit of ABU Teaching Hospital, Kaduna, as a focal point, comes up with the findings that psychiatric patients in the age group 25-34 constitute 39.5% of the total sample, followed closely by the 15-24 age-group, constituting 38.5%. The preponderance of the former is due to the fact that this falls within a period during which the individuals concerned are prone to be engaged in social activities and to indulge in drinking, smoking, and other forms of luxury more than at any other time of their life. And all of these contribute to mental problems. One unique finding is that females are extremely low in their proportions of psychosis and neurosis, while they are not vulnerable to conduct disorder.

This study seeks to alert the authorities of the Psychiatric Unit to the prevailing inadequate system of collecting patients' histories, urging them to make good this deficiency, so as to enhance future research endeavors.

The research into health care organization at the ABU Health Center (Dokotri, 1977) is an evaluative study of the day-to-day operation of this health center located on the Samaru main campus.

The findings show that 68% of students and worker respondents have to miss work or lectures as a result of undue delay at the center while there for treatment. However, most people seem to be generally satisfied with the medical treatment received.

The study in Kaduna State on primary health care delivery services, comparing Nigeria's primary health care delivery services with those of other developing countries like China and Cuba, etc. (Yahaya, 1979) uses library source, general observation, and informal interview methods. Rather than being merely analytical, the study is prescriptive because of the involvement of the basic health service scheme with planning.

This study comes up with the findings that in many rural areas one health center serves 129,487 people and one dispensary serves 21,581 people, while (as many as) two to three hospitals are established in most urban areas of Kaduna State. Even then, the attitude of the rural populace and certain physical constraints prevent maximal utilization of available health care facilities. The situation in other developing countries like China and Cuba is much better than this.

The study on socioeconomic correlates of malnutrition among preschool children, with Idah community as a case study (Omaji, 1980) comes up with the findings that the number of children of the respondents does not necessarily affect feeding of children with meat and eggs; and so there is no correlation between number of children and malnutrition. However, malnutrition is found to be a feature present among members of low-income group, who cannot afford to purchase sufficient nutritious foods.

Ringim Rural Health Center in Kano (Adamu, 1980) constitutes a study area in which it is found that within Ringim village itself about 76% of the patients are children. However, inaccessibility in terms of distance, discourages people living in the village south of Ringim from utilizing the facilities of the center. For they lack good road network.

It is also revealed that 81% of the respondents either attribute their ailments to the supernatural power or are ignorant of the cause.

The study in social interaction in a psychiatric setting with Makurdi General Hospital Psychiatric Unit as a case study (Dansoho, 1980) examines the interaction between patients and doctors against the socioeconomic characteristics of the former.

The findings reveal that males constitute 57% and females 42.66% of the psychiatric patients, thus countering the usual anti-women understanding in literature that female are more prone to mental illness than males. Also, 74.7%, 11.10% and 12.96% of the patients are functional psychotics, neurotics, and organic psychotics respectively.

The study on the evaluation of health care services with the Physiotherapy Department of ABU Teaching Hospital as a case study (Omokore, 1980) focuses on staff and patients in relation to other departments in the hospital and on physiotherapic facilities.

It is revealed by the findings of this study that physiotherapists are overworked, attending to 140 patients daily, with a doctor-patient ratio of 35:1. The facilities used are inadequate. Included in these are physical facilities, e.g. working space. Moreover, the status of physiotherapists are not regarded as being the same as that of other medical workers, with their salary not being commensurate with the magnitude of the service they render.

Interview with the patients and observation by the investigator revealed the need for the junior staff in the hospital to improve their attitude to patients.

The recommendations made by the study include the training of inpatients in some crafts right in the Department of Physiotherapy of the hospital, to enable them to work when discharged and the need, to be propagated by the mass media, for people to take a rest after hard work, in order to reduce disabilities resulting from much bending and lifting of heavy things by, for example, carpenters, farmers, and traders.

Oriented, in the main, toward inquiry into health-seeking behavior (otherwise known as help-seeking behavior) among hospital patients, the study by Aliyu (1981) is partly an evaluative study.

This study comes up with the finding that while some respondents in Sokoto town do not attend Sokoto General Hospital because their ailments do not appear to them to be serious, others do not attend hospital due to lack of trust on their part in the hospital.

On evaluation, like the study in the Physiotherapy Department of ABU Teaching Hospital, Zaria (Omokore, 1980) referred to above, facilities in the Sokoto General Hospital are inadequate. However, only patients treated in the junior staff section of the latter, as distinct from those treated in the senior staff section, feel the brunt of the inadequacy of the facilities. For the senior staff section (i.e., the elite section) is much better equipped than the junior staff section.

Doctor-patient relationship in a Nigerian hospital (i.e., University College Hospital, Ibadan, as a case study) has been shown by research study (Aboderin, 1981) as not being cordial and to the disadvantage of the sick, understandably in dire need of effective and prompt treatment and recovery. Instead of the needed cooperation, the doctor resorts to shouting on the patient. Worse still, because the sociocultural background of the patient makes him/her have a different idea from that of the doctor regarding the etiology of disease, the latter habitually ignores, rather than persuade, the former. The picture becomes uglier if both of them are not in the same social class.

It is, however, revealed that some patients fail to follow doctor's advice on drug taking, resulting in poor treatment and non-cooperation.

Theories tested against Nigerian situation are not suited to the various clinics in the University College Hospital (UCH). For example, the activity-passivity model tested shows that, contrary to the position of Zasz and Hollender, patients, and not doctors, are active, while doctors are passive. Also, the 'guidance-cooperation' and mutual-participation' models/theories turn out to overlap.

This study recommends, *inter alia*, that booklets containing useful information be introduced and given to patients, so as to reduce the number of questions (most of them unappealing) directed to doctors, and thus enhance doctor-patient relationship.

Survey of traditional healers in urban Zaria (Otesanya, 1984) comes up with the findings that middle-aged men and women who have undergone long periods of informal and unstandardized form of training render services at the primary level of health care. Unlike in the past, these healers hold that there is now a change in their attitude—in terms of each of them keeping his/her healing power secretly to himself/herself—to mutual cross-fertilization of ideas among them. There is also specialization among them, with any of them 'referring' a case outside his/her specialty to an expert colleague.

It is further revealed that the traditional healers admit that there are diseases (e.g., diabetes) which are better managed by Western doctors. They, according to them, are more competent than the Western doctors in managing malaria and mental disorder, for example.

Convinced that a neglect of the activities of traditional healers is detrimental to our health care delivery system, this study recommends integration of traditional medicine with Western medicine after a scientific study of the former has been undertaken and certified.

The above recommendation is perfectly in line with similar ones, prominent among which are those by the governments of Africa. Hence, the colloquium of the Second World and African Festival of Arts and Culture (FESTAC) has felt the need for setting up academies of traditional medicine in Africa as being imminent. For this is considered the most realistic way of reviving and developing traditional medicine—an important aspect of African cultural heritage—to its full bloom (Amoda, 1978). More empirically important, governments of Africa have released grant through the Organization of African Unity (OAU), now known as African Union, for systematic research in traditional herbal medicine. Obafemi Awolowo University, Ile-ife, Nigeria, has been a beneficiary of this grant. Other universities and national scientific research institutes, notably in Nigeria and Cameroun, have reportedly been engaging in similar research activities.

The desirability of the afore-mentioned practically demonstrated enthusiasm for research pursuits is readily discernible in the contents of Obanwu's public lecture (1984) at ABU, while, in particular, echoing Sofowora (1982), thus:

> The practice of traditional medicine varies from the highly organised and long established Chinese Ayurvedic forms to the largely herbalist type common in West Africa. From time immemorial the African has relied on traditional medical practice for prophylactic and curative purposes.

Hence, he (Obianwu) recommends, *inter alia*, the development of drugs from our traditional medicine, and also examines some of the main problems researchers in this area encounter. Prominent among these problems is unavailability of adequate funds. Worse still, according to him, the thirty or so pharmaceutical companies in Nigeria, majority of which are subsidiaries of the large multinational pharmaceutical companies, are not engaged in meaningful research on drug development.

Perhaps it is in a bid to give recognition to the practically demonstrated enthusiasm for research endeavor within a world-wide context that the WHO (see WHO Chronicle, 1985, Vol. 39, No. 4) has selected names of some pharmaceutical substances and included them in the lists of the Proposed International Nonproprietary Names (Prop. INN)[1]

The study on Kilba conception and treatment of stigmatized diseases (Hellandendu, 1981)[2] is a survey of the social institution of people, who live in a rural society and who are suffering from stigmatized diseases, which conspicuously project their sufferers, who, physically, are disabled and so glaringly different from non-sufferers in the society.

This study was conducted in Kilba District, Gombe Local Government Area of Gongola State. Interview method involving patients was utilized. The case history of each patient was always written immediately after the interview. The guides or village heads, who took the investigator to the patients, furnished him with some information, later utilized as corroborative evidence regarding the responses of patients.

This study reveals that the Kilba attribute some of the diseases to several causes, which vary from one community to another. For instance, enlarged abdomen (acytes) is attributed to eating of food—food eaten by two male who have already had sexual intercourse with the same women. Some people attribute the disease to naturalistic factors, particularly bad drinking water and consumption of strange foodstuffs introduced on the advent of colonial government. Further, the cause of enlargement of the scrotum (hydrocelle) is ambiguous: some communities do not know the cause or simply believe that it is contracted when a male sits on the bare floor of a granaries infested with some organism. The disease is said to be infectious, the victim being someone sitting on a seat just vacated by its victim. According to the indigenous healers, hydrocelle is no longer as stigmatized as it used to be due to its successful treatment by modern medicines.

Elephantiasis is regarded by the Kilba people as an alien disease, being believed as the side-effect of using magical medicines from non-Kilba cultural groups to enrich oneself. Consequently, it is also an index of wealth.

Blindness is believed in the north of the district—where blindness is endemic—to be caused by the filariasis fly vector. However, a man, blind right from infancy attributes his blindness to wizard. Altogether, six patients give human malevolence, four evil spirits and twenty three natural factors as the causes of their blindness.

It is unanimously believed that epilepsy is caused by the devil, with some communities holding that it is even contagious. The Kilba seems to not have a clear distinction between epilepsy and hysteria. The word for a frenzied, violent, and unconscious reaction is *ngumi*, occurring, however, in situations of intense, grief, delight, or sudden fright. *Ngumi* is ritualistically-biased: the soul of a person during his childhood and that of a wild animal, he possesses, are said to be united. The *ngumi* is thus reminiscent of the gait and mannerism of whatsoever animal the person's name is associated with. However, *ngumi* is not seen as a disease, but even cherished, since the union of man and animal spirits is symbolic of wealth, potentials, diligence, and clairvoyance. So this study regards the Kilba as people associating hysteria with epileptic seizures and reserve *ngumi* for the ritualistic type. To complicate the picture of epilepsy even more, there are several episodes regarded as cases of epilepsy, but which this study considers hysterical reactions. There are incidents recognized by some communities, in which they occur, as not being typical cases of epilepsy. But there is no other appropriate term for such incidents.

Leprosy is conceived in naturalistic terms: everyone is believed to have been born with the 'seeds' of leprosy in the body. Chronic ulcers are attributed largely to accidental cuts, boils, snake bites and guinea worm infestation, but, when beyond a reasonable period, casual explanations are sought in human and spirit-based factors.

Regarding occupation, most of the patients engage in some kinds of occupation, particularly farming. Even those who are blind do walk unguided around the villages or travel as far as nine kilometers as typified by the case of three itinerant Christian evangelists who claim traveling at times even beyond Kilba District.

This study further reveals that all the patients have sought help from either traditional or modern medical systems, with the majority believing more in the efficacy of indigenous medical system than in the efficacy of Western medical system.

It is suggested, *inter alia,* that the existing administrative set-up be used as an effective means for getting information regarding individuals: the village heads know everyone in the villages and messages through them are more promptly received than by radio, due to financial and/or physical barriers. Thus, patients can be better advised and encouraged as to how to get rehabilitated or treated.

Social correlates of mental illness with Kaduna State as a case study (Tuggarlergo, 1981)[3] focuses on first admissions at the Kaduna Psychiatric Hospital, owned by the state government, and at the Psychiatric Unit of Ahmadu Bello University Teaching Hospital. Both hospitals are located in Kaduna. The aim of this study is to examine the sociodemographic correlates of mental illness.

This study comes up with the findings that males constitute more than half of the respondents, thus confirming the findings of studies done in other African countries, e.g., that of the study by Orley (1970) in East Africa.

Other findings are that younger persons, more than the older ones, were frequency diagnosed for all disorders, since they are more mobile and thus migrate to the town, move about in search of jobs and fun and try to establish their identities, while at the same time exhibit youthful exuberance. Consequently, all of these, together with the effect of social change from the traditional to the modern, are most likely to expose the youths, normally in the process of making life-long commitments to the future, to factors precipitating mental problems.

Furthermore, this study reveals that admission was predominantly composed of person with little or no education, although it might be argued that, after all, there are more non-literate persons in the state than literate ones and that, therefore, by simple chance probability, they might be more represented in the admission than the literate ones. Nevertheless, there is no gainsaying the fact that, given the socioeconomic situation in Nigeria, higher educational achievement is more protective of mental stress, more so as education is a certificate to live well, i.e., to have less stressful life-style.

This study comes up with a number of recommendations. First, since young adults in Nigeria are confronted with psychological blocks on their ways to meet up with the economic expectations of the society and since, paradoxically, provisions are not made for the necessary economic and educational institutions, it is recommended that research into the effects of our present educational system on the mental health of the youth be conducted. Secondly, research into the mental health of the illiterate and educated persons is recommended. Thirdly, a re-examination and restructuring of some of our social institutions, especially economic and educational ones, are recommended. Fourthly, research into the belief systems of the people is recommended to be conducted.

Maternal education as a factor in infant and child mortality (Sanyu, 1983)[4] is a study in Gyallesu, a part of the Zaria metropolitan area, focusing on the effect of the education of the mother on infant and child mortality. It also examines the suggestion of Caldwell (1979) that maternal education is strongly associated with infant and child mortality, and even goes beyond this, examining the mechanisms by which education is associated with other factors that seem to affect mortality.

The unique methodological quality of this study lies in its sampling technique: a map of Gyallesu (the study area) was obtained and a five-millimeter square grid was plotted on it; the squares were numbered, and numbers ranging from 1 to 2,460 were plotted on the map. This procedure made possible the random points generated, using a calculator (H.P. 25), and the points at which the randomly-chosen squares fell were identified. Most of the houses around the two sub-areas of the whole study area were then identified on the actual site for three days, but without serial numbers to be plotted on the map. Since these houses did not have numbers, some descriptive identifications, made by writings found on the doors, colors of the houses, electric poles, and other available signs were used.

The results of this study reveal a moderate positive association between education and use of protein foods for weaned children of 1-4 years old. For example, respondents who indicate that protein foods are of importance to weaned children are mainly those with some formal education. On the other hand, the uneducated sample seem to stress the importance of *tuwo*' and this may be due to their consideration of quantity rather than quality. There is a substantial positive relationship between the knowledge of what causes fever and education, with those having some formal education mentioning mosquito bites as a greater contributor to getting fever. Further, some of the uneducated respondents associate kwashiokor with over-feeding and do not know the treatment for this kind of disease. Their educated counterparts indicated that better feeding and hospital treatment would be a remedy. More than half of those with formal education have tap water in their houses, whereas, as suggested by Harrington (1979), sharing of a tap water supply may increase the probability of diseases. Most of those with no formal education share pit latrines or flush toilets and one admits to using bush.

Whilst on the question of education and health, it is important to note that education and health complement each other. As Erinosho (1982) puts it:

> Health comes next to education in the development of human resources in many underdeveloped countries. It is valid to suggest that education and health complement each other in this context. On the one hand, education facilitates general enlightenment in the population as well as the acquisition of the varied and much needed skills which could be harnessed for the transformation of society. On the other hand, general enlightenment fosters a change in attitude and habits which may be conducive to the attainment of a high health status particularly amongst people in developing countries. Both are needed skills which could be harnessed for the transformation of society.

On the whole, the findings of the above-mentioned study by Sanyu are in accordance with Caldwell's (1979) suggestion that maternal education is strongly associated with infant and child mortality. And the data also seem to indicate that health-related matters and the health-seeking behavior of the respondents are associated with education and socioeconomic status.

It is suggested by this study that there is a need for vigorous educational efforts, especially among rural women and the urban poor, since it is not easy for the educated mothers to change the views and values of the uneducated; that policy makers should aim at improving living conditions of the rural areas and the slum areas in the urban centers; and that more research concerning children and their problems and needs should be encouraged, in order to understand the different mechanisms affecting their survivorship and health.

The study on the impact of health education on the personal and environmental health status of rural dwellers, with rural communities around Zaria as a case study (Awosan, 1984)[6], seeks to ascertain the impact of health education specifically on the health knowledge, attitudes, and practices (KAP) of rural communities.

Data-collection involved interviews with heads of households and health personnel (i.e., community health officers and nursing officers). Besides, personal observation and inspection of the study areas, namely, Hunkuyi and Danbami-and-others[7], constituted part of the data-collection. Data were also collected from the health records of the primary Health Centre located in Hunkuyi.

In this study, health and illness (or diseases) are conceptualized as being socially-derived. This sociological standpoint tends to derive its source from the sociology of knowledge, which attempts to locate all knowledge in its social context. Thus, ideas, if any, commonly accepted in principle, but not always, or at all, carried out in practice are most likely to stand the chance of being brought into a much clearer stream of understanding.

It is revealed by the findings of this study that the level of personal hygiene, as depicted by the source of food preparation and chances of contamination during dry season, is low both in Hunkuyi and Danbami-and-others, since the bulk of the people (81.3% and 90.7% respectively) do prepare food in the open air. Consequently, the chances of contamination are apparent as well as grave implications for the health of the rural dwellers.

Similarly, food preparation in Hunkuyi and Danbami-and-others during rainy season exhibits about the same pattern as that obtaining during dry season. The only glaring change in the pattern of food preparation exhibited in both communities is that, with the change of weather from dry season to rainy season, 'cooking in the open air' *ipso facto* gives way to 'cooking inside kitchen'. The connection between seasonal variability and source of food preparation is, therefore, established.

It is also revealed that, regarding human fecal matter disposal pattern in both Hunkuyi and Danbami-and-others, the use of pit latrine (96.7% and 99.3% respectively) is prevalent, thus portraying the rural dwellers as observing basic health rules at least at the village level. Nevertheless, the observation and inspection adopted by this study reveal that dwellers in both communities do defecate indiscriminately in nearby bush, while moving from one "street" to another. They may have been dissuaded by the prevailing purdah system from using pit latrines outside of their own homes.

Another finding is that the dominant characteristic of refuse disposal in both Hunkuyi and Danbami-and-others is that the bulk of the respondents (77.3% and 82% respectively) burn refuse near houses. One important point involved here is that as few as only 4% and 10% of the respondents in Hunkuyi and Danbami-and-others respectively use refuse as compost. Thus, the bulk of the dwellers in these rural communities dispose refuse in such a way that the disposal pattern adopted constitutes a menace to proper environmental sanitation.

Further, the higher level of formal education in Hunkuyi (3.3% are literate with one to eight years of schooling, as against 2% in Danbami-and-others)[8] seems not to have made positive impact on the rural dwellers in this village. The findings themselves do not reveal difference between the health KAP of the Hunkuyi people and those of their counterparts in Danbami-and-others, even though the village of the former is characterized by availability of health education facilities and that of the latter is not. The basic import here is that it is not enough merely to focus on formal education or health education alone as far as human health is concerned. Other intervening variables are, therefore, called for. These are sociocultural variables, as is evident in the purdah system referred to above, and socioeconomic variable, which is evident in the fact that the levels of income (in Nigerian currency) of both Hunkuyi and Danbami-and-others are low (1,145 naira and 898 naira per annum respectively)[9]. Clearly, this tends to indicate that the inability of the dwellers of both communities to own private wells rather than public wells, normally unhygienic, can be attributed to this index of low socioeconomic status.

It is, moreover, revealed that there exists differential access to health facilities between the adults and children in Danbami-and-others, since the latter are unable to trek long distance. Also, the help-seeking behavior of the rural dwellers in both communities is such that these people tend to shuttle from one source of treatment to the other and seem to exhibit similar use of multiple source of treatment for a simple illness.

Regarding the health education program itself, this study reveals inadequate or, in some cases, unavailability of equipment, lack of incentives to community health personnel, and poor staff development program.

On the whole, the findings of this study reveal, contrary to expectation, that there are no appreciable inter-village disparities as far as the KAP of the rural dwellers in both communities under investigation are concerned—a situation out of context with the process of attaining the target set by the Alma-Ata declaration of the World Health Organization, viz., "Health for all by the year 2,000". Precisely, then, the health status of the people is at risk.

This study recommends that adequate equipment be provided in primary health centers; that drug research units in some of our universities should intensify their efforts, while more of such units should be established; and that our local medical resources in the indigenous healing aspect of medication as well as human resources be tapped, with a view to integrating the indigenous system with the Western system. Also, the career structure of community health personnel should be reviewed and these personnel be paid 'bush' allowance.

An alternative operational program—easily a potentially acceptable simple program of action suitable at the village level—is also recommended by this study. This, in the main, involves a village health board with a coordination and research unit as well as the primary health center. All of these together with other groups of an external dimension (namely, teaching/full-fledged hospital, health institution, University's agricultural extension services institution and state ministry of education) will, in the process of agricultural production and rural life, use their expertise in their various fields to bring about an improvement upon the KAP of the people and upon their appalling health conditions, always stressing that utilization of health facilities is their inalienable right and not a privilege. The rural dwellers, themselves, backed up with the efforts of a village health committee (composed of elders, headmasters, teachers, etc.) and youth club will be motivated and will get involved accordingly.

Thus, the rural dwellers will develop an attitude toward shaking off the conflict between lack of health education and themselves in their poor health status. And, since this conflict stems directly from another, but more fundamental conflict—the structural conflict in the Nigerian society on account of its capitalist socioeconomic formation, which tends to favor the tiny minority to the total neglect of the overwhelming majority of Nigerians—that more fundamental, structural conflict will correspondingly be shaken off or, at least, will begin to crumble or will be weakened.

It is also recommended that a study, hopefully to improve upon the present more or less pioneering study, be conducted in the context of a distinctly specified period, to make for an adequate scope for the evaluation of health education. Furthermore, it is recommended that an interdisciplinary research into the chemical constituents of local medicinal plants by scholars in pharmacognosy, botany, chemistry, etc., be conducted, focusing particularly on plants with enough antisickling activity to prevent disease from escalating into a more serious extent or to prevent disease from getting a foot-hold on human body.

On a general plane, prevention is very significant. Little wonder, then, that this was the point being driven home when Adesuyi (1970,) asserted:

> Most of the morbidity and mortality in our community are due to communicable diseases, most of which can be prevented or readily treated, such as malaria, dysenteries, pneumonia, tetanus, tuberculosis, cholera and others.

Indeed, the popular saying "prevention is better than cure" is enough to expose the wanton nature of curative medicine in contradistinction to preventive medicine. And prevention is even cheaper than cure when considered within the economic context of cost-and-benefit analysis.

Nutritional status and socioeconomic background, with the under-five children attending ABU Teaching Hospital, Wusasa Hospital, Kofan Gaya Hospital, Tudun-Wada Underfive Clinics, Government Health Office and ABU Sick Bay, Samaru, all in Zaria, as a case study (Ujiri, 1985)[10] is a research involving anthropometric measurements of children and interviews on their socioeconomic background as well as dietary practices and attitudes of their parents. This research comes up with the findings that the majority of the malnourished children are underweight, compared to the normal children who are heavier, thus confirming the earlier work of Waterlow (1978), who observed that protein calorie malnutrition causes low weight for age and height, and also causes stunting. Besides, acquisition of primary education by parents does not seem to have advantageously affected the nutritional status of children. Acquisition of secondary and/or post-secondary education by parents, however, does. Better health and feeding knowledge and, better still, good jobs with adequate remuneration stand these parents in correspondingly better stead.

Other findings are that 55.6% of children given eggs occasionally are malnourished, as against 44.4% of normal children. Occasional giving of eggs aside, it is possible that the normal children have other sources of nutrients, not within the reach of the malnourished ones. 59.7% of mothers who give bones, skin, or intestine to their children are those children that are malnourished, as against 40.3%, who give flesh to their children and whose children are, consequently, normal, for, nutritionally, flesh or skeletal muscle contains more nutrients than intestine, bones, or skin.

Further, the incidence of malnutrition is lower among those having two meals per day than those having three, with the plausible reason that the quality of the meals had by the latter might be low or inferior. The incidence of malnutrition is high among children of rural dwellers, polygynous families, uneducated families, petty traders, and low-income earners.

It is recommended that nutritional education be given to all mothers, that family planning be encouraged and that the Zaria local government should encourage mothers to breast feed their babies up to one and a half years or two years, discouraging bottle feeding as much as possible, except on medical grounds.

Needless to say, the above recommendations seek to raise the health status of infants and children, who, according to Essien (1981), are the most susceptible groups to another disease—gastroenteritis—in nearby Malumfashi town. Likewise, they are the most vulnerable groups to malnutrition wherever they are found, given their infancy and childhood.

The study on traditional birth attendants in Zaria, with Jama'a and Koraye villages as a case study (Alti-Mu'azu, 1985)[11] focuses on traditional birth attendants, their clients, and their services, highlighting the implications which the accompanying interaction between these two groups and the interaction between each of them and Western medical professionals have for the health care delivery system in Nigeria.

This study utilizes interviews, both formal and informal, with traditional birth attendants (TBA's) and their clients, precisely those of child-bearing age. All women of child-bearing age in a selected household were, contrary to the original plan, interviewed. For it was originally planned to utilize drawing of lots, whereby any woman in a polygamous household and drawing positive (+) would be interviewed, while any woman in a monogamous household would just be interviewed. This original plan was dropped after the first few interviews. For respondents (co-wives) left out of the interviews started complaining and, consequently, made those interviewed suspicious and uncooperative, interrupting the interviews, just to show their displeasure at being excluded. Happily, interviewing every woman in a selected household, as a result of this interruption, turned out to enrich the data.

The findings of this study reveal that TBA's have high regard for the professional ability of modern medical doctors, particularly regarding obstetric case techniques, stressing, that, by virtue of the educational attainment of the latter, they are assistants to them. This is evidenced by the ability of the modern medical practitioners to successfully manage such child birth complications as hemorrhages, which, according to the TBA's, are referred by them to the hospital.

Following from these findings are others—seven of the TBA's indicate their willingness to undergo training in modern obstetric care, to be more efficient, while three favor such a modern training, with the proviso that this is done right in their own village and not in the hospital. Four do not favor undergoing such training on advanced age grounds, while the remaining one declines answering the question. The modern medical practitioners, according to the TBA's, do demonstrate their professional expertise in surgical operation (cesarean section, i.e., the delivery of a baby by making incision through the abdomen walls and uterus), in most childbirth complications, in the detection of antenatal problems, in the correction of the body's position, in the dispensation of effective medicines, and in effective antenatal care services. Though incapable of teaching modern doctors, the TBA's believe they are better than the former in squatting during childbirth, in waiting for the placenta to be born before cutting the cord, in washing babies thoroughly, in treating the cord area properly and in preparing as well as disposing the placenta.

Furthermore, as is the case with other Nigerian TBA's, this study reveals that the clients (pregnant women) on the one hand and the modern doctors and nurses in the hospital on the other are heterophilous with each other, i.e., the clients do not speak the same language as the medical doctors and nurses and do not share the same kind of educational experience, background, household organization, and marital status.[12] The doctors are mostly men, and some women complain about the hostility of nurses to them. By contrast, the TBA's have sympathy for their patients and, at that, in an environment not as depersonalizing as that of the hospital. In other words, the TBA's are homophilous with their clients: they both have the same attributes. Hence, even though they attend antenatal clinic and acknowledge the superiority of modern obstetric services, the patients prefer home delivery to hospital delivery. Understandably, therefore, these women are not against the utilization of obstetric services, but their own indigenous childbirth practices and beliefs run counter to the organization of, and practice in, the Western-type hospital, particularly regarding childbirth.

This study recommends that a TBA be employed in the maternity ward of the hospital for the purpose of disposing the placenta in an acceptable manner, using a separate piece of land. Also, TBA's interested in modern obstetric care should be trained, to minimize congestion in the hospital and harms sometimes caused to both the mother and child through ignorance. Such trained TBA's may be of immense value, particularly now that, due to economic crisis, hospital fees are being introduced in government hospitals. The government should integrate traditional healers and midwives into the health care system. In order to obtain crude birthrate and maternal mortality data, it is further recommended that the illiterate TBA in the village be given two tins, white and red, and that she drops in the white tin a pebble for every child of her client(s) delivered and, in the red, a bead or even a stone for every mother who dies during childbirth. An official from the health department can then check the tins every three or six months, recording the quantity of the contents therein. Moreover, the TBA's should be supervised and training conducted in the dominant language of the area concerned, with medical personnel respecting rather than belittling the TBA's, and a sociologist advising the medical personnel, while the government awards national honors to outstanding trained TBA's as well as adopts other measures in addition to these, in order to provide health care services for the people, particularly the majority of them in the rural area.

For future endeavor, investigation, involving interviews with husbands of the TBA's regarding their opinions on childbirth, is recommended.

The study by Kyom (1988)[13] focuses on the psychosocial consequences of urological diseases with particular reference to urethra stricture in the Urology Unit of Ahmadu Bello University Teaching Hospital. Urethra stricture is a universal urological condition which involves inability to pass urine due to a blockade in the urethra, the channel that conveys urine from the bladder to the penis for discharge. Catheter—an artificial tube into which urine flows and then emptied by the patients—is used to solve this medical problem. Respondents attribute the disease to various causes which include traumatic experiences, venereal infection, congenital malfunction, and diets.

Since their medical condition forces them to use catheter, each of the patients assumes an odd appearance and, in order to conceal the catheter, wears loose attire, which is a normal type of attire. This coping strategy rhymes up with Erving Goffman's dramaturgical perspective—that of likening social interaction to a drama. It involves preparing oneself backstage and then go on to present oneself as if onstage, in order to impress others with whom one interacts. In other words, one makes what is not as though it were! According to Goffman, no human behavior emanates from instinct or habit. It is all a presentation!

However, the findings of the study reveal that people, particularly wives, other family members, and close friends of the patients get to know about their medical condition, with some of them disseminating the information by gossiping. Another category of people who know about it are those with whom the victims travel on public buses during long-distance journeys, since urine accumulates in the catheter and there is no chance to empty it. Besides, the findings reveal that the conditions of the patients make them have a negative self-image, given the divorce experienced by them, social distance generally, and their inability to continue to engage in their regular occupations (e.g., motor mechanic, farming, etc.) and even leisure. This fits in with Charles Horton Cooley's (1964) the "Looking-Glass Self" concept, whose three components are how we think our behavior appears to others; how we think others judge our behavior; and how we feel about, or react to, the way others judge us, a combination of which makes us come up with our overall self-image.

To the medical doctors, who treated the patients, the use of catheter is not a problem. However, the social distance experienced by the patients at the hands of other members of their society makes them feel that the use of catheter is certainly fraught with a hug problem.

The study recommends, among others, that medical doctors be made aware to take into consideration not only the medical aspect of patients' conditions, but also their psychosocial conditions, since catheter constitutes a negative informer to non-users.

## Endnotes

[1] It is made quite clear, however, that "the inclusion of a name in the lists of proposed international nonproprietary names does not imply any recommendation for the use of the substance in medicine or pharmacy" (*Ibid.*). This is a pointer to the fact that the importance of further research and verification cannot be overemphasized. More important, this is a way of making a non-committal statement.

[2] This is a Master's thesis.

[3] This is a Master's thesis.

[4] This is a Master's thesis.

[5] *Tuwo* is a food, locally prepared from guinea-corn or maize powder.

[6] This is a Master's thesis.

[7] For convenience's sake, 'Danbami-and-others' is used in this study to mean villages and hamlets without health education facilities, as distinct from Hunkuyi with health education facilities. 'Danbami-and-others' is made up of Danbami, Kwa-Kwaren-Manu, Mararraba, Zabi, Jaja Baba, Unguwar Maikudan, Unguwar Dufadufa, Unguwar Mallam Bello and Unguwar Doka. Since these villages and hamlets are similarly characterized by unavailability of health education facilities, they are regarded as the same and one community, and referred to simply as 'Danbami-and-others', while Hunkuyi (with health education facilities) is regarded as another community.

[8] These findings do not tally with those of a study conducted by Caldwell (1979) in both new and old Ibadan, that the child mortality of a woman with only primary education was 30% lower than that of a woman with no formal education. Perhaps this is attributable to the fact that both new and old Ibadan are parts of an urban center, as distinct from a rural area, which Hunkuyi and Danbami-and-others are.

[9] Income per annum is calculated on the basis of guinea-corn sold per bag by the rural dwellers, who are predominantly farmers, since it is extremely difficult, if not virtually impossible, to obtain an accurate income. For a typical farmer loses no time in either refusing to declare his actual income or distorting it, for fear of its being used as a basis for personal income tax assessment, because tax paid is not recouped by self-seeking political leaders into bettering the socioeconomic condition of taxpayers.

[10] This is a Master's thesis.

[11] This is a Master's thesis.

[12] Heterophilous and homophilous are adjectives of nouns heterophily and homophily respectively. By heterophily is meant the degree to which pairs of individuals who interact differ in certain attributes (Sargent, 1982). Homophily refers to the degree to which pairs of individuals interacting are similar in certain attributes (*Ibid.*).

[13] This is a Master's thesis.

## DISCUSSION QUESTIONS/EXERCISES AND ESSAYS

1. What is the practical significance of the interplay of clinical and sociocultural factors?

2. Explain the meaning that medicine has come to have now, as distinct from the traditional English meaning of the art of healing.

3. What is the methodology used by medical sociology?

4. What is the effect of the pharmacy law of 1966 in Nigeria?

5. Briefly compare the rural health care services in China and Cuba with those in Nigeria.

6. Come up with a critique of the differential treatment accorded patients at University College Hospital, Ibadan.

7. Discuss improvement made by traditional healers and the areas in which they are more competent than Western doctors.

8. What are the rationales for integrating traditional medicine into Western medicine?

9. Examine the factors to which the Kilba attribute stigmatized diseases.

10. Enumerate the sociodemographic correlates of mental illness at the Kaduna Psychiatric Hospital.

11. Examine the effect of the education of the mother on infant and child mortality.

12. What is sociology of knowledge?

13. Discuss the intervening variables identified in the study in Hunkuyi and Danbami-and-others.

14. What is the target set by the Alma-Ata declaration of the World Health Organization?

15. Discuss the relationship between nutritional status and socioeconomic background.

16. Compare Traditional Birth Attendants (TBA's) with Western doctors and nurses. Discuss your experience with either or both of these categories of health providers in America and/or other parts of the world.

17. Explain the recommendation for the integration of traditional healers and midwives into Western health care system. At the same time, take into account your answer to question number 8.

18. Discuss the connection between Erving Goffman's dramaturgical perspective and psychosocial consequences of urological disease.

# ·VI·

# POLITICAL SOCIOLOGY AND RURAL DEVELOPMENT/RURAL SOCIOLOGY

**Political Sociology**
(a)  Political Sociology (generally)
(b)  Decolonization
(c)  The Military

As is evident from the way in which this subdiscipline has been further divided into three areas of study (political sociology, decolonization, and the military), it has gradually metamorphosed in light of the social realities of our times.

Political sociology studies the political structure of a given society. The sociopolitical processes that go on within this political structure are focused upon. As is the case with some other fields of sociological studies, some of the studies in political sociology overlap with other subdisciplines of sociology. These include sociology of mass communications, economy and society, and demography.

Of great significance to national unity and, therefore, political stability is the study on the integration of the lbo in Kano after the Nigerian civil war[1] (Ogbogu, 1973). This study observes, *inter alia,* that, even though it is difficult to make any conclusive statements or claims about the degree of their integration, the Hausa and lbo are now at "a well-advanced stage." This is particularly so when these two ethnic groups are compared to what they used to be in the pre-civil-war period.

The research into the effect of Kwara State 1968 local government reforms on Ilorin Division (Alade, 1973) comes up with findings portraying change from traditional to modern way of local government, whilst the elite, in an attempt to protect and maintain the *status quo,* and the citizens, due to ignorance, through no fault of theirs, are averse to a change.

This study observes that the relationship between Ilorin town and the rural areas can be considered within the context of Gunder Frank's metropolis and satellite relationship. For in terms of divisional administration, Ilorin serves as the source of policies over the rural areas, thereby occupying a position to exploit the surrounding rural districts.

This study takes cognizance of the political and economic interests of three groups in the division. First, the traditional elite who dislike the reforms which strip them of their erstwhile power. Second, the Native Authority Administrative Officers, employed because of their educational achievement and also because of kinship ties between many of them and the emir or the other members of the ruling traditional group; hence the change is viewed in the same light as is viewed by the ruling elite. Third, the *mekunnu* (or, put alternatively, *talaka*), meaning the poor or the masses, are averse to the change because, being illiterates and far away from the center of political power, do not understand the intricate nature of the whole set-up. And to them, any reform not entailing personal/physical participation by the common man serves no useful purpose.

It is further revealed by the study that gift-giving from the citizens to the rulers still exists, but in a different form: it is no longer compulsory, but voluntary.

It should be noted that, traditionally, the African revels in giving gifts but that "with changing political orientation as a result of modernization, gifts assumed another role (Utomi, 1978)." This sort of gifts has been described as 'political gifts', traced to white District Officers (DO's) who were at the receiving end during the colonial period, while Nigerians who took over from the DO's followed in the footsteps of the former. This has far-reaching effects on political stability in Nigeria. As Utomi epitomizes the ugly political scene:

> From this rather primitive stage, political exigencies evolved in the gift-giving of a new era. This reign of black district officer had begun. These new black "white men" went on extensive tours and at each stop, the villagers would present their…presents, sometimes brought out of heavy levies on members of the local community, including food stuff, items of clothing and traditional treasures like carvings or metal works.
>
> The motive behind these gifts were expected political favors the District Officer could cause…
>
> This aggravated the soporific effect of power on the earliest Nigerians to taste it. To a large extent *it became one of the greatly cherished spoils of office that made it difficult for the first generation of Nigerian leaders to leave* office. Relinquishing power became synonymous with abandoning the good things of life. (Emphasis added.)

"Continuity, conflict and change in Igala political system" (Braimah, 1973) constitutes a study focusing on a political system studied against its old and contemporary backgrounds, which tend to open the floodgate to continuity amidst conflict and change within the context of the interests, values, attitudes, and behaviors of the various groups in the Igala social structure.

This study traces the origin of British local administration to 1927, even though the colonialists had been in Igala land as early as 1902. It also reveals that economic 'development' leads to an appreciable change in the system of stratification prevailing in Igala land. Indigenous, religious rituals and festivals have been abolished following the introduction and establishment of Christianity and Islam and the structure and beliefs on which the royal rule was built are consequently weakened. Originally, members of the royal class were wealthier than those of the commoners' class. But, following the imposition of taxation in 1927, the colonial government introduced wage labor and cash farming, to enable people to pay taxes, and only the commoners chose to work, while the royalists considered it disrespectful to engage in these occupations. By 1940, this phenomenon had reversed the economic structure, placing some non-royalists (the commoners) at the top of the economic strata, the erstwhile exclusive preserve of the royalists. Consequently, the former easily gained political positions and membership of the local councils and, with the emergence of the educated as well as economic elite, each locality demanded the appointment of District Heads from among their own elite, instead of one normally sent from Idah, the administrative headquarters. This demand continued to be actively expressed through partisan political activities until the creation of states. Meanwhile, the traditional ruler, Ameh Oboni, was dethroned in 1956, and the Native Authority gave priority to community welfare over law and order, while simultaneously increasing taxes and concentrating development at Idah.

The nation-wide local authority reforms came in handy. For on December 17, 1968, the government announced the reforms, whereby the former Igala Division was divided into three separate local authority units in line with the structures and welfare program of the federal government, with a view to bringing the government to the people.

This study claims that its findings run counter to the hypothesis of Evans-Pritchard and Fortes (1940) that 'people will over-throw a bad king but not the kingship.' As can be seen from the foregoing, both were overthrown in the Igala society. Indeed, the dethronement of Ameh Oboni in 1956 and the coincidence of the people's long protest with the reforms, culminating in the split of the kingdom in 1968, are hallmarks of the double overthrow. The people have since been obliged to work physically and financially hard toward the development of their respective local authority areas rather than for an amorphous or a remote unit.

The study on title succession from the perspectives of structure and functions, with Kabba District (Owe) as a case study (Gefu, 1977) focuses on the underlying principles of the traditional title system in the context of the social structure existing before the indirect rule.

Interviews were held with respondent with the use of a tape-recorder, which helped with recalling any point made, especially minute details, which might otherwise have gone unrecorded for fear of risking interruption of the natural flow of the conversation. On the completion of each interview, some part of the discussion was played back, often leading to a further interview between the respondent and the investigator.

This study comes up with the findings that the traditional title system was fairly rigid: people were engaged in economic activities, affording a living at the subsistence level; the social structure and its underlying religious structure were rigid, with the ranking of the title-holders being clear-cut and their functions well defined along with the religious obligations and practices; the interdependence of every member of the community did not allow for the independence of any section of the community from the rest of the society; and, consequently, the title institution was in a state of complete harmony with the social structure, thereby maintaining balance.

Nevertheless, such external factors, introduced together with indirect rule, as the monetization and the resultant commercialization of the economy, according to this study, fetched the people (predominantly farmers) a fairly "heavy purse" with which they could, unlike hitherto, afford to take ('buy') titles. The would-be title-holders outnumbered the existing titles and so limitless numbers of offices were created, with title-holders turning out to have little or no leadership qualities and the title institution being dominated by the 'haves' to the chagrin of the 'have-nots', despite their possession of leadership qualities.

Following the introduction of indirect rule, leadership structure and the allocation of authority changed, with power now coming from above and advice from the masses no longer flowing up the system, as was the case in the traditional system. One of the clans—Ilajo clan—attempted to 'usurp' the traditional rulership, namely, *Obaroship,* while members of other clans objected, culminating in a dispute and the 'intervention' of the external body (based on indirect rule) within which the traditional system becomes a subsystem.

This study concludes that, since we can no longer think solely in terms of lineages, age sets, and social groupings, appropriate to a traditional economy and society, and with the increasing changing principles of governance in the local community and equally changing economic system, both being swept up into the nationalization process of a modern industrializing country, it would appear that the traditional title system will cease to function, unless it is drastically changed in tune with the new set-ups.

The research into reform and power in the Nigerian local government system, with, as a case study, the Habe ruling dynasty 1900-1976 (Bawa, 1977)[2] examines the process of political development in the northern part of Nigeria from the period prior to the indirect rule, the periods of civilian rule, and the military regime.

The data collected and utilized were mainly archival, oral (historical) testimonies, ethnographic material, and historical as well as political documents, supplemented by intensive interviews. The National Archives in Kaduna served as a source of data-collection. Relevant government gazettes, colonial political memoranda, and historical, economic, political, and quarterly journals of administration were used. One relevant analytical approach adopted by this study is the concept of social networks[3], itself a theoretical framework of exchange and communication.

This study comes up with the findings that the Habe claims that the chiefdom of Abuja land had formed the south west part of the ancient Zazzau Empire, and that these chiefdoms occupied vassal status *vis-a-*vis Zazzau (i.e., present-day Zaria).

Using the work of Yahaya (1975), this study makes it clear that the traditional political authorities and institutions in the Northern Emirates of Nigeria were 'developed' into units of Local Government from the early days of British administration, that they had been based on emirs and chiefs and that by the end of the Second World War, they had evolved into 'powerful' political institutions and forces, initially called Native Authorities. Further, the administrative acumen of the traditional rulers is clarified—that much of the protectorate of Northern Nigeria established in 1900 by Lord Lugard, the first High Commissioner, was ruled by powerful chiefs, known as Emirs. Since the Emirs had a highly developed system of administration, he recognized their authority and retained them as rulers rather than abolish them. The Habe dynasty, being a part of the northern area of Nigeria, was a part of this highly developed system of administration.

Having situated the traditional political authority of Abuja Emirate within the context of the social networks concept, this study reveals that Lord Lugard utilized social connections to maintain his status, power, and influence, successive local government reforms, apparently aimed at reducing his power, notwithstanding. Implicit in the relationship between the traditional ruler and his subjects is the principle of reciprocity, whereby whilst the latter conform to the norms and values of society and remain loyal to the former, deserving subjects are rewarded with chieftaincy title.

Concerning the position and future of the traditional political authorities generally, this study, in light of the foregoing, asserts, as did Tugbiyele (1965), that it is wrong to say that the traditional political institution is no longer desirable, emphasizing that emirs and chiefs are individual personalities around whom society is 'woven'. Similarly, the concept of *sarki,* associated with indigenous, supernatural power, is indicative of the fact that our traditional political institution was a symbol of leadership and authority for over a thousand years before colonization, but that, strictly speaking, its existence has continued to be on the basis of religion and custom of the people.

This study argues that the merger, in February, 1966, of the Native Authority Police Force and the Native Authority Courts (hitherto within the jurisdiction of emirs) could be viewed only as a removal of formal powers vested in the chieftaincy institution by the colonial administration. For, after all, emirs and chiefs had maintained perfect peace among their subjects using the political mechanism of the chieftaincy institution for over a thousand years in the pre-colonial period.

It is suggested that before the central government can successfully remove the chieftaincy institution from the political processes of Nigeria, an alternative administrative set-up, equally reflecting the different cultural backgrounds of our people, has to be provided. Precisely, the only alternative adequate administrative system is one in which political processes emphasize total political and social mobilization of the citizens, thereby discarding the present situation in which only the elite largely wield political power to the chagrin of the majority, consequently rendered apathetic.

The study on the social interpretation of the Satiru revolt of C. 1894—1906 in Sokoto Province (Mohammed, 1983)[4] seeks to contribute to the existing knowledge of a famous but fundamentally obscure event in the political sociology of Sokoto in particular and Nigeria in general, and to offer new explanations.

This study utilizes the historical materialist and dialectical framework on account of its advantages over other approaches, which advantages pave the way for new, convincing explanations.

Data-collection involved interviews with people mainly in the immediate geographical area around the old, albeit now unoccupied, settlement of Satiru and other parts of Sokoto State. Some of the interviews were done with the aid of tape-recorder and members of both classes of the rich and the poor were interviewed. Songs and poems were collected from the informants and from the archives. Data collection also involved visits to the Nigerian National Archives, Kaduna; Arewa House, Kaduna; Nigerian Army Museum, Zaria; the Northern History Research Scheme Library, ABU; the Sokoto State History Bureau; and the Department of History at the University of Niamey in the Republic of Niger.

This study thoroughly criticizes the existing interpretations of the Satiru revolt offered by some authors. It criticizes Mani's (1970) interpretation for attempting to present the revolt merely as an inter-ethnic war; Al-Hajj's (1973) for seeing the revolt within the colonial context and as a religious conflict between Muslims and Christians; Ukpabi's (1976) for failing to explain the revolt within the prevailing social structure from a historical perspective; Adeleye's (1972) for viewing the revolt mainly from religious standpoint and as a fight to protect the Sokoto Caliphate from imminent destruction; and Tahir's (1975) for offering an explanation, not only confusing, but also contradictory, and, therefore, inadequate. Overall, the various authors offer their explanations exclusively within the context of colonialism and the perspectives from which they view the revolt are ahistorical, unscientific, undialectical, and inadequate.

The new explanation of the Satiru revolt offered by this study is that it is an uprising of peasants and slaves initially against the Sokoto aristocracy and later against the British colonial rule, with a view to overthrowing the latter. And a number of indications discernible in the next few paragraphs are as much plausible as they are convincing.

The word *Satiru* can be interpreted as a sort of fortress (or haven), protected from the exactions of the ruling class. For the word *Satiru* is a noun, with its root being *Satara*, itself a verb, meaning "To cover, veil, to hide, conceal, to disguise, to shield, guard, protect" (Cowan, 1961, p.397).

The Satiru community was established in the pre-colonial period. Although historical records seem to have given prominence to Mallam Mai Kaho, having been popularly referred to as the 'headman' of Satiru, yet this study's oral sources tend to present a different picture. For, as is customary for most of the towns and cities of Hausaland which have a praise-song *(Kirari)* that often identifies the founder of a given town or city, there is a praise-song for Satiru, which clearly portrays Mallam Siba as the founder of Satiru.

From all indications, Satiru was a politically autonomous community, situated very close (twenty kilometers south of Sokoto) to the seat of the caliphate—Sokoto—unlike other rebellious communities which were situated merely on the periphery.

The leaders of the Satirawa (i.e., people of Satiru) used Mahdist ideology (i.e., a kind of religious ideology) as a weapon of their struggle, itself a practical expression of their objective to seize political power in a revolutionary and forward-looking manner. This is in sharp contrast to most peasant revolts, merely tending to be reformist and backward-looking, sequel to their objective to merely make economic demands. And, what is more, women, too, were in the struggle.

After most of the Satirawa had been killed at the battle, following heroic, albeit unsuccessful, resistance against the combined British and native, aristocracy-sponsored troops and with a few British having suffered casualties, the remaining (surviving) Satirawa were driven from Satiru and pursued, leaving the community completely annihilated. Not all the Satirawa leaders were killed at the battle: those that were not killed were publicly executed later in Sokoto market.

The significance of the revolt, therefore, was that it was a peasant struggle against the aristocracy and British imperialism. It is revealed that the Satirawa were also involved in acts of banditry, violently burning and looting neighboring peasant communities not in support of them. (This is a tactical mistake, providing justification for their being condemned by opponents.)

Interestingly, the sort of tactical mistake just highlighted is a trend, which, according to this study, seems to be typical of peasant movements even in contemporary Nigeria, e.g., the Maitatsine riots of December 1980 in Kano and the Bulumkutu riots in 1982 in Maiduguri, whereby displaced peasants resorted to attacking innocent workers and petty traders instead of soliciting their support.

This study concludes that, since colonialism, together with its capitalist mode of production and amalgamation of Nigeria in 1914, is instrumental in the transformation of the erstwhile Sokoto Caliphate and other kingdoms and societies into what Nigeria is today, the ideology of Mahdism will be inadequate for our emancipation.

Marxism-Leninism, as a new ideology, is, therefore, suggested together with the necessity for a vanguard party of the working class offered by Lenin (1964). And it is opined that the future generations and history will condemn intellectuals failing to raise the political consciousness of all oppressed groups including women. Indeed, they should expose the hollowness of bourgeois ideology and propagate the proletarian ideology. And, whilst the Satirawa will forever remain a shining example, the struggle continues.

## (b) Decolonization

Sociology of decolonization is concerned with the interaction between political and other social variables. Its analytical tools are directed towards colonialism and the techniques and strategies employed in the process of decolonization. The application of these techniques and strategies varies from one country to another. Correspondingly, the resultant variability experienced by the countries concerned tend to color the political and socioeconomic realities of their post-decolonization period. This basically explains, as is indicated in the opening paragraph of this chapter, that political sociology has gradually metamorphosed in the light of the social realities of our times.

So far, only a few research studies, which utilize library source of data collection, have been conducted exclusively in this sub-field. Its relative novelty accounts for this paucity. Of course, it was just being developed by Patrick F. Wilmot, whom, according to Omafume Onoge (1983), "we would single out for his pioneering scholarship which has made possible the founding of a Sociology of Decolonization." Onoge, himself, had previously been writing on decolonization.

The studies on the theory and practice of national liberation in Nigeria and Mozambique (Ado, 1980) and on decolonization in Angola and Uganda (Danmallam, 1981) make comparative analyses of the processes of decolonization, with a view to identifying the processes which usher in a genuine and meaningful independence. The studies make it quite clear that when the liberation/decolonization struggle is elitist, the instrumentality employed is peaceful negotiation. When, however, it is non-elitist, the instrumentality is large-scale violence. Lack of a sound ideology on the part of African liberation movements is emphasized. This disturbing situation is inimical to meaningful decolonization.

### (c) The Military

This sub-field has, as its main focus, the role of the military as a professional group. However, the military is a professional group with a difference: it is an institution of warfare. Yet, in peacetime, the military has dramatically surfaced and is known for holding on to power for a long time, particularly in Africa. This situation has its very root specifically in the politicization of the military in Africa or, put differently, in the militarization of African politics.

While on the question of the militarization of African politics, it is important to note that the selfish attitude of African politicians (and, by inference, Nigerian politicians) on the attainment of independence serves as an unfailing invitation to the military to participate in politics. The parties within which these politicians function are fond of making empty promises to the electorates. Since they benefit maximally from the existing social order, structural re-organization of our society, based on a revolutionary approach, is none of their business. Besides, they see politics both as a career and an opportunity, having tasted power and realizing their low-level educational attainment. Hence, holding on perpetually to power, especially through incredibly massive election-rigging, is the order of the day as far as a given government in power is concerned. And the fact that the government controls power and the means of coercion tends to enhance the possibility of this, at least initially.

Worse still, even some Africans who, on account of their high-level educational attainment, should not be expected to regard politics as a career, turn out on the political arena not only to be political careerists, but also political opportunists of the most enlightened order. Precisely, in their capacity as hand-picked advisers to the government and as commissioners or ministers, they either 'misadvise' the government or engage in evil machinations with the government against the masses, even when the latter warn that the consequences of their policy and action do not augur well for the society. They choose to dismiss all fear of imminent doom for the economy of the nation. The motives behind the choice of this ignoble line of action are no doubt made quite clear in the assertion of Chukwudum (1981) that runs thus:

> We acquire knowledge mainly to place chains of diploma and degrees after our names for self-aggrandizement; and the certificates are used as stepping-stones for money or fame. These motives defeat the essence of knowledge which is the advancement of the human race and real enjoyment for the individual.

And, highlighting the ultimate end of knowledge, Chukwudum *(ibid.)* quotes the English philosopher Francis Bacon, who said:

> The greatest error of all is mistaking the knowledge; for some men covet knowledge out of natural curiosity and inquisitive and entertain the mind with delight; some for ornament and reputation; some for victory and contention; many for lucre and a livelihood; and few, for employing the divine gift of reason to the use and benefit of mankind.

Now that attention has been focused on the politicians and some academics that are hell-bent on holding on perpetually to power, it is important to know what the position of the military that is known for taking over the reins of government with a view to correcting the ugly situation really is. On the African continent, the military is not infallible. A classic example is provided in Nigeria by the Gowon regime, popularly believed, at least on a comparative basis, to have shown concern for the masses. This example was graphically epitomized in the words of a Nigerian social critic, Tai Solarin (1974). As he pungently and metaphorically committed his words to writing:

> The army came to power because the people wanted it in power. It is in the interest of the army itself that it should quit power when the people thought they have had its fill. An actor steps off the stage whilst the ovation from the audience is loudest. To wait for that ovation to peter out to nothingness before stepping off is, to put it the crude way, allowing the latrine fly to meet the bush toileting man yet toileting. Tafawa Balewa's government waited until it was forced out, Ironsi's government waited until it was shown the way out... Unless the military government has the courage to call it quit on January 14, 1976 [as promised earlier on by it], a chain of events might be set in motion... It would not be the end of our beginning; it would be the beginning of our end.

Since the Gowon regime continued holding on perpetually to the reins of the government of Nigeria for upwards of nine years, it was, true enough, overthrown, albeit in a bloodless *coup d'etat*, while Gowon was himself away in Kampala, Uganda. The Gowon regime is nonetheless generally regarded as one in which resources were not confined exclusively to the elite.

The study of "Civil-Military relations: the soldier's perspective" (Usman, 1977) is an inquiry, as the title clearly shows, into the relations between civilians and soldiers from the standpoint of soldiers.

This study utilizes interview method, involving soldiers in the Nigerian Army Depot, Zaria, and the Garrison Organization, Kaduna, both towns having had military establishments dating back to the early part of colonial era and having experienced co-existence of civilians with soldier after the Nigerian civil war.

An examination of the literature on civil-military relations by this study shows that the military is the same everywhere (with a few exceptions) and that relation between the army and the public is always very poor.

This study comes up with the findings that the rating of soldiering as an occupation is a determining factor in enlistment into the army. For the army provides secure employment and better chances of promotion and economic advancement *vis-a-vis* the civil service. Also, the relations between civilians and soldiers are relatively harmonious during military regime, since the latter, unlike during the civilian regime of the first republic, reside outside barracks—a situation in which they both live together, with the possibility of making friends and getting along well with each other. Nevertheless, conflict does frequently occur between civilians and soldiers. This friction would seem inevitable between the two parties. To borrow the words of de Tocqueville (1968), the soldier feels that he is disrespected and that "he occupies an inferior position and his wounded pride.... stimulates his taste for hostilities."

Another finding is that fights in clubs or hotels have been attributed to drunkenness and prostitution. Yet another finding is that when the soldier appears in uniform, the chances of his getting involved in a brawl are quite high. However, the civilian is endeared to the military profession on ceremonial occasions, which bring together the society, and on which the public ignores the uniform and usually get carried away by the pageantry characteristic of the parade, display, etc. Further, it is found that competition and antagonism exist between the higher ranks of the army on the one hand and the educated elite generally, civil servants and merchants/contractors on the other. However, the lower ranks identify and sympathize with the masses, members of whose class they, too, are, thus leading to the belief that they are like civilians or rather are laborers in uniform. Their attitude toward university students is negative, denoting jealousy on their part.

On the whole, it is concluded that the aggressive behavior of soldiers toward civilian is a direct reaction to the way civilians view and treat soldiers.

## Rural Development/Rural Sociology

Rural Development/Rural Sociology is obviously concerned with rural development. It focuses on the social structures of rural communities as well as on rural development strategies.

It is of great interdisciplinary significance that the studies undertaken in this field of Rural Development/Rural Sociology are intimately connected with those in the field of Development Studies.

The sociological, rural-oriented research studies undertaken focus primarily on the farmers, who are no more than the hewers of tree and drawers of water for the undeserved benefit of the elite. This situation, ugly as it is, has been most blatantly masked in the name of 'development' executed by the successive Nigerian, and some other African, governments.

Relationship between family size and land utilization for agricultural purposes (John, 1980) has been empirically crystallized. And Kamuru Station in Kachia Local Government Area of Kaduna State is the study area.

The findings of this study show a general tendency toward large families, which need not necessarily be conjugal families; ownership of farmlands by the whole production unit, with instances of members using some parts for individual purposes; growing of local food crops is accorded priority; and the existence of a hand-labor economy.

The study also undertakes a comparison of its findings with those of another study by Norman (1972) in a different setting, namely, in rural communities around Zaria. The comparison reveals glaring similarities. The glaring difference is that, while women in the Zaria rural communities play less significant roles in farming, their counterparts in Kamuru Station play glaring, significant roles.

An approach to the study of solutions offered to farmers, with the Lafia Agricultural Development Project (LADP) in Plateau State as a case study (Lobadungze, 1980), is a research whose findings reveal that only 8.3% of the farmers use the crop introduced by the project due to high resistance from LADP authorities, and that 85% of them receive no response regarding loans for which they have applied.

The findings also reveal that only 15% of the 'capitalist farmers' would want collectivization, presumably due to a strong feeling of individualism. Besides, farmers who lose their land as a result of the project are given no compensation, thus turning them to migrant job seekers or apprentices. This study recommends a labor-intensive technique.

The study on the potential mechanization of agriculture in Nigeria and the role of the peasantry, with some aspects of the Chad Basin Development Authority (Abba, 1980) as a case study, focuses mainly on the World Bank philosophy of raising the 'purchasing power' of the Nigerian peasant through an ideology of 'integrated rural development'.

The findings of this study reveal that a decline in the agricultural productivity in the basin of the Lake Chad is accelerated by the world system of imperialism. Since wheat (covering 60% of a ten-acre plot) and cotton (covering 20%)

are exported, while only rice (covering 50%) is for home consumption, the project is, in essence, intended to meet the food requirements of the advanced capitalist countries. This deplorable situation where more export crops are grown than crops for local consumption was highlighted by Olayide (1976) when he asserted that:

> The agricultural policy of Nigeria… has in general been skewed in favor of export in the belief that food production will take care of itself. This *laissez-faire* food policy has tended to progressively aggravate the problem of food production.

It has also been revealed by this study that the problem lies in the 'pattern' of mechanization envisaged, as outlined by the World Bank, rather than mechanization *per se*.

Moreover, this study recommends total 'structural shift', which, of course, is possible only in a revolutionary situation, and explains that it only makes an attempt at generating further studies rather than being an absolute documentation of the project.

The study on the socioeconomic impact of the 'Green Revolution' (Othman, 1981) demonstrates that the green revolution (as it obtains in Daudawa under Funtua Agricultural Development Project like in any other place) is an integral part of agricultural development project package in Nigeria. And it is an examination of the 'Green Revolution' as a solution to the problem of food-shortage and that of rural poverty.

According to the findings of this study, landless peasants increased from 44% (before the introduction of the Funtua Agricultural Development Project) to 73% (after the project was introduced in 1975). Farmers were turned to laborers, with no appreciable improvement in their standard of living.

The research into rural proletarianization, with the lake region in Mali as a case study (Balobo, 1981) portrays the peasants in another African country, where their sufferings have assumed staggering proportions. Two study areas are covered, namely, the industrial center, which is also the capital city (i.e., Bamako) and a group of seven lakes surveyed among the nineteen lakes constituting the 'lake region' in Mali, itself a semi-arid country.

This study is quite revealing of the fact that the entire farmers in the sample pay different kinds of taxes, namely, income tax, cattle tax, tax on revenue, 'petrol tax', and 'welcome tax'. The 'petrol tax' is given by the dwellers (the farmers) whenever an administrator pays a visit to the rural areas, paying for the petrol used by his car during the journey. The farmers also pay 'welcome tax' whenever a delegation of officials arrives. Other taxes are paid in addition to all of these.

The findings of this study also show that 84.87% of farmers interact among themselves, 64.10% with the rural agent and only 3.84% with the administration. This very low level of interaction with the government is vividly indicative of the extermination of the peasantry from decision-making process.

All this goes to confirm that the rural lake region (the periphery) is dependent upon Bamako (the center, that is, the metropolis), with the consequent neglect of the rural lake region. And this lopsided situation created by the Mali's national elite and the French elite is a direct reflection of the same pattern of dependency between Mali as a whole and its metropolis, France—a situation reflecting the dualist nature of the dependency paradigm.

Believing that it is imperative for 'development' to improve the lot of the masses and to enhance respect for human dignity, this study recommends inter alia, mental decolonization of the Malian elite and, on a more basic note, smashing of the world capitalist system.

The opticom farm system established in 1980 in Ogun State is the focus of another research into a strategy for solving the problem of food-shortage (Ogunkoya, 1984).

The word 'opticom' is a combination of two words—optimum and community. So, the opticom farm system is one whereby members of a community, occupying a particular territory, engage in productive and social activities for the optimum well-being of the populace. This system is an integrated approach to rural development, but one with a difference: it is also cooperative in nature. And cooperatives, as Igbozurike (1976), asserts:

> ...create the necessary atmosphere of trust which is a precondition for successful organization. In this way, governments and agriculture credit banks can advance loans, for when they insist on security (as the Federal Agricultural Bank rightly and understandably does) which individual farmers cannot offer, multi-purpose cooperatives can still get loans and other supplies such as transport and equipment.

This research study indicates that the principle behind the establishment of the opticom farm system is the development of rural areas, with a view to providing enough food for all, not only in Ogun State, but also in the country at large.

The findings reveal that pensioners, who join the opticom farm system merely to keep them busy and to exercise their body, constitute the majority of the opticom farmers. Furthermore, 25.3% females engage in farming. This proportion is nonetheless an improvement. For farming activities are usually associated with men, rather than with women, in the study area. Besides, there are accusation and counter-accusation between the farmers and the government: bureaucratic bottlenecks, the farmers say, constitute a barrier to their getting loans; inability on the part of the farmers to repay loan, the government argues, leads to unavailability of loanable funds. It is further revealed that some corrupt officials mismanage the funds, concentrating them in the hands of a few farmers. The objectives of the opticom farm system are, therefore, not achieved.

It is instructive that the findings of the foregoing research studies become more crystallized within the context of the following assertion of Igbozurike (1983):

...Our current agricultural policy and practice are reducing the mass of small-scale peasant producers to subsistence farmers, wage workers and gangs of the jobless walking the street of our urban areas. It is creating a class of landless peasantries of the Latin American kind. All these peasants form the majority. They are not just being neglected, they are being ejected from their farmlands in the name of large-scale agricultural development.

Given the findings of the research studies in both the fields of Development Studies and Rural Development/Rural Sociology, the common scapegoats are the impoverished, small-scale farmers, who, according to Igbozurike, constitute the yeomanry proper of Nigerian agriculture.

The research into agro-industrialism in the Greater Zaria (Agbonifo, 1974)[5] examines the introduction, and evaluates the effects, of dry-season tomato on river valley[6].

Regarding sampling, before a village was included, it had to have a comparative number of farmers not involved in the tomato project. This was necessary to allow for an evaluation of the socioeconomic impact of the project on rural life. This study utilized participant observation: the researcher was present and participated in some of the farm operations.

It is revealed by this study that the tomato project is not a success, since farmers have decided to sell their produce on the Zaria fresh food market instead of delivering all their produce to Cadbury. The data emanating from this study indicate that there exists a general dissatisfaction on the part of the change-agents, with the way the project is organized at the local level. For instance, on the one hand, plots and supplies from the change-agents are, through local leadership influence, not shared equitably by farmers, who in some cases are compelled to pay extra for project supplies. On the other hand, there exists as well dissatisfaction, on the part of the individual farmers, with the change-agents regarding supply of inputs and the inefficiency of the officers. Low yield sets in. Cumulatively, the poor farmers are led into taking advantage of the higher price on the fresh food markets, rather than delivering their produce to Cadbury.

An analysis of the situation in the entire villages—covering the previous dry season (1972-73)—provides evidence supporting the generalization that wherever and whenever the farmers are organized into the existing political structure, which is fundamentally instrumental in the above-mentioned dissatisfaction, delivery to Cadbury will tend to be low. Furthermore, the analysis reveals that a strong cohesiveness in the group of growers will tend to lead to high delivery to Cadbury, as is evident from the excellent case of Ungwan Talmuwa (one of the sample villages).

More important, further findings indicate that there exists a general resentment among farmers against being organized under the existing political system and, therefore, against the leadership of the political head of the village.

The recommendations by this study are, among others, that government and other change-agents should reconsider the efficacy of using political system, headed by traditional rulers, for economic undertaking; that farmers should be given the opportunity to organize themselves under a popular leader, and that field workers should be stationed in the smaller villages, with constant supervision by higher officers.

Regarding possible future direction of research in this and similar projects, it is suggested that a study primarily on the effectiveness or efficiency and on the actual productivity of various forms of organization and agro-industrial project be undertaken, thus extending research endeavors to such other agro-industrial projects as fish processing and groundnut processing, with direct linkages to the factories concerned.

The political economy of food dependency in Nigeria, with the Lafia Agricultural Development Project (LADP) Plateau State as a case study (Tukura, 1985)[7] is a study which attempts to ascertain the origin, nature, and causes of food dependency or food crisis in Nigeria.

This study reveals that there is a direct correlation between the introduction of the LADP and the phenomenon of land consolidation. For example, an overwhelming majority of the sample (i.e., 66%) constitute the class of small-scale farmers, 9% constitute the class of medium-scale farmers, while only 25% own land of 10 hectares and above. Worse still, whilst the dominant average land size is between 0.10 to 5.99 hectares, the average land-size for the class of large-scale farmers alone is 54.14 hectares. It is also revealed that prior to the LADP's introduction; farmers managed farms within the labor power of their households, using the hoe as the main farm technology and surpluses gained from farming to hire labor. However, the present large-scale land holdings imply that source of extra farm inputs and extra farm capital exists. And the LADP constitutes this source through the tractor services provided by its Tractor Hire Unit, and the capital through credit (both in cash and in kind) it provides. Consequently, the LADP has, as have other such projects of multinational corporations, fostered Nigeria's dependency on the technology of the Western capitalist countries. Consolidation of land itself has been privatized by the LADP in the hands of local exploiters—members of feudal aristocracy, ex-politicians, bureaucrats, and businessmen.

In order to arrest the creation of landed aristocracy and a landless and pauperized peasantry, it is recommended that land review policy be implemented and that, in order to achieve self-reliance, the LADP be transformed and based on local resources and on the creative energies of the peasantry.

The research into the political economy of rural development with the effects of the Funtua Agricultural Development Project (FADP) in Bakori District of Kaduna State as a case study (Kungwai, 1983)[8] focuses on the agrarian aspects of rural (under)development, with a view to identifying and understanding the real causes of rural underdevelopment.

This study utilizes the Marxist-Leninist theoretical political economy perspective, which differs fundamentally from the essentially static mode of analysis typical of the organic intellectuals of imperialism, who not only conceive of underdevelopment as a natural state of thing, but tend to reduce "the central task of the theory of development to answering the question 'how to spread capital-ism?' rather than 'how to transform fundamentally the underdeveloped econom-ics in favor of the masses?'" (Wambadia-Wamba, 1982).

Both formal and informal interviews were used during the course of this re-search. Interviewed were officials of the Funtua local government, some officials of the FADP, district heads, and farmers in Tandawa (without formal presence of FADP), Bakori, Kabomo, and Yankwani (where FADP dams had been con-structed and farm service centers established).

The study comes up with the observation that, over the past two or three decades, United States Imperialism has tended to gradually supersede British imperialism through the medium of her cultural values which have psychologi-cally influenced the Nigerian elite. Hence, 'development' is tied not only to the British, but also to the American, monopolies. Other findings reveal that farmers in Bakori district indicate that, during the Second World War, farmers were forced by the colonial authorities and the Emir of Katsina to cultivate cotton or else face being jailed. The 'cotton culture' seems to have been well entrenched into this rural society, as is evidenced by the fact that of the 100 farmers, 65 ad-mit that cotton is one of the major crops still being cultivated . Likewise, of 23 of the 30 farmers in Yankwani, 19 of the 30 in Kabomo and 28 of the 40 in Tan-dawa mention cotton to be one of the most important crops as well as the major and favorite crop being cultivated. This confirms the observation of Gavin and Oyemakinde (1970) that the avowed object of the British colonial powers was "to direct cotton from local Nigerian industry to the textile mills of Lancashire."

It is also revealed that the capitalist and 'progressive farmers' have easy access to loans from banks in Funtua and Kaduna and from the FADP itself. Further, the bulk of the capitalist farmers live in urban Kaduna and Zaria and merely engage peasants to work on the farm for them. For the peasant's farm-land have been seized from them. 12% of farmers in Bakori have had their land seized; 12.5% of farmers in Tandama are faced with the confiscation of some part of their farms; and 13% of farmers in Kabomo confirm that their plots have been confiscated.

Given the nature of property relations in agriculture analytically handled by it, this study comes up with the finding that the penetration of capitalism into agriculture necessarily results in expropriating the peasants and enriching impe-rialist monopolies like the World Bank, International Minerals and Chemicals, International Harvester, Massey Ferguson, etc., as well as the local bourgeoisie and the middle peasants.

It is recommended that FADP and similar organizations be democratized; that the Land Decree of 1978 (now Land Act) be amended, to make land expro-priation and confiscation strictly prohibitive and put a limit to the amount of land leaseable to any one individual or family in Nigeria; and that confiscated and seized land be returned to the owners. In the final analysis, it is, however, argued that only social and national liberation of the peasants, the workers and all the oppressed groups can end poverty, uneven development, and other related problems. This is possible through socialism—an alternative to the prevailing capitalist-oriented system.

Social relations of production in peasant commodity production in Kaura Namoda Area of Sokoto State (Abdullahi 1983)[9] is a research into the nature of production relations in peasant agriculture among farmers in Birnin Magaji, Kasuwan Daji and Yankaba.

This study uses archival records of the National Archives Kaduna, and documents from the Ministry of agriculture and the Sokoto State History Bureau. It also uses interview method. Above all, it adopts downright Marxian approach.

This study comes up with the findings that the nature of labor and property relations existing in peasant agriculture best facilitates maximization of the exploitation of the peasants. For the institutions involved are associated with industrial capitalism. This maximization of the peasants' exploitation is evident in the progressive break-up of composite families as the basis of production organization. Consequently, fragmentation of land-holding and destruction of free communal or cooperative labor in its entirety set in. Moreover, labor becomes drudgery and is time-consuming on account of its being individualistic, isolated, and subjected to being purchased and sold.

Other findings are that the conventional role of commerce in the developed capitalist economy is not the same as in the peripheral formations. For, regarding the latter, the commercial sector is the nucleus of the relations of exploitation (via extraction of peasants' surplus) and the attendant capital accumulation within the domestic economy for the benefit of the bourgeoisie (both petty and international) at the expense of agriculture and those directly engaged in agricultural production. Worse still, the small producer is forced to maximize his own exploitation in a bid to cover his expenses and meet his mounting debts: he is powerlessly confronted with low prices for his produce, but with high prices for whatever he buys.

Furthermore, it is revealed by this study that the failures of agriculture to develop and its stagnation as well as the poverty and abysmal misery of its producers are not as a result of its being 'traditional', but as a result of its backward internal characteristics and organization and of its subordination to exploitative relationships with foreign/domestic commercial and industrial capital. The backwardness of agriculture also facilitates the smooth functioning of this exploitative system: underdevelopment is peripheral capitalism, and *vice versa*. All the foregoing findings culminate in a major crisis in the agrarian system, as evidenced by an appreciable sharp decline in cultural production and consequent massive importation of food and agricultural materials. It is concluded that current development policies and strategies are designed to facilitate vertical integration of the agricultural sector with agribusiness, controlled by foreign multinational corporations, while the state subsidizes the process of capital accumulation and the progressive pauperization and marginalization of the peasantry.

This study recommends a progressive social change, i.e., structural and institutional transformations leading to the elimination of the structures of domination and institution of exploitation. Thus, the Marketing Boards and Licensed Buying Agents will be dismantled from agricultural marketing and be replaced, at the local government area, district and village or settlement levels, with democratically constituted producers' marketing cooperatives, which must be solely responsible for agricultural production in all its various ramifications, both internal and external.

The cooperatives should, thus, evolve into centers of popular control of political power in their respective areas eventually, while the state will provide banking facilities, heavy industry, assistance to the cooperatives and general coordination of the activities of the entire cooperatives.

Establishment of large and self-sustaining collective farms is also recommended. Similarly, rural-based processing and other industries can be established. Thus, surplus labor, which may be occasioned by farm mechanization, may be industrially absorbed, with the potential added advantage of stemming the tide of rural-urban migration.

It is confidently opined that the present exploiter and their foreign allies and masters, who, among other things, see the whole problem of underdevelopment in technical terms, are bound to oppose the proposed set-up, even with force, if need be, but it is equally confidently opined that such an opposition can be broken by people's power. So is the climate of opinion that it is contended that fundamental development presupposes the elimination of the current structures of political domination and economic exploitation and the emancipation of our society and national economy from the shackles of world capitalist imperialism.

The political economy of farmers' cooperatives in the Jemaa area of Kaduna State (Nkom, 1983)[10] constitutes a study examining the extent to which cooperatives in Nigeria have served as an agent of rural development, given the overall Nigerian social structure.

The methodology adopted by this study is the political economy approach[11], which studies the continuous struggle of man to transform the resources of nature into useable and consumable forms and the intricate relationships which emerge between men in the process of satisfying their material needs—an approach focusing on concrete socioeconomic formations of a given society. Precisely, this approach is resourcefully applied to the analysis of cooperatives within the context of the overall national economy of which they form an integral part, highlighting how they are conditioned by the historical and structural character of the overall national economy.

Data collection methods utilized were the historical-documentary method (involving a careful scrutiny of government files, documents, and policy statements, archival and other historical materials, articles and papers, and records kept by the secretaries of the various co-operative societies in Jemaa); the survey method (involving interviews with farmers consisting of 161 cooperative members and 155 non-cooperative members in Kagoro, Moroa, Kafanchan and some other districts); and the observation method (involving personal observations by the investigator of the activities, operations and problems of both the cooperative societies and their farmer-members, with the added advantage, on the part of the investigator, of being opportuned to attend several meetings of the societies and a few special meetings where cooperative loans were distributed to farmers).

Using data from the archives, this study reveals that the major beneficiaries of the credit and marketing facilities of cooperative societies are not the peasant producers, but the state agents serving as the middlemen (or 'buying agents') between the actual producers and the state-owned Marketing Boards.

Using data from sources other than the archives, this study reveals a clear tendency for cooperative farmers to own more large farmlands than non-members. Also, 97% of both cooperative and non-cooperative farmers use modern fertilizer, with the average use of fertilizer being 14 bags for cooperative farmers as against 11 bags for non-members. The distribution of farmers shows that 37% of the cooperative members as against 12% of non-members earn between 201 naira and 1500 naira (Nigerian currency) from the sale of agricultural produce. The mean of 197 naira for cooperative members contrasts very sharply with a mean of only 88 naira for non-members.

Thus, the potentials of the cooperative members to produce more and to acquire more income are proved. This higher degree of commercial-oriented agricultural output among cooperative members tallies with the thesis that cooperatives tend to attract the more enterprising and capitalist-oriented members of rural society, who lose no time in maintaining the *status quo*. More important, it is revealed that cooperative membership is heavily skewed in favor of the wealthier and more influential members of society. For instance, about 56% of the cooperative members as against 14% of non-members occupy positions of authority and influence in the local political system, in the church, or in the school.

It is concluded that in spite of obvious failures and shortcomings of cooperatives, Nigeria and many other African countries (this study covers other parts of Nigeria and Africa in its review) have continued to retain the existing model of cooperatives, even in post-independence period, and that government efforts have merely concentrated on the infusion of modern technology into the structure of private production and ownerships in a bid to increase the output or productivity of the private producer.

Further, this study cherishes a realistic approach by Nigeria to societal organization and development, namely, one that involves a complete transformation of the rural and national economy along more egalitarian lines rather than a consolidation of the existing capitalist arrangements. This is so since a policy that emphasizes an *improvement* rather than a *transformation* of the existing socioeconomic formation is in line with the ideology and class interest of the ruling bourgeoisie in Nigeria.

It is, therefore, recommended that a completely new cooperative model, reflecting the interest of the masses and emanating from their own creative abilities in the struggle to free themselves from the clutches and exploitation of the national bourgeoisie and its international allies, be adopted. This people-oriented model of cooperatives calls for conscience-raising strategy of cooperatives and mass education. To this end, progressive intellectuals are to pay a leading role, regardless of their ambivalent position within the dynamics of class identification and action (i.e., of being sellers of their mental labor and so are being exploited and of being performers of mental and managerial functions and so are in high socioeconomic status).

Precisely, the progressive intellectuals have to provide the peasants with useful guidelines and organizational principles, drawn from the experiences of such societies as China, Cuba, and Tanzania. The peasants will then be educated to realize that the evolution of people-oriented cooperatives must form part of a wider program, which is committed to, and works toward, the fundamental reorganization of the entire society along the line of collective ownership and production. In this way, the peasants will see their salvation as being tied up with the collective struggle of all exploited classes against reactionary forces.

## Endnotes

[1] The Nigerian civil war lasted thirty months—from July 6, 1967 (when fighting actually broke out) to January 15, 1970 (when the war ended).

[2] This is a Master's thesis.

[3] According to this study, the usage of social networks as an analytical tool in the British tradition of social anthropology and sociology dates back to 1954, when it was used by Barnes. The concepts were developed, assuming popularity due to dissatisfaction with structural-functional approach to the analysis of society and the desire for precision in the social sciences. It refers to an individual's total social relations and the links involving him with others in the society, laying emphasis on the characteristics and values of such interpersonal links both within and outside that individual's own social group. Since implicit in the structural-functional approach is the notion that the behavior of the individuals in the interrelated units (parts) of society is predetermined and since, contrarily, no known human society functions in this manner, the adoption of the concept of social networks would seem to be an improvement on the structural-functional approach.

[4] This is a Master's thesis.

[5] This is a Master's thesis.

[6] The sample-villages (Garu, Dan Dako, Mahuta, Kaura, Dan Ayamaka and Tamowa, or Tamuwa) are located along the Kubani and Shika *river valley* in Makarfi district of Zaria Province of the North Central State (now Kaduna State). Makarfi district is located in the Northernmost part of Zaria Province —the Greater Zaria. And the tomato processing project was jointly introduced by the state government and Cadbury Nigeria Limited (Cadbury for short) approximately five years prior to the time of this study. The existing political system, headed by rural traditional rulers and some local leaders, was the system under which the whole activities were performed.

[7] This is a Master's thesis.

[8] This is a Master's thesis.

[9] This is a Ph.D. thesis.

[10] This is a Ph.D. thesis.

[11] This study holds—and quite rightly so—that the methodology adopted here derives from Karl Marx's method of "successive approximation" by which social phenomena (e.g., inequalities) are empirically verified through a step-by-step progression from a more general and abstract level to the concrete and observable level (Lange, 1966). And such abstract but important phenomena are substantiated through logico-deductive and historical methods (Magubane, 1976) rather than being merely subjected to empirico-statistical verifications which normally do no more than grossly trivialize these phenomena. In other words, the analysis is not unnecessarily bogged down by the empiricist necessity of reducing everything to the observable level. For certain propositions can be verified only at the logical, deductive, and historical levels rather than at the statistical level, whose verification has been turned into a fetish by Western social science.

## DISCUSSION QUESTIONS/EXERCISES AND ESSAYS

### Political Sociology and the Military

1. What is political sociology?

2. Explain why the relationship between Ilorin town and the rural areas can be considered within the context of Gunder Frank's metropolis and satellite relationship.

3. Discuss the political and economic interests of three groups in Ilorin Division.

4. Discuss the various factors involved in the continuity of Igala political system in spite of conflict and change.

5. Examine leadership quality, the introduction of indirect rule by the British colonial power, traditional rulership and the economy.

6. Why does the study on the Habe ruling dynasty utilize mainly archival, oral testimonies, ethnographic material, and historical as well as political documents, among others?

7. Why does the study on the social interpretation of the Satiru revolt utilize the historical materialist and dialectical framework?

8. Critique Mahdist ideology, while comparing the efforts of its adherents with those of most peasants that revolt against local and colonial authorities.

9. Why is the military a professional group with a difference?

10. What factors are responsible for the politicization of the military in Africa or, put differently, the militarization of African politics?

## Rural Development/Rural Sociology

11. Explain the dissatisfaction on the part the change-agents and individual farmers.

12. With particular reference to the study on the effects of FADP in Bakori District, discuss the 'cotton culture' well entrenched into rural areas.

13. Explain why the conventional role of commerce in the developed capitalist economy is not the same as in the peripheral formations.

14. What is political economy approach?

15. What are the consequences of the maximization of the peasants' exploitation? Compare these consequences with those of labor in America, England, or France.

16. Why is it that a policy that emphasizes transformation rather than improvement is what is needed in Nigeria (or other African countries or, indeed, all Third World societies)?

# ·VII·

# SOCIAL INEQUALITY, SOCIAL PSYCHOLOGY, SOCIAL WORK AND SOCIAL WELFARE

## Social Inequality

Social inequality refers to inequality that exists in society. And this inequality is in terms of unequal access by the members of society to resources.

Social inequality has been defined by Headrick (1977) as differences in social prestige, based chiefly on differences in family backgrounds, social conventions, wealth, income, political influence, education, manners, and morals. He goes on to explain that the differing degrees of social power, prestige, and influence possessed by the diverse social groupings in society indicate the extent and kinds of social inequality. He further explains that differences in degrees of social prestige are largely transmissible from parents to children through, *inter alia*, social networks and the institutions of property ownership and inheritance.

Differences in education offer a noteworthy and illuminating example of social inequality that continues to be decisive and of paramount importance. The educational background of an individual determines to a large extent the class to which that individual belongs in society. Take, for instance, the legal fund scheme, established by the federal government on November 25, 1976, under which poor Nigerians involved in criminal cases would enjoy the services of counselors free-of-charge. Aside from attendant bureaucratic bottleneck, which itself requires some degree of enlightenment to be surmounted, high illiteracy rate tends to prevent the poor from availing themselves of this opportunity. Indeed, the social stratum, to which the non-literate individual belongs and which is indicated by the stratigraphic position of his class, is no match for that of his educated counterpart. For there is the possibility of the latter securing relatively lucrative occupation, itself a culmination of education. Education thus accords him double opportunity.

In Africa in general and Nigeria in particular, social inequality in terms of unequal access to resources finds practical expression in the distribution or provision of health care facilities which are largely urban-based, with the health care delivery system itself being curative, rather than preventive, and elitist. Consequently, the overwhelming majority of our people in the rural areas and the urban slums are deprived of access to these much needed health care facilities. Worse still, such basic human needs as education (dwelled upon above), nutrition, water, and shelter are denied these poor people. On the other hand, people in high socioeconomic status, usually resident in the city and, ironically, are the minorities, monopolize these health care facilities.

Those in the minority just referred to in the preceding paragraph constitute what Segun Osoba (1970) called the "Nigeria 'Power' elite (1952-65)", portraying the powerlessness of this class regarding the control of the economy of their country, even on the attainment of political independence, with far-reaching consequences for them and the entire country. Osoba puts his portrayal of the powerlessness as follows:

> The tragedy of the Nigerian power elite and of the country arose primarily from the obsessive concern of the Nigerian political decision-makers with the illusion of *personal wealth and power* to the extent that they did not fully appreciate the obvious fact that real power in any polity belonged to those who controlled high points of its economy. Because the crucial control of the Nigerian economy continued to reside in the hands of foreign business concerns, backed by their home governments, the Nigerian power elite robbed *themselves and their country* of power and initiative, without which Nigeria could not be modernised rapidly and efficiently. (Emphasis added.)

Even though Osoba focused attention on the power elite of 1952-1965, his portrayal of this class is as true today as it was in that period. The lust for personal wealth and aggrandizement has, indeed, come to be more of a vogue than an exception, having increased in incredible heaps and bounds. Moreover, one is inclined to be under the impression that it was not that the elite "did not fully appreciate" the implication of their action and that, assuming they really did not, their successors in Nigerian society no doubt do fully appreciate. The attempt being made by the Nigerian government at the privatization of such public corporations or concerns as the Nigerian Railway Corporation, Nigeria Airways, National Electric Power Authority, etc., would further exacerbate too glaring an inequality already in existence. This *laissez-faire* attempt would equally further exacerbate the existing corruption which, to borrow the words of Zakari Kano (1982), is generated as a result of scarcity of resources caused by some groups and "the inability of the system to re-distribute resources equitably."

Mainly concerned with social inequality, Huxley (1937) proposed some solution in terms of what he called "income tax and duties", asserting that:

By any government which so desires, such taxation can be used for the purpose of reducing economic inequalities between individuals and classes, for imposing a maximum wage and for transferring control over large-scale production and finance from private hands to the state.

Much as income redistribution enunciated by Huxley can be said to point the way to some solution to the problem of inequality (a fundamental structural change would, however, be quite welcome), the government might not oblige. The assertion of Dudley (1975) is instructive in this connection, as stated below:

> ...ultimately, it is the state which defines which of the varied issues that confront a society at any given time are to be regarded as societal problems, how such problems are to be solved, with what tools and what are to count as solutions.

The solutions offered by successive Nigerian governments are not only cosmetic, but are also sabotaged by the very people charged with the responsibility for effecting them. A good case in point is the Nigerian Enterprises Promotion Decree 1972, otherwise known as the Indigenization Decree, which was prevented by this class of people from 'indigenizing' the numerous foreign business enterprises in Nigeria. Of course, enactment of a given law (or promulgation of a given decree) does not *ipso facto* guarantee the achievement of the objective of that law (or decree). As Omaji (1985, p.16) makes it crystal clear:

> Experience has shown that law does not function automatically to bring about [social] change, just because it is legitimately issued and marked by valid authority.

As it will be clear to us later in this chapter, the instruments of state power are used to maintain the *status quo*, whereby inequality is correspondingly maintained. In this regard, the assertion of Ikenna Nzimiro (1985) is relevant. He says:

> The instrument of state power is effectively in the hands of a social minority which is ever willing to sell out the masses' interests to the multinational corporations. Workers and peasants are irrelevant to the political process and to the administrative procedures which are licensed politically: the products of their labor do not find their way into their own hands.

It has been observed, regarding the restrictive and repressive role of the Nigerian state in the development of trade unionism, by Zasha (1985) that there is now a strong tendency towards portraying the state in a neutral light. As he puts it in his paper:

> There is a powerful tendency in the Nigerian industrial relations literature to treat the state as a more or less neutral referee in the game of industrial relations. This paper rejects this view and argues the thesis that far from being a

neutral referee, the Nigerian state (colonial and post-colonial) has consistently played the role of capital in the development of labor movement in the country. It is only from this perspective that one can understand the policies and actions of the state as they relate to the development of trade unionism in Nigeria.

Obviously, if governmental policies and actions are consistently inimical to the development of trade unionism, then inequality will continue to rear its lop-sided head and will even be aggravated. A favorable situation might obtain if trade unionism is spearheaded by a militant, indomitable, truly committed, and sincere leadership capable of dealing a death-blow to inequality. The African governments (the Nigerian government in particular) had better borrow a leaf, on this score, from the Swedish situation, which Forsberg (1984) has explained thus:

> The first trade unions were formed in the second half of the 19th century. The employers tried to gain the support of the authorities to declare strikes illegal. They pointed out to the old vagrancy system as expressed in the bonded servitude ordinances, the most recent dating from 1833. But in 1885 parliament made it clear that the vagrancy system could not be used. (Emphasis added.)

Ultimately, however, one would expect a situation where those conditions warranting strikes are wiped off within the context of a new, relevant social order, truly beneficial to the masses. But the problem with the successive Nigerian governments is that they abhor criticism, which cannot be ignored if we really want development. No wonder, then, that Dudley (1975) asserts that:

> Stability is not only desirable; it is the very antithesis of progress, and progress comes about only through continuing change, which in turn arises from struggle and criticism or, to be more accurate, from criticism and struggle.

Indeed, it is because the Nigerian governments abhor criticism that they, particularly the military regimes, are known for quelling student crises or even demonstrations by sending soldiers (as in 1978) and the police to fire live, rather than rubber, bullets at students, massacring them in cold blood. One's memory is not so defective as to forget the killing of Kunle Adepeju (the first Nigerian student killed) in 1971 at the University of Ibadan, the massacre of many defenseless students in the country's universities during the Ali-must-go episode in 1978, the killing of students at the university of Ife in 1981, and the massacre of students at Ahmadu Bello University in May 1986, all during student crises or demonstration! Worse still, students were, all along, mercilessly wounded. And we lose no time condemning killings, albeit much more serious and well entrenched, in apartheid South Africa, particularly the Soweto massacre of June 16, 1976, during which unarmed school-children protesting against an obnoxious educational system, completely biased against the black, were shot dead *en masse*. The Nigeria police are so intoxicated with lethal weaponry that their catalog of barbarism and brutality is extremely disturbing. The merciless killing of hundreds of farmers by the police in Bakolori in 1980 provides us with a clear example (see p. 51). This leads us to the consideration of a kind of inequality which finds a most gruesomely practical expression in racial discrimination. That kind of inequality is expressed within the framework of apartheid. A vivid portrayal of apartheid by Patrick Wilmot (1980) given below would suffice:

> Apartheid is a system that spells affluence for a white minority and abject poverty for a black majority. A mere 17 percent of the population, the white man gets over 70 percent of the country's income while a black majority of over 70 percent struggle to get even a pittance of 17 percent.
>
> There are, thus, two faces to the economic realities of apartheid, one shining, white and radiant, the other ravaged.

It is worth noting that social inequality is in sharp contrast to Nigeria's national principle of justice and egalitarianism, contained in the section on the national objectives in the Second National Development Plan 1975-80, and reaffirmed in subsequent plans. The study of job-seeking experience amongst school leavers in Sabon-Gari, Kaduna (Dawodu, 1977) is one which examines the differential obstacles with which school leavers (up to post-primary level) are faced in their job-seeking efforts in Kaduna. Being a study conducted in a cosmopolitan town, this study selects its sample in such a way as to be representative of the ethnically, occupationally, religiously, and educationally heterogeneous primary and post-primary school-leavers of Sabon-Gari, Kaduna. This study comes up with the finding that the relationship between parental socioeconomic status (SES) and employment among school-leavers is mediated by the educational attainment of the respondents. That is, parental SES enhances or inhibits educational attainment of respondents. Educational attainment also influences job opportunities. Other related finding is that school-leavers from low SES with higher educational qualifications are small relative to their counterparts from high SES origin. Similarly, the latter is better off in terms of duration of unemployment and social connections as job-securing mechanism. Class consciousness among the elite, with Minna, capital of Niger State as a case study (Zubair, 1977), is aimed at studying the activities and attitudes of the elite toward one another, ascertaining whether or not class consciousness exists and, if so, the indicators of the prevailing class consciousness. Of three hundred people constituting the elite in the study area, one hundred respondents were chosen by accidental sampling method rather than by random selection, since it was impossible to obtain a list of the elite. This study comes up with the findings that class consciousness exists among the elite as evidenced by commonly-used recreational activities and facilities as well as membership of clubs or associations. Also, the existing unequal distribution of social goods and services and consequent differential access to these would make the privileged group feel it is superior to other groups. One important factor revealed by this study is that, due to horizontal, social relationships among them, the bureaucrats (i.e., state commissioners) and the educated elite (i.e., lawyers, judges, magistrates, doctors, and lecturers) see themselves as being more distinct and class-conscious than the business elite (i.e., businessmen and contractors) and traditional elite (i.e., traditional rulers in charge of local government affairs). For the type of class consciousness among the business elite and the traditional elite is not expressed in form of club association, which is not cherished by their culture. However, by living among their kin and relations in town rather than in Government Reservation Area-type, secluded location, and by simultaneously maintaining a large number of dependents in form of patron-client relationship, on which their social prestige lies, the business and the traditional elite, too, do exhibit some form of class consciousness.

The study on wage differentiation between the public and private sectors, with Ministry of Works and Housing, Federal Super Phosphate and Fertilizer Company, Kaduna, for the public sector and D'Alberto and Giampaoli Company Limited, Kaduna, long established since 1940, for the private sector (Akubor, 1981) focuses on wage disparity from both individual and national standpoints. The findings of this study reveal that there is an appreciable difference between the two sectors in terms of service conditions. This obviously follows from the fact that each of these two sectors operates a distinct salary structure and peculiar remuneration policies, with the pay structure tending to favor private employees *vis-a-vis* their public counterparts. Nevertheless, further findings reveal that fringe benefits are paid by, and general employment conditions are relatively satisfying in, the public sector. Wages can, therefore, be considered to be equal at an aggregate level in both sectors.

From the individual standpoint, knowledge of whether or not there are real differential wages and salaries in both sectors can serve as a guide to ordering one's priorities as a prospective or full-fledged worker. Also, a greater percentage of the middle-aged (say, 40-50-year olds), one would have expected, would dominate the public sector, to be able to enjoy retirement benefits. Conversely, this age-group dominates the private sector, thus convincingly proving that the Nigerian working class is more likely to be interested in readily-available financial benefits than in any long-term consideration.

From the national perspective, an adequate knowledge of differential wages and their socioeconomic dynamics will serve as a guide to accurate formulation of wage policy, e.g., a minimum wage policy for Nigeria as a whole. Much as the economy is generally categorized into the public and private sectors, this categorization gives rise to some problems for Nigerian universities. For, strictly speaking, they are neither a public nor private sector of the type implied by this categorization. Clearly, this is fundamental to the anomalies inherent in the Udoji Commission (or the Public Service Review Commission, as it was officially called) regarding inadequate handling of the submission of Nigerian universities in 1973. For, although the commission accepted a large proportion of the universities' submission to it, it could not cover the whole ground in its own report[1]. Consequently, the salaries recommended by the commission and approved by the government were far from being commensurate with the magnitude of the work done by the academic staff-members of the universities. Closely related to the question of wage differentiation between private and public employees is that of private and public goods and services. Hence, in terms of inter-sector resource allocation, what the economist calls 'social indifference curves' reflect "The aggregate preferences of the individual members of the society for private and public goods *as made effective* by the distribution of income and wealth in the private sector and political representation in the public sector" (Herber, 1975). Specifically, private sector allocation is characterized by the forces of demand and supply and price mechanism, as determined by consumer sovereignty and producer profit motives. Public sector allocation is, however, effected through the revenue and expenditure activities of governmental budgeting. It is instructive to note that both forces of demand and supply as well as price mechanism and public sector allocation are in the interest of a tiny minority. For the price mechanism is what Adam Smith (1776) called the 'invisible hand'—which no doubt is unreliable—and public sector allocation falls within the context of the political model of David Easton (1965), involving political system and its environment, whereby, apart from the political authorities and their functionaries, everyone is outside the political system, with the citizens making demand on it. Too many demands, according to this Eastonian model, could undermine the stability or the regulative capabilities of the political system. This situation has been portrayed as one where many people are dominated by the few, with political science serving as an instrument of domination. As Claude Ake (1979) puts it:

> We have seen that, strictly speaking, only those who authoritatively allocate values[2] belong to Easton's political system. In the Estonian system the avenue of participation available to non-elites is the inputs. Insofar as Easton is interested in inputs, his interest centers on the point that inputs place stress on the political system and could conceivably destabilize it or undermine its ability to regulate behavior...his framework makes the central interest of political science the establishment and maintenance of domination over men. We may now legitimately modify this statement and say that in the context of his framework, the main interest of political science is the establishment and maintenance of domination of the few over the many.

As a consequence, social inequality becomes a glaring feature. It is worth noting, however, that the point is not so much the use of power by the government over its citizens as the unilateral and obnoxious conversion of power into coercive instrument. This was made clear by Harold Laski, who was a leader of British socialist thinking in the first-half of the twentieth century and "who rejected an organic view of the state or any claims to divine right by its rulers" (Barber, 1970), when he wrote:

> ...It [the state] exerts power over us that it may establish uniformities of behavior which make possible the enrichment of our personality. It is body of men whose acts are directed to that end. If the state is known by the rights that it maintains, clearly it needs the power to maintain those rights. But there is al-

> ways present the danger that a power which exists to secure good may, from its very strength, be used to frustrate it. Certainly, the assurance of good intent is no longer adequate. Those who sit in the seat of government must be judged by their elevation of humble and ordinary men.

According to Barber, Laski looked around the governments of the 1920s and decided that many of them were not promoting the 'good' referred to in the above quotation, and that their failure rested on the *social order from* which they sprang and which, in turn, they defended. The social order, he maintained, was based on grave inequalities—of wealth and property, and of opportunity and rights. An examination of the role played by governments in the 1980s would reveal even graver social inequalities. The study on the victims of crime, with Ajegunle and Victoria-Island in Lagos as a case study (Adewale, 1984), focuses on two residential areas which are polar opposites, the one being a slum for people of low socioeconomic status, and the other well planned, largely with tarred roads and, indeed, a GRA (Government Reservation Area) provided under governmental auspices, with 24-hour police check-point security.

A systematic probability sampling technique was adopted in interviewing. Streets in Victoria-Island were categorized into main, middle, and back streets, with the aid of a pathfinder map. Every second or third house was then chosen out of every three streets in each category. Owing to its planlessness, no map of Ajegunle was available, but, with the assistance of someone living there for about fifteen years, a categorization, similar to that of Victoria-Island, was made. This study comes up with the findings that person victimization is much more rampant in Ajegunle than in Victoria-Island. For person victimization results from disagreements between co-tenants in the common use of such amenities as toilets, kitchens, etc., in contradistinction to separate and exclusive use of these amenities by the residents of Victoria-Island, characterized by self-contained households. Also, residents of Victoria-Island experience property victimization more than those of Ajegunle. For household electrical appliances like television, stereo-sets, refrigerator, video-recorder, etc., which the former can afford to, and do, possess, attract burglars. Burglary is fostered by the fact that relatively very few people live in each household, and those whose households fall within the 'back street' category are more vulnerable to property victimization. Males, rather than females, tend to have a high rate of property victimization, since they are more likely to keep late nights, with consequent danger of night marauders. Based on further findings, this study explains that respondents of low socioeconomic status hesitate to report criminal victimization to the police, mainly because the police serve only the interest of those in high socioeconomic status. Suggestions made are that, to reduce property victimization, burglary-proof iron-bars be fixed on windows and doors in addition to dogs and night guards (who tend to connive with thieves); attendance of night parties be minimized and, when traveling, one or two member(s) of the household be left behind by the traveling member(s); the police be requested to intensify patrol efforts, especially at midnight/early morning and be vigilant during celebration of such important festivities as Christmas and Sallah (i.e., Muslim festivity); and hotels, motor-parks, and bars—hideouts of men of the underworld in Ajegunle—be constantly raided by the police.

## Social Psychology

Social psychology is one of the areas of studies, informed by a variety of conceptual approaches, within the discipline of psychology. The other areas are, at least theoretically, regarded as 'non-social psychologies'. The conceptual approaches of the other areas of study, together with which social psychology is within the discipline of psychology, include behavioral, cognitive, psychoanalytical and neurobiological approaches, while that of social psychology is sociological. Hence, as the term implies, social psychology is 'social', while, by virtue of their behavioral, cognitive, psychoanalytical and neurological approaches, the other areas are 'nonsocial', merely retaining their distinct status of psychology. But, sociologically, in a situation where one deals with humans, who are social animals and who, by their very nature, are gregarious, no useful or practical purpose is served by putting an artificial line of demarcation between what is 'social' and what is 'nonsocial'. Psychology is the scientific study of mental processes, while *social* psychology is the scientific study of the mental processes of man, regarded as a *socius* or social being. The distinction between psychology and social psychology is ambiguous and so untenable. This situation, devoid of distinguishing factors, has been elucidated by Phelps (1977). He writes:

> Social psychology: The scientific study of the mental process of man, regarded as a *socius* or social being. The distinction between social psychology and any other psychology is essentially abstract and academic, since it is impossible to study any human being entirely detached from social relationship.

Historically, it has been said that the first two books bearing the title of social psychology made their appearance in 1908 (Mann, 1969). One was written by William McDougall, a psychologist, and the other by E.A. Ross, a sociologist. On balance, Mann describes social psychology as representing "a curious amalgam of its parents, psychology and sociology" and further explains that "any attempt to define social psychology must recognize the different approaches to social behavior of these two disciplines."

Social psychology is categorized into two types, namely, 'psychological' social psychology and 'sociological' social psychology, both reflect their unique objects of study—individual and group respectively. Hence, 'psychological' social psychology studies the attitude, feelings, perception, learning, and motives, as shaped by society and its groups. On the other hand, the sociological school of social psychology studies the group as the unit of study and is concerned with *person and the social context*, dealing with what happens between people (Mann, 1969).

Nevertheless, this is not to say that the two types/categories of social psychology (i.e., 'psychological' social psychology and 'sociological' social psychology) have nothing in common. For instance, they both study social behavior within a framework of interacting influences, make positive efforts through cross-cultural and intergroup comparison to achieve a perspective necessary to guard against ethnocentrism in drawing conclusions and make increasing use of scientific methods and techniques (Sherif, 1963).

Even in a situation where there is an appreciable dichotomy between the two categories on the basis of one studying individuals (i.e., internal factors, namely, motives, feelings, attitudes, etc.) and the other studying groups (i.e., external factors, namely, person-cum-the-social-context), the fact still remains that the personal mannerism or idiosyncrasy of the individual concerned is not focused upon. If anything, it is the influence of a group on an individual that is focused upon, and not the influence of one single individual on himself/herself. For individuals are studied in relation to the social environment, and not in isolation from it.

What, more than anything else, lends credence to the validity of focusing on the influence of a group on an individual is the fact mentioned above that, as social animals, humans are, by their very nature, gregarious, i.e., like the company of others. This explains that sociology—a scientific study of man in his social relationship—is itself concerned primarily with social interaction (or the aggregate of individuals), and not with the unique or isolated aspects of individuals. The study on attitude toward abortion (Ahmed, 1977) starts off with an explanation that, when the word 'abortion' is mentioned, what readily comes to mind is the fact that a conscious and deliberate effort is being made to intervene in the process of natural development, thereby bringing to an end the life of a would-be human being, with the implication that the child is not wanted.

The purpose of this study is to measure the opinions of students on the main campus of A.B.U. on what they feel about abortion. And, in order to overcome the problems inherent in attitude measurement, 'attitude' is equated with 'opinion.'

On data collection, consideration was first made of the need to have the data as representative of sex distribution as possible. Thus, quota sampling was used. Cluster sampling was also used to make good the potential deficiency noticeable in the reluctance of the respondents to fill in and return the questionnaire on schedule.

This study comes up with the findings that 61.1% of the respondents indicate that, in the event of pregnancy, after having had the required number of children, they would prevent it; while 30.6% indicate they would not. 15.4% of them associate possession of children with sign of respect and 19.2% give economic reason as a motivating factor. Other findings are that only 30.5 % of the respondents are favorably oriented toward abortion, while 57.1 % think it is a sin against God and so undesirable. Still on the finding, 48.6% of them hold that abortion should be allowed to anybody needing it. It is further revealed that people are afraid of death and so do not like abortion. Regarding its validity, this study, like any attitude studies, is not easily replicated for the obvious reason that different elements will tend to fall into the replicated sample and hence give different revelation.

Achievement motivation and education in the development of sex-role differentiation in Zaria (Agum, 1977) constitutes a study with a somewhat special approach to the study of child-rearing practices, focusing on sex-role development in the process of socialization. The findings of this study, which utilizes open-ended questionnaire, show that the personality or behavior patterns respondents think are most important for their daughters to have are, in order of importance, good manners, house-keeping, excellence, moral uprightness, altruism, and intelligence. However, only 44% of them think that intelligence is important for their daughters, presumably because intelligence is commonly associated with boys rather than with girls. Hence, this study further reveals that practically all the respondents indicate intelligence as the most important single attribute anticipated for their sons.

This study also comes up with the findings that only 6% of mothers from polygamous marriage indicate that women should seek employment outside the home. On the contrary, 86% of mothers from monogamous marriage indicate the necessity for women to seek employment outside home primarily for financial purposes and for such social reasons as mixing with people which consequently reduces boredom and frustration.

This study asserts that the right to vote, the right to seek employment outside the home, and the right to education, particularly in the context of the Universal Primary Education (UPE) introduced in the 1976-77 academic year, are all parts of a new freedom for women, but, nevertheless, that the core of the problem of sex-role differentiation lies in the socialization practices embodied in our culture.

It is strongly recommended by this study that further research into the problems of sex-role differentiation be carried out by those with the time and wherewithal to do so.

The study on rank and file apathy among Nigerian trade union, with Nigerian Tobacco Company Limited, Zaria, as a case study (Adebola, 1978) is aware of the established four major problems of the Nigerian Trade Union, namely, problems of leadership, rank and file apathy, size, and financial insolvency, but singles out rank and file apathy for examination. For, as a study focusing on psychological-cum-industrial factors, rank and file apathy is the only one of the four problems with psychological overtone. And, what is more, the question of apathy is one of behavior, which is not in most cases as physically viable or demonstrable as are the remaining three factors. The major hypotheses of this study, portraying apathy as a dependent variable, are that (1) "Low educational level increases apathy and high educational level decreases apathy to trade union, (2) "apathy increases with younger age and decreases with older age". (3) "the lower the occupational status of a worker, the higher his apathy, and the higher his occupational status, the lower his apathy", and (4) "workers are usually more confident in ethnic union than in trade union, and this increases workers apathy to trade union".

The findings reveal that there is no significant difference in terms of apathy to the union among respondents of low and high education. Education is not, therefore, a sufficient factor to prevent one from being apathetic. Similar findings are obtained in the case of the remaining three hypotheses, that is, that these hypotheses are all rejected. It is logical to expect a similar result regarding both variables (education and occupation), since they are causally-related variables. Concerning possible affiliation to ethnic union and anticipated apathy to trade union, it is found that most of the workers still hold some allegiance to their ethnic unions. Besides, the incidents of increased urbanization and industrialization—which have triggered fundamental changes in our sociocultural behavior—have affected the variables used to test apathy in this study. It is concluded that, being a variable with multicausal factors, rather than with monocausal factors, apathy can be regarded as a difficult variable to measure. Deductive method is, therefore, necessary for a final analysis.

## Social Work and Social Welfare

Social work and social welfare are basically the same. They are distinguished from each other, in order to delineate the characteristics of them both. The distinction between the social welfare institution and the profession of social work has "accompanied the general professionalization of social work and the rise of experts in an increasingly complex, bureaucratized, and scientifically-oriented society" (Tomanyshyn, 1971). Social work studies people who are prepared to help other people resolve or eliminate problems in social functioning. Interestingly enough, social welfare is the organized effort of a society to improve people's well-being by tackling and solving social and economic problems. Both are no doubt two sides of the same coin, the sameness of the coin being portrayed in the end-product of them both—the improvement of people's well-being. Whilst, through the use of knowledge, skills, and values, there is a helping relationship between social work (or, more correctly, the social worker) and other people in society, social welfare distinctly "represents society's formal effort exclusive of the family and private enterprise, to maintain or improve the economic condition, health care, or interpersonal competence of some or all of the population" (Hasenfeld et. al., 1974). Social work and social welfare are of paramount importance to Nigeria, where "There is some evidence to show that under the impact of the new changes, the traditional family and community system is breaking down...It is usually in conditions or situations such as these that a country finds the need to substitute a state system of assistance for what was traditionally provided by the family and the local community" (Kazah, 1981). However, it is eminently worth noting that the institution of the family in Nigeria in particular and Africa in general has not really broken down. The relative paucity of the efforts of the various governments in the area of social welfare in particular is eloquent testimony to this. One of the crucial areas social work focuses upon is children's home. One of the empirical studies undertaken in this area is that on the Zaria Children's Home as a social institution (Otowo, 1974). Like any other children home, the Zaria Children Home was established with a view to catering for maternally-deprived children. It is a pioneer of this kind of project in the northern part of Nigeria. The first person to translate this into practical experience was Mrs. Barrett, a Jamaican wife of one of the lecturers on the staff of the former School of Pharmacy, Zaria. She and some voluntary persons decided to set up the home on August 24, 1964.

Mallam Idris Morrow, a keen supporter of this project, loaned his compound, opposite the Provincial Secondary, school (later Government Day Secondary School and now Al-hudahuda College), Zaria City, to be used for housing the children's Home. In response to public appeal by Mrs. Barrett, some voluntary bodies donated generously both in cash and kind. The Chapel Committee of Ahmadu Bello University, which employed a qualified midwife and was paying her salary, was a typical example on this score. The Zaria Local Government Authority has taken over the Home from the voluntary agency. The Home is still forging ahead. The Home did, and now the Zaria Local Government Authority does, rehabilitate children to individuals desirous of fostering children. This is complimentary to the Home's activities. All the foregoing constitute the findings of this study on the Zaria Children's Home. This study illuminates the complexity of the day-to-day function of anyone acting as a substitute mother to the maternally-deprived child. As it illuminatingly puts it:

> Fostering needs somebody who has a deep understanding of the twisted nature and the hidden sorrows of the deprived child and would be prepared to try to bear them with sympathy and patience...Another aspect of social welfare that has attracted research endeavors is the destitute factor in Kano, with a view to exploring scope for rehabilitating beggars.

This research study proposes that rehabilitation is not an end to begging, but the beginning to an end of begging. It also categorizes beggars as the physically deformed, the old-aged, and supernatural believers, e.g., mothers of twins. Other categories are traditional musicians and praise singers as well as flatterers and rumor-mongers who, according to Adamu (1974), make their living by flattering people and spreading rumors. This study stresses an ardent need for rehabilitating destitute in Nigeria. However, some problems in rehabilitation do rear their heads. One is how to convince beggars, with success, to go to the rehabilitation center. Another is how to keep them there and cater for them. Concerning the former, 56.1% of the respondents (i.e., beggars) in the rehabilitation center wanted to be sent to their relatives and receive monthly allowances from the government. With regard to the latter, government's efforts are thwarted through unnecessary bureaucratic maneuvers and embezzlement on the part of public officers. The appalling situation is in sharp contrast to the Ethiopian and British situations, to which, in passing, this study refers. In Ethiopia, 600 disabled people are employed by the government to work in an umbrella factory, while another batch was engaged in manufacturing batteries. In London, the Orthopedic Division of Reemploy Limited engaged the services of 8,500 disabled people who produced goods worth equivalent of 24 million naira (Nigerian currency) a year (Babalola, February 2, 1977). This study, on the whole, recommends the cooperation of both the general public and the Nigerian government in establishing massive welfare service, and that those who are beggars at present should be properly rehabilitated.

## Endnotes

[1] For detailed information on Nigerian Universities' submission, see *The Nigerian Universities and the Udoji Commission*, published by the Committee of Vice-Chancellors of Nigerian Universities (1975).

[2] It is said that coercion is what is euphemistically referred to as 'authoritative allocation of values.'

## DISCUSSION QUESTIONS/EXERCISES AND ESSAYS

### Social Inequality

1. Define social inequality.

2. Suppose the status which Bob occupies now has been bought by his father for him. Name three factors, through one or all of which the status that Bob occupies must have been acquired by him. Then discuss the three factors and relate personally to them, if applicable.

3. In what aspect does social inequality in health care services find practical expression? What are the consequences of this social inequality?

4. How would you characterize the Nigerian power elite?

5. What is the solution offered by Huxley? Do you agree with this? Why or why not?

6. Discuss the relationship between law and its implementation.

7. Examine the catalog of barbarism and brutality perpetrated by the Nigeria police. Relate these to similar phenomena in America and/or other countries. Regarding America, it is widely acknowledged that it is the minorities, particularly African-Americans, who suffer at the hands of police officers. What differences can you pinpoint between the brutality perpetrated by police officers in Nigeria and their American counterparts?

8. What is apartheid? What are the two faces of apartheid?

9. Inequality in Nigeria is said to be in sharp contrast to her national principle of justice and egalitarianism. Discuss this in relation to America's principle of freedom and civil liberty or a similar principle cherished by any other country.

10. What factor mediates the relationship between parental socioeconomic status and employment among school leavers?

11. Enumerate the indicators of class consciousness among the elites.

12. Explain wage differentiation between the public and private sectors.

13. Examine the salary-related problems of Nigerian universities in terms of their being neither a public nor a private sector.

14. Distinguish between private and public sectors in terms of demand and supply as well as price mechanism. How would you relate this to public higher education in America or any other country?

15. In the context of the Eastonian model, expatiate on the statement that "the main interest of political science is the establishment and maintenance of domination of the few over the many". What has this got to do with the use of power as a coercive instrument?

16. As is contained in this chapter, an examination of the role played by governments in the 1980s would reveal even graver social inequalities. Can you relate to this as an individual or a family member who is prone to be vulnerable to such inequalities?

17. Carefully examine the suggestions made regarding reduction of property victimization. What is your evaluation of these suggestions? What lessons can you learn from these suggestions?

### Social Psychology

18. Make a clear distinction between social psychology and 'non-social psychologies.'

19. Discuss the statement, "Social psychology is an amalgam of its parents, psychology and sociology".

20. Distinguish between 'psychological' social psychology and 'sociological' social psychology.

21. Why is sociology concerned primarily with social interaction (or the aggregate of individuals) and not with the unique and isolated aspects of individuals?

22. What are the findings of the study on abortion? You and your mates might divide yourselves into two or more groups, each with different opinions regarding abortion. Then each group should come up with its points in an atmosphere of academic discourse.

23. Discuss the role of intelligence in sex-role differentiation.

24. Distinguish between social work and social welfare.

25. Discuss rehabilitation of beggars. Is there any connection with the homeless in America?

# ·VIII·

## SOCIOLOGY OF EDUCATION

S ociology of education is concerned with the analysis of educational institution or organization. Educational sociology, as it is sometimes called, is also
concerned with the functional relationships between educational institution
and the rest of the social institutions—the familial, economic, religious, and political institutions. Moreover, this subdiscipline of sociology deals with both formal and informal learning processes in a given society.

Education, like any social institution, provides for basic needs. It is, indeed,
the means by which society perpetually creates the condition for its existence.
Since the existence or survival of a given society is not unconnected with some
kind of norms, values, language, knowledge, and skills, educational institution is
one of the agents engaged in the transmission of these from one generation to
the next.

The form, in which the various functions of education are performed, however, varies from one stage of societal development to another. For instance, in
the simple, pre-industrial society, social skills in anticipation of adult life are for-
mally taught to children. But in the modern, industrial society, formal specialist
and systematic approach is adopted in tutoring or instructing people with a view
to imparting knowledge and skills. This is because the modern, industrial society is
characterized by heterogeneity, high degree of specialization and high-level technology *vis-a-vis* the simple, pre-industrial society with little specialization and characterized by low-level technology. The implication of this state of education is
that, while the educated in the simple, pre-industrial society is not prone to be
substantially productive, his counterpart in the modern, industrial society is.

It is important to note that education need not necessarily be confined exclusively to a formal, systematic process of learning. In fact, education can take
place in the home, on the farm, and even during the celebration of a particular
festival. Argungu fishing festival in Sokoto State, Nigeria, is quite a good case in
point. As contained in the *ABU Bulletin* of January 31, 1969, this festival, which
dates back to the latter part of the nineteenth century, is a colorful fish 'drive' in

the River Sokoto. And its origin "is rooted in the economic need for food conservation during the period of plenty to cater for the people's demand at the time of scarcity." In this way, a learning process, whereby food conservation is being learned, is readily identifiable. The activities, in which the learning process is identifiable, are equally readily identifiable within the context of a descriptive account given by the *ABU News Bulletin* under reference. As it vividly portrays them:

> ...Every man and boy in the area, armed with a large fish-net scoop, enter the water and, to the accompaniment of canoes filled with drummers, and rattling the huge gourds filled with seeds, drives the fish into shallow waters. Many and strange are the piscatorial specimens caught in the drive...

It follows, then, that education is not something existing only in a formal, water-tight compartment, but something normally rooted in the sociocultural environment of a given society. Indeed, its original or maiden concern was with the latter, not only in Africa, but also in all known societies. All known societies have one form of education or the other. For any total absence of education in any known society simply means that that society will be swept out of existence.

On a purely academic note, one area, among others, generally believed to be a possible and viable direction of expansion when historians at the University of Ibadan were discussing academic programs around 1972 was the history of the professions (Fajana, 1982). By the history of the professions was, for example, meant the history of Science, Law, Music, Education, and so on. This idea was given a second thought amidst "whisperings here and there but the protest was not loud enough to change the situation" (Fajana). In 1982, the chair of history of education was inaugurated in spite of the protest.

Formal education is a latecomer in all societies. For example, this is what obtains in the Western society. And it was not the government that started formal education in Britain. It was, indeed, the church and some individuals that introduced formal education there. Just in about the same way, it was the missionaries that brought Western or formal education to Africa for evangelism. It was later that the colonial authorities embarked on educating Africans in a formal manner, to enable them to recruit Africans at a relatively little cost for the civil services or bureaucracy in their colonies in Africa.

This leads to the issue of educational system (otherwise known as 'education system'). Since formal education is systematic, purposeful, deliberate, and conscious, there exists a structural aggregate of its activities and interests in phases as well as in an orderly arrangement. This structural aggregate is known as 'educational system', and its type is defined or determined by the kinds of action with which it is specifically identified. For instance, the kind of action with which a given educational system is specified may be of a technical or scientific nature, in which case that educational system eminently merits being called 'technical/scientific educational system' or, simply, 'technical/scientific education'.

In Nigeria, as in some other African countries, what obtains is Western (or colonial/neocolonial) education, which largely turns out people only suitable for white-collar jobs, which are not adequately available. The implication of this is that we have inadequate manpower base for technical/technological and scientific advancement. Worse still, Western (precisely, neocolonial) education, which is our own type of education, makes us socially, economically and psychologically subjugated to the whims and caprices of the technologically advanced countries. Basically, all this is tantamount to the fact that our educational system fails to meet our needs!

It is in a bid to remove the defects in the educational system in Nigeria that a new educational system has been formulated and adopted. This is a change from a 6-5-2-3 to a 6-3-3-4 educational system. Although the same total number of years is spent within both the old and the new educational systems, yet the end-products differ. The new educational system is designed in such a way that it is expected that the imbalance inherent in the old educational system, and which is in favor of liberal arts against offerings in technology, will be removed.

However, problems abound regarding successful implementation of the new educational system. These problems include funding of education (Omojuwa, 1982). Needless to say, this problem of funds is prone to lead to, and has even started leading to, unavailability of teaching equipment and non-payment or erratic payment of teachers' salaries as well as discouragement of people from making teaching a career, all of which will give rise to a fall in standard, thus defeating the purpose for which the new system is introduced.

Much thornier and fundamental are the problems of pedagogic orientation and movement from one level of education to another within the system. Figure 1 shows the various levels, with each number constituting the number of years each level entails. The crux of the matter lies in the second level (i.e., Junior Secondary School), at which brilliant pupils are required to move on to Senior Secondary School, while those not very brilliant, "but are good with their hands" are to move on to trade centers and the like to learn painting, brick-laying, carpentry, etc. A criterion based on merit though this would seem to appear at first sight, the obvious fact that the parents of the pupils are of differing socioeconomic backgrounds, with the pupils consequently attending schools of correspondingly differing standards, convincingly proves that only a relatively few pupils will find themselves move on to Senior Secondary School. This is because both private and public schools do exist. Therefore, the scale is *tilted in favor* of a relatively few pupils, whose parents *can afford* to pay exorbitant school fees, characteristic of private schools, or, through some social networks, in favor of pupils, whose parents are of high socioeconomic status. The overall effect of this is that the removal of the liberal arts-science imbalance – so much desired – will be impossible. Thus, technological advancement and emancipation will continue to elude the Nigerian populace.

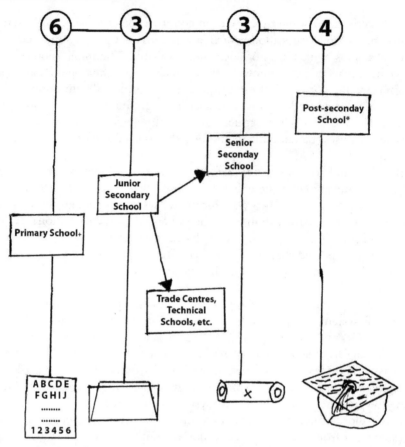

**Figure 1 – The new 6-3-3-4 educational system, based on the National Policy on Education (1977) in Nigeria**
(The artistic layout, constituting this figure, is conceived and designed personally by the present author.)

**KEY**
+ Pre-primary school is included.
* Polytechnics, colleges of education, universities, and other institutions of higher learning.

The question of language and educational attainment in West Africa in general and Nigeria in particular is a crucial one. This is all the more so as "... while it may be said that some changes have subsequently been effected in the orientation of the educational system, it still remains the case that, fundamentally, the syndrome of alien cultural domination continues to plague the entire educational system" (Onwubu. 1976). The "syndrome of alien cultural domination" finds practical expression in English Language, which is the official medium of instruction in Nigeria to the neglect of our own Nigerian languages, numbering 395.[1] Indeed, the problem arises from our inability to be unanimous in our choice of one of the Nigerian languages as our own *lingua franca*. Moreover, according to

Adeyanju (1986), it has been empirically proved by Akinde and Omolewa (1982) that having only one language as a national language is not a *sine qua non* for national unity. As Akinde and Omolewa put it:

> ...the use of two or more languages in a country does not necessarily create division, nor is the use of only one language a sufficient condition for ensuring national unity. Disunity derives less from the language(s) in use than from the lack of integration of a people's economic and political interests and from conflicting religious and other value systems.

In this connection, Adeyanju (1986) resorts to cross-cultural factors to explain possible dynamics of disunity, thus:

> It may very well be that the mastery of another person's major language (i.e., subtractive bilingualism) does not necessarily make us more unite to him, especially if he makes no effort to learn our no less valued "minor language (additive bilingualism)". In other words, authentic cross-cultural understanding must be reciprocal to be attainable.

Our inability to choose one of the Nigerian languages as our own *lingua franca* exhibits two problems, namely, that of choosing from among the three main ones (i.e., Hausa, Yoruba, and Igbo) and that of choosing from among both the three main ones and those spoken by the various Nigerian minority groups put together. (The Nigerian constitution guarantees, without mincing words, the rights of minorities, particularly regarding the development of their languages.)

How does language used as a medium of instruction fit into the context of the New Policy on Education (NPE), i.e., into the new 6-3-3-4 educational system? Adeyanju has provided us with a recommendation, whose focal point is the Junior Secondary School (JSS) stage within the context of the NPE, i.e., that within the new 6-3-3-4 educational system. Now, let us hear from the horse's mouth:

> ...If as the New Policy on Education states, some 70-100% of the pupils completing primary education would move on to the JSS stage, this would allow more flexibility in the introduction of English as a medium of instruction. Thus, schools which are favorably disposed to start in the mother tongue, while teaching English as a subject, may decide to opt for a partial transitional policy, using English as a medium in only a few subjects in the fourth year of schooling, for example, rather than changing over to English all at once. A few more subjects may be added in the fifth and sixth years. Another school may decide to teach half of the subjects in the third year in English and the others in the mother tongue and make the total change in the following year or subsequent years. Such flexibility is not only educationally sound, but it also eases the frustration of a sudden change over. It also combines the advantages of a transitional policy with those of maintenance one...

Fundamental to the above-stated recommendation is the fact stated, again, by Adeyanju that people, who decide to learn languages other than theirs, are far more likely to consider instrumental economic and social advantages first before such abstract political concept as 'national unity'.

Just as in the case of the proposed Nigerian languages as a medium of instruction in our schools, so the same Nigerian languages can conveniently serve as a means for learned communication. Indeed, the time for making this a possibility has definitely come. And this view is being held by the most senior Nigerian sociologist, Akinsola Akiwowo (1983). As he convincingly puts it:

> We believe the time has definitely come when *Nigerian Sociologists* should begin *to write short sociological essays in Hausa, Igbo, Yoruba, Edo, Efik, Ibibio and Fulfulde or Ebira* and that our journals should accept such essays with parallel translations in English. In short we need *bilingual or tri-lingual journals of sociology.* There are great benefits to be derived from this practice of writing. One is that it compels us to think sociologically in Nigerian languages, and opens avenues for the sociological enterprise to be enriched by concepts and propositions in our languages. (Emphasis added.)

Looking into the future of the sociological enterprise on the African continent, Akiwowo also anticipates the time when great and significant works in Africa will be published in Zulu, Xhosa, Yoruba, Igbo, Luo, Hausa, and Fulfulde, for example; or the time when inaugural lectures will be delivered in the dominant language of the area in which a university is located.

Closely related to the laudable practice of writing in African languages is the important question of publishing works in African and English languages on the African soil. For example, in the introduction to the first volume of *Ibadan Studies in English,* a journal founded in June 1969 at the University of Ibadan, with a view to serving as a vehicle for the publication of original and scholarly articles on research and criticism in English studies for the universities of Africa, the editors (John McVeagh and Peter Young) made some assertion regarding the belief in which the journal has been founded, as follows:

> The journal is the only one of its kind in Africa outside the Union of South Africa.... It has been founded in the belief that the universities of Africa can and should be able to maintain a journal of English studies...; that research or critical writing being undertaken in Africa should indefinitely not be forced to go elsewhere to be published.

As citadels which, in effect, are a conglomeration of the most enlightened, articulate, and intellectually distinguished population in any society, having drawn their staff members from the topmost strata of intellectual ability, universities eminently and unequivocally merit being duly considered within the context of sociology of education.

A consideration of universities, particularly in societies where their origin is normally traced to outside societies, entails, as a matter of necessity, following up that origin historically to its logical conclusion. Hence, the few paragraphs that follow are copiously replete with the history of universities in the United Kingdom and of those in colonial territories, among which were African universities, as written by Lord Fulton. The foundation day lecture by Lord Fulton at the School of Oriental and African Studies, University of London, comes in handy in this connection. Lord Fulton (1972) said:

> Let us first recall the special features of our [British] university system: the broad picture includes the ancient universities, some six hundred years old; joined after a relatively short gap by the medieval foundations north of the Tweed. Then a long, long interval separating these from the first of the newcomers—in the nineteenth century, the University of London, followed by the first of the civic universities and the National University of Wales. Then the reinforcement in the first quarter of this century of the civic universities in two stages: thereafter, in the 1960s, the 'new' universities; followed by the generation of those which began life as Colleges of Advanced Technology.

Lord Fulton explained that each of these geological strata, as it were, came successively into being, largely to provide something thought to be missing in the system. It may as well be said that each of them came as an improvement on its predecessor—a situation reminiscent of the Comtean law of three stages.

Concerning universities in the British colonial territories, the history involved here revolves around the popular Asquith Commission on Higher Education in the Colonies. Following the report of this commission and its recommendation, which was accepted by the then British government in 1945, the latter invited universities of the United Kingdom to set up a representative body to advise on the establishment and the development of universities in the colonial territories.

This commission, according to Lord Fulton, saw an unparalleled opportunity in the colonies for "a close partnership in the realm of university education" and "in the development of institutions of higher education (overseas) a peculiar opportunity for the forging of intellectual links which are so desirable in the world today." Centered around all of these are some functions of the proposed universities in the colonies which include the production of graduates, definition and maintenance of all that was best in local traditions and cultures, and the maintenance of so high a standard as to enable these graduates to enter on a footing of equality into the worldwide community of intellect. The commission, therefore, recommended that the universities should be (a) of first-class standard; (b) fully residential; (c) multi-faculty institutions; and (d) center of research.

In order for the goals set for the universities in the colonies to be realized, the Asquith Commission saw the need to enlist the interest and the support of the home universities. To this end, it recommended the establishment of the Inter-University Council for Higher Education Overseas, popularly known, for

short, as the Inter-University Council (IUC). Consequently, the IUC was established in the following year (1946). At this time, there were only two universities
in the colonies one in Hong Kong, recently relieved from the Japanese occupation, and the other the Royal University of Malta. Besides, there was also one
college at Fourah Bay in Sierra Leone, which was affiliated to the University of
Durham. The IUC was responsible for recruiting academic and other staff. It
also consulted with governments in the United Kingdom for funds and generally
advised the British government, the colonial governments, and the colleges in
the colonies on academic matters.

It is eminently worth noting that the history of university education and so
of research endeavors in West Africa dates back to the founding of the popular
Fourah Bay College in Sierra Leone. For it constituted a veritable citadel of university education for that African sub-region in its entirety.

In Nigeria, university education originally had its root firmly established in
the founding of the Yaba Higher College, started by Hussey in 1931. In 1948, the
products of this college, on the completion of their studies, moved on to the
newly-established University College, Ibadan, affiliated to the University of London under a scheme of special relation and was the college (later referred to as
university of Ibadan) established by the British colonial government in the colonies, following vociferous agitation by the nationalist movements.

After a decade had elapsed, interest in African education, particularly at the
higher level, was gathering momentum in the United States of America, as evidenced by the unique composition of the Ashby Commission on Higher Education in Nigeria (1959/60). For, out of a total of nine members, no fewer than
three were from the United States. Besides, the existing universities in the United
Kingdom were expanding rapidly, with new foundations of a different orientation emerging and post-war challenges making the conventional affiliation of
new institutions with a collegiate status give way to full-fledged university right
from their very inception. Accordingly, the Ashby Commission paved the way
for the next generation of universities, namely, University of Nigeria at Nsukka,
Ahmadu Bello University, University of Ife, University of Lagos (all in Nigeria),
University of Nairobi and University of Kumasi (in Kenya and Ghana respectively). Specifically, University of Nigeria, Nsukka (now known as Nnamdi Azi-
kiwe University) was modeled on both the British and American patterns, with
Dr. Nnamdi Azikwe, who himself had studied in the United States, and so endeared to the American pattern, as the prime-mover. The brains behind the
founding of Ahmadu Bello University and University of Ife (now known as Obafemi Awolowo University) were Sir Ahmadu Bello and Chief Obafemi Awolowo respectively.

Today, there has been an enormous increase in the number of universities in
Nigeria and a corresponding increase in student population, although it is being
held, particularly in the academic circles, that, rather than engage in establishing
new universities, the government should give adequate support to the existing
ones. But, with the politicization of university education coupled with the un-

bridled lust for contract award (which has been called 'the contract illusion' by Teriba, 1978), this view against the proliferation of universities in Nigeria has fallen on governmental deaf ears.

In Nigeria, as in other parts of the world, universities are a distinguished and leading citadel of scientific production of knowledge. The obvious notion of the inevitability of interaction between scientific production of knowledge and sociocultural factors in the community is of paramount importance. Indeed, universities in this part of the world deliberately and dynamically address themselves to this issue rather than serve as mere ivory towers. For, borrowing the words of the Committee of Vice-Chancellors of Nigerian Universities (1975):

> The term "ivory towers" may have been appropriate for the unreformed European universities of the 18th century, but it probably does not truly apply to universities as a whole anywhere today, although it does indicate a danger to be constantly guarded against. By and large universities are too much open to the public view and public demands upon them, to want or to be able to shut themselves off in ivory towers...

Indeed, African institutions of learning have to be conscious of the importance of the interaction between scientific production of knowledge and sociocultural factors. In so doing, science and technology will be made more responsive to our own peculiar needs. In this regard, the older Nigerian universities have blazed a trail. A few examples would suffice. The University of Ibadan conducts community health projects, involving teaching, research, and health care programs at Igbo-Ora and Ibarapa; and is well known for its extramural studies. At Obafemi Awolowo University, there is the Oriolokun Center, located right in the heart of the ancient town, one where gown and town meet. The University of Nigeria, Nsukka, is eminent right from its unique inception for its concern for local, peculiar circumstances. Ahmadu Bello University, Zaria, is likewise eminent for its unique commitment to the local community, as eloquently evidenced by the establishment and functioning of its Center for Adult Education and general Extension Services Unit, Center for Nigerian Cultural Studies and the Extension and Research Liaison Services, charged with the responsibility for disseminating knowledge of the most modern farming techniques to farmers. The University of Lagos has distinguished itself in continuing education, which goes beyond its confines, in music cultural activities, and in running evening classes for degree courses. The University of Benin, itself strategically located in a historic city endowed with rich indigenous African heritage, is known for its unique endeavor in the area of fine arts, and of a motley dimension at that.

The issue of transfer of technology merits our attention while on the question of scientific production of knowledge and sociocultural factors in the developing countries such as those in Africa. Transfer of technology, as the term implies, is the transfer of technology from one country to another, the latter being dependent on the former. This, in essence, means that technology is being transferred from one social milieu to another different social milieu and that the sociocultural dimension of the latter is not taken into account when that technology is being designed. The inapplicability of imported machines to African tropical soil (since they grow out of temperate environment) is a good case in point.

Indeed, experience continues to show that countries such as India, Iran, and Brazil to which technology is transferred, rather than being developed and designed internally, do not derive appreciable benefit from such a technological transfer. The Nigerian case poses a gloomier and more pathetic picture. For example, one of the benefits which a host country is expected to derive from the activities of the multinational corporations is the 'transfer of technology', but what goes on in the Nigerian construction industry is a negation of such benefits (Fadahunsi, 1977). A good case in point is that of Julius Berger, a German construction company awarded contract to build a second bridge linking Lagos Island and Mainland. Contrary to expectation, Fadahunsi laments, this company has failed to show concern in transferring technology within the construction industry to Nigerians. Experience continues to show, however, that the opposite is the case in countries where transfer of technology is not the order of the day. China, in this connection, not only provides us with an admirable example, but also serves as a potent eye-opener to other emergent nations of the world that generating technology side by side with the sociocultural background of a society is a right step in the right and productive direction. In other words, the fact that such technology would have to be developed within the social milieu of a given society in which it would be used does not necessarily mean it has to be of the same size, specification, and complexity as that of the developed country which has enjoyed popularity of a long standing in Africa. And the developing societies do not necessarily need to tread the tortuous and painful way the advanced countries trod before they (the advanced countries) reach their present height of development.

However, the erosion of the autonomy of universities in Nigeria is perhaps by far the gravest problem with which Nigerian universities are blatantly confronted. The origin of this dates back to the take-over of universities by the federal government, made possible by the transfer of university education in the early 1970s from the concurrent list to the exclusive list (i.e., whereby university education becomes the responsibility, or is within the jurisdiction, of the federal government). Consequently, universities are unduly subject to the dictates of policy-makers within the government. And this constitutes an impediment to socioeconomic development. As a matter of fact, the products of scientific studies are used only if the powers-that-be are convinced that such products or results are appealing to them.

Still on the question of the erosion of the autonomy of universities in Nigeria, the big question that arises is: How is the government to secure the cooperation it needs without infringing on university autonomy? This question has been asked by the Committee of Vice-Chancellors of Nigerian Universities (1975)[2]. In the extreme event of degeneration or obstinate narrow-mindedness in a university, a government, according to the committee, may be right to intervene. The committee has asserted that there must be checks and balances between the govern-ment and the universities, but that these should not mean detailed or day-to-day involvement in university management. The National University Commission (NUC) has an important role to play in the much desired cooperation between the government and the universities, serving as an intermediary between the government and the universities, explaining the government's development needs to the universities and the universities' needs to the government and trying to bring about a fusion of the two.

One area the erosion of the autonomy has affected and which is more than being of secondary importance is the appointment of Vice-Chancellors. For the effective powers of the appointment of Vice-Chancellors have been transferred from the University Councils to the Visitor, who invariably is the head of state. Lamenting this situation and elucidating the potential resultant reaction from the universities, the Committee of Vice-Chancellors of Nigerian Universities (1975) writes:

> ...Even in countries where a Minister or the Sovereign does make such ap-pointments the effective choice is almost always made within the university. If in future appointments are made which do not command acceptance in the uni-versities, the governments may find themselves embroiled in conflicts and the work of the universities would suffer.

It is very important to note that before concluding this introductory aspect of sociology of education we need to recall the type of the educational system we earlier on understood is ours, namely, Western (colonial/neocolonial) education (p.123). It is worth recalling that we understood, *inter alia,* that, as a consequence, we have inadequate manpower base for technical/technological and scientific advancement. Little wonder, then, that some African leaders like Kwame Nkru-mah of Ghana, Julius Nyerere of Tanzania, and Samora Machel of Mozambique have signified their preference of technical/technological and scientific educa-tion to colonial/neocolonial education, which merely turns out white-collar 'job-bers'. More important, these African leaders are mainly concerned about how our own education can be genuinely productive. In particular, while delivering his speech following the conferment on him of an honorary degree of Doctor of Laws of Ahmadu Bello University at the fifteenth convocation ceremony of the university on December 10, 1977, President Samora Machel emphatically dwelt on how our own education could be genuinely productive. He vehemently asserted:

> ...we want, in our Ahmadu Bello University, that knowledge and science should be instruments of progress, instruments of liberation...

In a similar vein, Amilcar Cabral of Cape Verde has asserted that education is an instrument of mobilization and liberation within the context of culture and identity.

Obviously, the contradictions in our capitalist-oriented socioeconomic forma-tion have, first of all, to be truly resolved, to be able to have a productive educational system. For example, the anomalies and inequalities in Nigeria's new 6-3-3-4 educational system, earlier on discussed on page 123, are a reflection of those in the wider Nigerian socioeconomic order. The same obtains in the case of other African countries operating similar counterproductive capitalist-oriented socioeconomic order.

Functional literacy as a factor for development with Kagoma farmers as a case study (Yakowa, 1972) is the focal point of a research which sets to find out about the economic and social activities of a group of farmers with a view to preparing a literacy primer appropriate for their work. It is also a research which seeks to ascertain the uses to which what has been learned by members of rural literacy classes is being put and to explore the possibility of incentives.

On the results of this study, some of the farmers interviewed claimed not to have enough time, to enable them to attend literacy classes. Others claimed that their already acquired knowledge and skills, through informal education, were adequate.

Further findings reveal some correlation between literacy and acceptance of new farming techniques. Also, most of the graduates of adult literacy classes make use of reading and writing, mainly for religious purpose, and there are primers to improve their skill.

This study suggests that literacy primers be tailored to suit the nature of farm work, that adults be taught how to write alphabets and that incentives be given to them through demonstrations and pilot schemes all over the area. These suggestions are no doubt a reflection of new attitude towards adult education. And they fit into "some of the international trends in ideas of what Lifelong Learning and Adult Education are about", referred to by Lalage Bown (1977) at her inaugural lecture. One of the international trends, in this connection, was a part of the final declaration of the 1960 UNESCO conference on adult education held in Montreal, Canada, as follows:

> We believe that adult education has become of such importance for man's survival and happiness that a *new attitude* towards it is needed. Nothing less will suffice than that people everywhere should come to accept adult education as normal, and that governments should treat it as a necessary part of the educational provision of every country. (Emphasis added.)

The study which focuses on a comparison of urban and rural primary schools' performance in NCEE (National Common Entrance Examination) and the migration of the school leavers in Fika Local Government Area, Borno State (Alkali, 1977) comes up with the findings that there is a very strong correlation between the pass rate of the school and the degree to which its leavers migrate and that there is a strong association between the pass rate and the size of the settlements in which the school is situated. Regarding the latter, urban schools (with 81.4% passes in the NCEE) perform better than their rural counterparts (with only 38.1% passes), for example.

Still on the findings, teachers with lesser years of experience (just between 1-4 years) are teaching in the rural schools, as against teachers (between 5-9 years) in the urban schools.

This study recommends further research into the impact of UPE (Universal Primary Education) specifically on the migration of young school leavers.

The research into "home influence on school performance in Igbiraland" (Yesufu, 1976) comes up with the finding that, on introduction of education in Igbiraland, Western education was perceived as a threat to the prevailing societal values. For children were to be kept away from home for the greater part of the day, thus making male children unable to help on the farm and female children unable to assist with home chores. Another finding is that the socioeconomic status of parents and home factors do influence the performance of children in school.

This study recommends that educational planners or policy makers as well as educational institutions should undertake parent education on a large scale; that the activities of Parents-Teachers' Association (PTA) should be extended to include discussions or courses on such topics as child development, problem of adolescence, learning, etc., in respect of which educational psychologists, sociologists, and social workers should be invited to participate; and that government and other education-oriented organizations should undertake to sponsor further research on the home-school factor.

The study on the development, organization and current status of the Islamiyya schools in Kano City and on the social origins of the pupils and teachers (Kabiru, 1980) has been undertaken due to the concern over lack of sufficient studies on sociology of education in Nigeria. Expectedly, the main focus of the study has to do with social factors, though both historical and religious aspects of the study are important components of sociological analysis,

Interview, together with the simultaneous use of tape-recorder, was the method of data collection adopted by the investigator.

The overall finding indicates that, of the 761 sampled pupils, the highest percentage come from the business elite, thus pointing to the conclusion that this class and the upper strata of Kano City and perhaps its surrounding communities dominate the Islamiya schools. And this class constitutes two-thirds of the categories/groups that hold the monopoly over sponsorship and proprietorship of these schools in Kano.

Furthermore, most of the Islamiyya schools do not have concrete plans for post qualification and occupational opportunities for their products. There seems, however, to be an awareness on the part of school proprietors, and some of them have started tackling the problem.

Included among the many suggested alternatives by this study to the existing arrangements are the take-over of the Islamiyya schools by the Kano Local Education Authority; or the maintenance of the *status quo*, but with more funds and all necessary assistance from the state government; and the operation of double session per day, to enable the pupils to attend both Islamiyya schools and primary schools.

## Endnotes

[1] Various estimates have been given, ranging, for example, from 250 to 400 plus (Onwubu, 1995).

[2] Vice-Chancellors of African universities, and of British and other countries' universities are the equivalents of Presidents of American universities/colleges, since they are the chief executive officers of their respective universities.

## DISCUSSION QUESTIONS/EXERCISES AND ESSAYS

1. What is another term for sociology of education?

2. Define education.

3. Discuss the functions of education in simple, pre-industrial society and modern, industrial society.

4. It is said that education can take place in the home, on the farm, and even during the celebration of a particular festival. Identify and discuss educational components, if any, during the festivals of minority/ethnic groups such as Puerto Ricans, Mexicans, Jamaicans, Haitians, etc., in the U.S.

5. What is the role of the church and some individuals in the introduction of formal education in Britain? How about your own country?

6. Discuss the implications that Western (colonial/neocolonial) education has for African countries.

7. Critique the transfer of technology in Nigeria and other developing nations.

8. To what factor can the erosion of university autonomy in Nigeria be attributed? What are the effects of the erosion?

9. Explain why the removal of the liberal arts-science imbalance might be impossible as a result of the problems of moving from one level of education to another within the new Nigerian educational system.

10. Discuss the new Nigerian 6-3-3-4 educational system, and relate it to standardized tests and tracking in the U.S.

11. What is your view regarding the statement that adopting a language as a *lingua franca* is not a condition for national unity? If your group has a view that is different from that of other group(s) in your class, then this may be turned into a debate.

12. What do you know about subtractive bilingualism and additive bilingualism? Relate these terms to the debate on bilingual education and foreign language program in the U.S.

13. Discuss the merits of having bilingual and tri-lingual journals of sociology. How about publication of great and significant works in Africa in Zulu, Xhosa, Igbo, Yoruba, Luo, Hausa, Fulfulde, and so on?

14. What were some of the functions of the proposed universities in the British colonies? Enumerate the recommendations of the Asquith Commission.

15. What was the role of the nationalist movements in the establishment of the first university college in Nigeria?

16. "After a decade had elapsed, interest in African education, particularly at the higher level, was gathering momentum in the United States of America." Discuss.

17. Judging from the examples given, do you agree that the term "ivory tower" does not apply to the universities in Nigeria? How about universities in America and those in Europe? If you agree, to what extent does the term apply to any or all of these universities?

18. Discuss the erosion of the autonomy of universities in Nigeria.

19. Explain the final declaration of the 1960 UNESCO conference on adult education held in Montreal, Canada.

20. In the U.S., some schools are located in wealthy districts, while others are located in poor districts, with resultant, differing standards of education. Is there a parallel as far as the findings of the study on urban schools and rural schools in Borno State are concerned?

# ·IX·

# SOCIOLOGY OF INDUSTRY

Sociology of industry (otherwise known as industrial sociology) studies industrial structures and, in particular, attitudes, values, and experiences of human individuals in an industrial setting.

Specifically, the main concern of the industrial sociologist is with the social facets of human behavior in a given industrial setting as well as with relationships within and outside that industrial setting. Relationships among human individuals at various stages of their working-cum-social life are focused upon and emphasized. In other words, an industry is not focused upon in isolation, but together with the relationships of human individuals therein to the society within which that industry subsists.

There are varying approaches to the study of a given industry, each approach reflecting the interests of the discipline of the scholar adopting that approach. Hence, for instance, an industrial psychologist, a management scientist, and an industrial sociologist view industry from different perspectives.

The research into productivity and industrial workers, with Norspin Industry, Kaduna, as a case study (Isa, 1973) examines the socioeconomic conditions of industrial workers, i.e., the semi-skilled and unskilled workers.

This study comes up with the findings that factory work in Norspin Industry, Kaduna, is centered on a 'shift system' classified into three periods, namely, morning, afternoon, and night and that workers are fixed permanently into a single shift work-group. This, however, has culminated in a strong avenue for companionship and 'covert competition', i.e., the result of concerted effort by workers of a particular shift to always achieve high productivity, *vis-a-vis* other shifts, with corresponding reward from the management.

Other findings are that the workers are faced with poor wage increase prospect, superficial/inadequate job satisfaction and ineffective union management. Ironically, there is an appreciable increase in the monthly productivity rate of yarn and cord per worker from 33 in July to 854 in December. This is due to night shift, coupled with good and effective supervision.

This study recommends, inter alia, improvement of the existing production opportunities for factory workers, an increase in night inducement allowance, and a reduction of night hours.

The social organization of crafts, with the pottery craft among the Attakar of Jema'a area of Kaduna State as a case study (Dandien, 1976) is aimed at showing how the processes of pottery are dependent upon the 'convenient social patterning' of the people concerned. It is a study also aimed at how this 'convenient social patterning' of the people has led to the organization of the craft in such a way that it has continued to persist among the people to this day.

This study traces the origin of pottery to the Neolithic period, thus:

> Archaeological findings prove that pottery must have been a world-wide craft during the Neolithic period; for remains of early pottery have been dug up in Egypt, China, Japan, Southern Russia, Europe and as far north as the Baltic Sea and Mesopotamia.

*Open firing ground for pot-making*

The findings of this study on the pottery craft among the Attakar show that 86% of women who are engaged in this craft depend entirely on it for their economic needs. Therefore, even though rapid educational development is anticipated, abandoning the craft completely is unlikely. Also, having got involved in craft, through the process of childhood socialization, for intrinsic reasons of satisfying the creativity urge and the desire for self-expression of their skills, the chances for the potters to abandon the craft are slim. Indeed, the craft is not only a craft, but also a cultural expression giving meaning to life.

This study recommends the conversion of traditional (i.e., indigenous) crafts in Nigeria into small-scale industries, thus creating an industrial base in the rural areas as well as a hybrid of traditional and modern production techniques.

*A typical market scene in a section of Kagoro market*

The study on pottery in Abuja as a case study of convergence of tradition and modernity (Akoshile, 1977) is similar to that on the same craft among the Attakar discussed above. It considers the traditional way of making pots and the imported Western style, with a view to seeing the ways by which these two cultures have produced the new synthesis. It is indeed, a case study of the Pottery Training Center, Abuja, founded in 1952 by Michael Cardew, a classic graduate of Exeter College, Oxford, and St. Jude's Pottery (where he learnt pottery for four years).

This study indicates that the convergence is made possible by the availability of suitable local clays treated with the Western-adopted machinery. There is a possible indication of the existence of what could be called 'a modern Nigerian technocultural tradition', just as modern medicine is 'a modern Western scientific tradition'. However, since the Pottery Training Center is merely an on the job-training one as well as a business concern, with a relatively few traditional potters training and working exclusively there, it has not been possible to impart what has been learned to other potters, potential or real, in the wider open society.

The research into the social aspects of production and marketing of traditional cloth-weaving in Ilorin town (Folorunsho, 1977) portrays cloth weaving as an age-long occupation, involving hand-woven cloth as the finished products. As in the case of the studies on pottery craft among the Attakar in Kaduna State and on pottery in Abuja, referred to above, the step-by-step production process is clearly spelt out.

Demand factors which tend to foster continuing production include the fact that, in Yoruba life, family gatherings and ceremonies are very important, entailing wearing of the same style and pattern of cloths. Looked at from the standpoint of Peter Lloyd (1958) that in the traditional craft industries a father hands

*Top: A warp on a sledge*
*Bottom: A man operating a loom, with his colleague beside him*

on his knowledge and skills to his sons, thereby making some crafts the preserve of certain lineages, one gathers from the findings of this study that there is a significant relationship between father's occupation and child's occupation. It is, however, anticipated that with the turning out of the Universal Primary Education (UPE) products, this situation will change. Besides, there was no production unit that did not lose some weavers to other occupations like manufacturing and building industries, taxi-driving, etc., a year prior to when the respondents were interviewed.

This study recommends the formation of voluntary weavers' association and government's initiative in taking decisions concerning new industrial ventures which will cater for labor likely to be diverted from its traditional skills.

Recruitment, training, and self-employment in the photographic trade in Kaduna (Masapara, 1979) typically constitute a research focus on foreign service industries, thus proving that the socioeconomic life of the people of a given so-

*Top: A boy winding thread*
*Bottom: A boy warping threads in a warp*

ciety like Nigeria is characterized by dualistic employment types, variously referred to as 'organized' or 'unorganized', 'structured' or 'unstructured', and 'formal' or 'informal'.

A number of things which can be observed or conceptualized from this research are, among other things, that photography, as a profession, tends to have a strong pull for people with some, rather than without, educational background; that expansion and prosperity of service industries generally tend to be favored by the growth of the economy; and that there is the likelihood that self-administering craft associations will develop into interest groups to be geared towards collective trading, as exemplified by the existence of craft unions.

The study by Opaluwa (1978) on motivation among Nigerian industrial workers, with Nigerian Fertilizer Company Limited, Kaduna, as a case study and which is an empirical verification or Frederick Herzberg's theory of motivation, serves as a local empirical means by which the validity of this popular theory is tested against Nigerian industrial background.

Focusing on Herzberg's theory of motivation, itself concerned with how to motivate workers, in order to raise the level of industrial production, this study reveals that many primary and secondary school leavers tend to be less permanent on their jobs, but are always looking for better jobs and educational opportunities, since no avenue of self-realization and fulfillment is provided for them. Interestingly, Herzberg's classification of such variables as salary and supervision as 'dissatisfiers' does not fit into Nigerian situation or, more specifically, the situation of the Nigerian Company being studied and under consideration. For, on the contrary, salary and supervision feature prominently as satisfiers and, therefore, as motivators. Given the low standard of living of workers in such a neo-colonial society as Nigeria with relatively low salary, monetary incentive is a great motivator.

On the whole, this study reveals that it is financial factor and societal evaluation, which vary from society to society, rather than intrinsic value in work itself (as maintained by Herzberg) that determine job-satisfaction or motivation. This study views the diametrically opposed positions, just highlighted, as a challenge constituting an agenda for further research.

Motivation of the Nigerian worker with NTC (Nigerian Tobacco Company), Zaria, as a case study (Ingbiankyaa, 1977) is the focus of a study which has traced the history of NTC back to the sixteenth century when the Portuguese explorers and merchants were in Nigeria. Since tobacco and tobacco-smoking were probably not known in what are now Nigerian communities, it is surmised that these were introduced by the Portuguese explorers and merchants.

On the findings of this study, it is revealed that wage incentives in terms of wage increase have failed to motivate workers, since wage increase does not mean increase or improvement in the standard of living of the recipients. And this is as a result of a decline in their purchasing power in the face of inflation in the wake of the wage increase. In this connection, while financial factors (i.e., wage incentives) have failed, working conditions potentially supersede them as satisfiers. The Adebo and Udoji salary increments, which have failed to improve the conditions of workers, are a good case in point. Alternatively, this study recommends that the management turn their attention to problems that instigate workers to demand higher wages and find solution to such problems. Those problems are unavailability of NTC housing facilities and drugs in the clinic, prevention of workers' families from attending the clinic and unavailability of bi-cycle, motor-cycle, and car loans – an availability of which would make them all satisfiers or motivators, contrary to Herzberg's position.

It is worth noting that those problems that instigate the NTC workers to make a demand for wages are included in the humanist psychologist Maslow's (1954) need satisfaction (namely, physiological, safety, belongingness and love, esteem, self-actualization, and cognitive needs), which, according to Oloko (1982), Oloko and Oloko (1980) have pointed out is surprisingly similar to what, in many of the United Nations agencies, is currently called the 'Basic Needs Approach to Development'. Quoting the Director-General of the ILO (1977), Olo-ko and Oloko have further pointed out that basic needs include two elements:

> First, they include certain minimum requirements of a family for private con-sumption; adequate food, shelter and clothing are obviously included as would be certain household equipment and furniture. Secondly, they include essential services provided by and for the community at large, such as safe drinking wa-ter, sanitation, public transport, health and educational facilities.

It is also worth noting that it is because wage incentives have failed to moti-vate workers, as pointed out earlier on, that the study under consideration, i.e., that by Ingbiankyaa (1977) makes, *inter alia,* basic-needs-oriented recommenda-tion.

The findings further reveal that the physical and mental health costs of jobs, as they are designed, are considerable. For the work involved is both dull and demeaning, and workers do not have control over it. Thus, this can contribute to an assortment of mental health problems. A re-design of jobs is, therefore, recommended.

The research into the development, organization, and functions of taxi and taxi-drivers' union (Adeyemo, 1980) focuses on Bida where these development and functions are given practical expression, revealing that taxi drivers have three sources of income, namely, monthly salary, 'chew-cash' (subsistence money giv-en to them by taxi owners whenever they work), and money for feeding, which they take out of the money collected from passengers.

Furthermore, it is also revealed that increase in the price of fuel and also in the value of insurance is one of the factors giving rise to corresponding increase in fares. Some drivers confessed when interviewed that there were some of them who did drink alcohol and got intoxicated while driving, maintaining that this is a stimulant.

The study on the employment process of the junior workers in ABU, Main Campus, Samaru, Zaria (Matanmi, 1981) mainly focuses on the processes of se-curing employment in the university as junior workers. They are lower clerical and technical personnel, library and laboratory assistants, drivers, cooks, ste-wards, messengers, cleaners, etc., all of whom are unskilled personnel.

The findings of this study reveal that the majority of the junior workers in the sample (60.7%) reside in Samaru village, while only 14.3% of them live in the villages around Samaru, since some of them possess no vehicles and cannot afford paying transport fare in the event of their living far away from the university. It is also revealed that a good number of the junior workers (51.2 %) have no primary education. The possible explanation for this is that these are people who could have been in full-time farming, but for the fact that they do not have enough encouragement to do so.

Further, some of the workers originally got the jobs through people they refer to as their 'brothers' who, strictly speaking, particularly given the Nigerian usage of the word 'brothers' which need not necessarily entail blood relationship, turn out to be such non-relatives as Alhajis and high officials of ABU. However, other findings of this study tally with those of the study in Lagos by Gutkind (1977), coming up with what has been called employment "brotherization". For many of the workers in the ABU Main Campus had to use kinship networks (or, precisely, their real brothers) before getting information about vacancy and even before securing employment itself. This is all the more important as between 200 and 250 applications a week are received by the university from unemployed people.

It is recommended that farmers be encouraged by the government by providing agricultural education for them and popularizing agriculture through agricultural shows, thereby discouraging farmers attracted by wages to join the bandwagon of salaried workers.

One needs to note that unemployment problems have assumed staggering proportions. The unprecedented unemployment problems do not only affect young school leavers, but also people already employed. The genesis of this is clear in the explanation offered by Ishola (1985), while on the question of cash management in a period of economic crisis. As he puts it:

> The poor balance of payments position has seriously affected importation of essential raw materials so much so that industrial activities have been curtailed and in some cases companies have been closed down resulting in loss of jobs and unemployment...

Retrenched (laid-off) workers are daily finding it difficult to cope with the ever-increasing inflation which has caused untold hardship to them and their families.

Worse still, unemployment is no longer confined to school leavers, but has extended at an incredible rate to university graduates, thereby landing one in a quandary as to whose unemployment problems to focus upon—whether those of school leavers or those of university graduates.

The study on sociology of calabash-carving in Gombe Division (Essang, 1974)[1] is a survey of some crafts, namely, calabash, smithing, leather-craft and pottery, with predominant, special reference to calabash-carving. The study was intended to be practical and problem-solving as well as descriptive, in that it was originally intended, to throw light on a problem posed to the researcher in the course of a previous fieldwork for the Federal Department of Antiquities in the area.

This study utilized quasi-participant observation: what craftsmen did on market days from home to market was observed, and some evenings were spent with blacksmiths, to be able to witness what they did. Data were collected from several sources—interviews with craftsmen, departmental files and field notes of research workers like ethnographers, anthropologists and sociologists, associated one time or the other with the museum. Also, utilized were library facilities in the Federal Department of Antiquities both in Jos and Lagos.

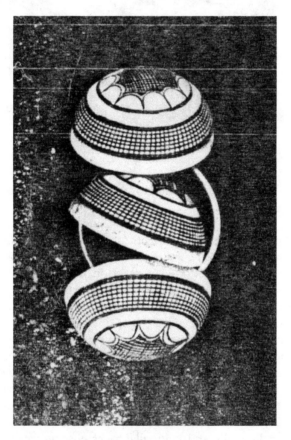

*Market display of calabashes*

This study reveals that no preferential treatment is given to calabash craftsmen over other ordinary citizens. According to this study, unlike the "Igun" brass-smiths in Benin who produced exclusively for the Oba (i.e., King) in the past and were recognized by the award of traditional titles in Benin, no such guild existed among the calabash craftsmen to have earned them a kind of status recognition in Gombe.

*Another market display of calabashes*

Other findings are that calabash vessels are used more by the Fulanis than by other ethnic groups; that only 12% of the total craftsmen surveyed paid for training; that most of the craftsmen do not copy, and do not use models, but always have in mind certain ideas, which are creatively expressed in their work; and that similarity of patterns on mats, wall decoration, textiles, decoration on hides and leather, and cicatrization (tattoo-like mark) on human body admirably express the cultural taste of the people. The faceting on calabashes is produced by a flat gouge or chisel to give alternated patterns. The tiny chip of circular shape, with a U-shaped groove, gives the rounded form. It clearly follows, therefore, that the use of tools goes hand-in-hand with the imagination of the craftsmen.

It is further revealed that 60% of the craftsmen put together have no difficulty selling crafts produced, while 40% of them have difficulty selling crafts. The latter attribute this difficulty to lack of such means of transport as bicycle, donkey, and motor. Besides, calabash is cheaper than other containers (i.e., wooden, plastic, or enamel) and so the poor and the rich alike can afford to buy. Users, traditionally and culturally conscious, prefer the decorated ones which, according to them, remind them of their past and present culture. Various reasons for use fall under three main considerations, namely, durability, aesthetics, and satisfaction. The could be seen in practice when Fulani women hawk eggs, garden eggs, butter and gruel in beautifully decorated calabashes: observation in this study reveals that several individuals could be lured into buying decorated cultural items because of their taste for decorative works.

This study concludes that the ensuing modernization in Gombe Division does not erode the cultural values the people place on traditional crafts. Moreover, these crafts are cheap to buy and easy to dispense with. Evident is the fact that cultural heritage continues to be fostered by the government and tourism promoted both at the federal and state levels.

The study on textiles workers and trade unions in Kaduna (Goshen, 1976)[2] is an exploratory and comparative study of the workers and trade union in four largest factories of the Kaduna textiles industry. Specifically, it focuses on the workers' perception of the union organization and their relationship to it.

Field research began with a brief survey of industries in Kaduna. Preliminary interviews were thus conducted with the state Ministry of Trade, Industry and Cooperatives, to gain some overview of industrial development in the town, and with personnel managers in several small-scale industries as well as the textiles. As much detailed information as possible was obtained concerning date of establishment, size of work-force, and several other areas relating to staffing and the day-to-day operation of each of the industries. During the actual period of interviewing, attitudinal and hypothetical questions were, on the advice and request of the researcher, minimized, although workers comments were fully noted where they elaborated on their responses.

This study reveals that the reasons given by the workers for joining a union are their perceptions of formal affiliation, although influence of workmates are not indicated by most of them, Further, a large number of workers see the union, whose power is centralized in its executive, as a 'problem-solving body'. In comparing the four factories and union situations, a number of factors and even inter-related factors seem to influence variations in formal union participation and perceptions of the union as workers' own organization. Such factors include conceptions of membership, payment of union dues, and attendance at meetings. Interestingly, there is no indication in the comparison of the four factories that any particular factory situations significantly affect workers' responses to the unions. Factory situations may, however, only be significant in combination with the nature of union leadership.

According to this study, the ambiguity as to whether unions are actually worker organization notwithstanding, the factors (mentioned in the preceding paragraph) that seemingly influence variations in formal union participation and perceptions still remain part of the few legitimate options through which workers have to express their demands and grievances without fear of losing their jobs. Above all, provided there is responsible leadership, coupled with workers' effective, not merely formal, participation, normally occasioned by genuine interest and sense of belonging, the centralization of power in the executive is not necessarily problematic.

The study on some problems of industrial labor with particular reference to efficiency and productivity in relation to labor turnover and management techniques (Koripamo, 1979)[3] focuses on the causes of labor turnover at Nigerian Tobacco Company (NTC) in the northern states of Nigeria, and its effect on worker efficiency and productivity. Essentially, the study shows that, contrary to earlier views which saw poor performance or efficiency as resulting from labor turnover caused by factors in the individual and the cultural environment (i.e., factors outside the work-situation), inefficiency results from the work-situation, especially those related to management practices.

A preliminary survey, entailing a tour of the factory in the company of the factory guide during which the production process was explained, was undertaken. Data collection was effected through the use mostly of the information contained in the personnel records on who had left and for what reason(s), and, to a lesser extent, on absenteeism, merely for counterchecking management's view that unauthorized absence was not as much a problem as labor turnover.

This study comes up with the findings that out of the total number in the sample, 26% indicate having close supervision, while 74% indicate having open supervision. To ascertain whether the workers responses are related to their efficiency grades, the two variables—efficiency grade and worker's perception of supervisory method—are cross-tabulated. The results reveal striking differences in the number of responses between those indicating they have open supervision and those having close supervision in the different efficiency grades, with a weak association between these variables. It is explained that, given the fact that machines control the workers' work-pace, they are efficient in relations to the speed of the machines.

At NTC, labor turnover rate is calculated monthly (elsewhere it may be calculated quarterly or annually), as follows:

$$\frac{\text{Number of leavers during the month}}{\text{Average number in employment during the month}} \times 100$$

This measure has been criticized, since it ignores the reasons for separation and the categories of workers (i.e., skilled or unskilled, male or female, and married or single). It is better to relate the separation rates of workers to their length of service on the job.

Concerning remuneration, this study reveals a weak association between salary level and workers' efficiency grades. Also, 52.1% of the workers hold that the reward system, in terms of partial promotion policies, is what dissatisfied them the most about their work. Clearly, then, it is not a person's salary level *per se* that determines or maximizes his efficiency, but rather the way he attains promotion or increment to a particular salary level. Generally, it is possible, given the results of this study, to conclude that the efficiency grades of the workers are not good indicators of either labor turnover or the standard of workers' performance. Chief among the reasons for this is that the efficiency appraisal of all the workers is done by a single foreman, irrespective of differential grades and types of job performed by the former, thus resulting in under- or over-rating, with a tendency to filter the biases of the latter into the decisive appraisal. It is, therefore, suggested that a method, whereby a group of foremen—rather than just a single foreman—appraise the performance of certain categories of workers be devised by the company.

Socioeconomic determinants of interpersonal interaction among rural-urban migrants (Verenyol, 1978)[4] are a study or factory workers in Northern Nigerian Fiber Products Company Limited, Nigerian Bottling Company Limited, and Plateau Confectionery in Jos with a somewhat unique approach. For it mainly focuses attention on actual behavioral and attitudinal characteristics of the labor force, rather than on the political activities of trade union officials that have so often overwhelmingly captured the attention of many a researcher.

Collection of data was both formal and informal. The informal data collection included informal discussions of issues with workers, especially outside the factory premises. The questionnaire was left open-ended, in order to make room for informal discussion, should the need arise. Most of the informal data were recorded as footnotes and have been incorporated into the thesis in form of reported statements.

Concerning the hypothesis of this study, ethnic beliefs, as expected, are negatively associated with trade union participation, while the strength of association is weak. Also, ethnic beliefs are positively associated with ethnic union, but, similar to what is the case with trade union, the strength of association is weak. This means that the hypothesis is weakly upheld. Perhaps, those with weak ethnic beliefs are those with class beliefs and *vice versa*. Overall, the patterns of participation in both trade and ethnic unions are not very much differentiated. Workers, in general, maintain higher ethnic contacts than class contacts.

This study also reveals that workers with full primary education and above maintained high level of ethnic contacts, while those born and bred in the urban centers maintained comparatively high level of class contacts.

Further, it is revealed that there is a dependency of rural relatives on urban workers. Participation in ethnic union should not, therefore, be seen as a concrete expression of ethnicity, but as a conscious way employed by rural-urban laborers (migrants) for solving the problem of economic dependency with which they are confronted. This is evidenced by the linkage being maintained between these laborers and their relatives back home through remittance of part of their hard-earned wages to support their dependents back home in their rural areas (villages). Lack of trade union participation could be blamed on desire for economic security. For fear of victimization in form of dismissal from job has often made many workers sit on the fence—to see who will bell the cat—more so as both federal and state governments are seen to be playing the role of suppressing industrial crisis.

This study comes up with the recommendation that empirical study of typical career histories, patterns of skill acquisition, rural-urban networks, and attitudes of workers to industrial work—which will make for more assessment of the process of working class formation and the basis of the rank and file support for trade unionism—be conducted.

Supervisory style and worker productivity, with a focus on the Nigerian Bottling Company, Kano (Oko,1982)[5], is a study whose main objective is to identify the productivity level of both the production and sales departments of the company in juxtaposition with the supervisory style and productivity of both departments.

This study reveals that two supervisory styles, namely, (1) a 'hard supervisory style', characterized by tough, strict supervision, that constantly suggests that the worker should not just sit around wasting away his valuable time on the job; and (2) a 'soft supervisory style' which is more person-oriented, showing warmth and concern for the individual. The first style of supervision was identified in the production department, where workers produced with the aid of 'process-technology' machines. The second style was identified in the sales department responsible for marketing and selling the company's products.

Regarding the relationship between the worker and the supervisors in both departments, it is revealed that 67% of the workers in the production department indicate that their supervisors always listen to their complaints, while only 22.7% indicate that the supervisors do not. The corresponding responses in the sales department are as high as 88.5% and as low as 11.5% respectively. The reason why complaints are more tolerated in the sales department is that interaction with more people—mostly customers—in the performance of their duties exists in the sales department than in the production department dominated by the use of machines. More important, the complaints are in the interest of the company, since customers, to whom the complaints pertain, have other business connections in Kano, itself the commercial nerve-center of the northern part of Nigeria, and so pose varied problems to the salesmen. In the production department, on the other hand, the preponderant use of machines entails complaints that mostly concern machines and so supervisors are likely to consider any other complaints merely as ones bordering on frivolity and dereliction of duty on the part of the workers. Therefore, the nature of the job or work in each department determines the style of supervision.

Nevertheless, this study suggests that the role of supervision in the activities of any organized laborforce should not be de-emphasized, that the knowledge, overall attitudes, and outlook of the supervisor should be broadened and that the trained supervisor should be given adequate and conducive opportunity to try out some of his new knowledge and techniques. Further, it is suggested that more attention be given to the relationships between the leaders and the led, since the nature of the relationships is likely to determine other resources or inputs and how these would be profitably utilized.

It is worth recalling that the research finding on page 137 reveals that, since it is operationally centered on a 'shift system', the industry under investigation obtains increased productivity through competitive, concerted effort by workers of a particular shift *vis-a-vis* workers of other shifts, because any workers whose shift produces the highest rate of productivity are rewarded by the management accordingly. This is another way in which increased productivity can be achieved. Yet another, albeit related, way revealed by the same study is that through 'night shift', and it is coupled with good and effective supervision. Into this the findings by Oko (1982), referred to in the preceding paragraph, fits, though stressing that style of supervision is determined by the nature of the job or work involved in a given industrial setting. On balance, both studies are not oblivious of the significance of the role of supervision in the activities of an organized labor-force.

## Endnotes

[1] This is a Master's thesis.

[2] This is a Master's thesis.

[3] This is a Master's thesis. Kwara State is not included, since, for the sake of effective administration, it is merged by companies with the states in the western area of the country. Turnover means the rate of replacement of workers in a work-place. By way of digression from the study under discussion, turnover also means the total amount of sales made during a given period by a company or an industry. This study defines separation of labor turnover as the termination of the period during which a worker is employed for whatever reasons.

[4] This is a Master's thesis.

[5] This is a Master's thesis.

## DISCUSSION QUESTIONS/EXERCISES AND ESSAYS

1. What is sociology of industry?

2. Describe the centralization of Norspin Industry on a 'shift system', and identify its beneficiaries.

3. Based on archeological findings, in what world geographic locations have the remains of early pottery been found?

4. What is the implication involved in craft through the process of childhood socialization?

5. Discuss Herzberg's classification of salary and supervision as 'dissatisfiers' within the context of Nigerian industrial situation.

6. Explain the similarity between Maslow's need satisfaction and the basic Needs Approach to Development.

7. Highlight the role played by employment "brotherization" and kinship networks.

8. Examine the patterns on products and the cultural taste of the people who use calabash vessels.

9. Discuss the conceptions of workers' union as (a) a problem-solving body and (b) an instrument of collective action and 'conflict insurance'.

10. How does the recommendation regarding the efficiency appraisal of all workers sound? Give your reason(s) for how it sounds.

11. Which of the two supervisory styles do you like, and why?

12. Discuss the extent of interaction in a machine-dominated work environment. Relate this to the issue of complaints.

# ·X·

# SOCIOLOGY OF LAW,
# SOCIOLOGY OF MARRIAGE AND THE FAMILY,
# AND SOCIOLOGY OF MASS COMMUNICATIONS

## Sociology of Law

Sociology of Law is the study of the social context of law. Its importance lies in the fact that it is concerned with the mechanism for encouraging and maintaining regular behavior in society.

It is against this background that any legal system which is worth its salt has, of necessity, to be suited to the peculiar circumstances of the society, within whose jurisdiction it operates. Sociology of law studies the contents of the law itself as well as the legal systems both at the national and international levels. The areas of its study become much more increased in a society, like Nigeria, characterized by legal pluralism, i.e., multiple legal systems.

The preliminary survey of Kagoro criminal law of substance and procedure (La'ah, 1976) attempts to assess and determine whether the present system in Kagoro is better appreciated than the indigenous one it has displaced.

This survey utilizes structured and unstructured interviews and archival data (from the National Archives, Kaduna).

The findings of this survey reveal that premeditated murder was a punishable offense in Kagoro society, but that punishment neglected the kinship ties between the offender and the victim. Also, it is revealed that theft settlement reflected the umbrella connection between litigants: the elder would simply demand the restitution of the stolen item and, regarding theft involving people of different clans or communities, elders of both litigants would arrive at the payment of fine.

Furthermore, adultery was a punishable offense, whereby the accused would be ordered to pay a ritual fine, with the adulterer, if he was from a different clan, paying a fine of two goats and beer, and part of the meat sent to the relatives of the woman involved, as proof of her worthlessness. The offending male would be ostracized, with consequent emigration by him.

This survey, however, comes up with the finding that, following the British expedition in 1905, a new social order with far-reaching effects, including judicial ones, displaced the hitherto existing order. Consequently, the informal and community-based judicial procedures disappeared, thereby making accessibility to the new courts extremely difficult. Power was also shifted from the elders to a new crop of colonial appointees, namely, village heads, *magaji,* and *waziri,* thus rendering the elders unproductive. Other findings are that in the pre-colonial period, issues involving misunderstandings between individuals and groups were the dominant feature. However, in the 1940s and early 1950s (the colonial period), property offenses became prevalent. The capitalist-oriented nature of the new social order, which normally encourages individual competition and capital accumulation, accounted for the prevalence of property offenses. This sharply contrasted with the pre-colonial period in which property was communally owned—a situation incompatible with individualism and private accumulation. The continuing existence of the new social order attests to the operation of the new judicial system in Kagoro to this day.

"Problem of choice of Law in a pluralistic legal environment" (Abdul-Qadir, 1987) constitutes a study focusing on the factors that might influence one's choice of one or another of the different legal systems in a particular case and also on the reasons advanced by individuals for choosing any of these systems.

This study comes up with the findings that about 48% of the respondents who choose the Customary and Islamic Laws do so, basically because the law is either that of their ethnic groups or that of their religion.

Further, the majority of the Hausa-Fulani (85.9%) choose the Islamic law, while only 4.1% of them choose General Law and none Customary Law. On the other hand, members of other Nigerian ethnic groups (Yoruba, Ibo, Idoma, Gwari, Kanuri, and Nupe) spread their choice: 27.6%, 24.1% and 48.5% of them choose Customary Law, Islamic Law and General Law respectively. The historical explanation of this two-fold trend is that a given law becomes preferred in the geographical area of its first appearance (e.g., the Islamic Law was first introduced to the north and the General Law was first introduced to the coastal areas). Additionally, regarding the Islamic law, the impact of the Danfodio Jihad makes possible the greatest acceptance of this law by the Hausa-Fulani.

Other findings are that the socioeconomic status of an individual influences his choice of law. For the higher one's status, the more likely one will opt for the General Law.

This study concludes that religion and ethnic origin will nonetheless tend to remain 'decisive factors in the choice of law for some time, recommending, *inter alia,* that efforts be made towards uniform legislations in personal matters, particularly as we now have uniform legislations in criminal matters and land matters.

The study on "The Nigeria Criminal Law: A sociological examination of the form, content and operation" (Omaji, 1985)[1] constitutes a preliminary contribution aimed at stimulating interest in critical investigations into the substantive law with particular focus on the criminal and penal codes. A pioneering research endeavor in Kaduna, Zaria, Makurdi, and Idah, this study is designed specifically to serve as a stepping-stone to further thought and research.

Purposive sampling method was adopted by this study, with the samples comprising of barristers/solicitors, legal scholars (university lecturers), magistrates, policemen, prison inmates, and the public. Data-collection involves the use of documentary sources (legal literature, court records [including 'minute books' and case file]), prison records, interviews with all the respondents and direct observations at police station, courts, and prisons.

The theoretical perspective used is the Marxist perspective, since it does not only seek to say what law there is and when it evolved, but also to explain how the law originated and why it is what it is. It also holds that an examination of law should be done through concrete historical and sociological methods of investigation.

This study comes up with the findings that two-thirds of the lawyers characterize the structural organization of the law as incoherent and haphazard. For example, 'goat-stealing,' conceived as a felony, in the law, should, according to 65% of the lawyers, be a simple offense in the Nigerian setting, while 'personating', according to 50% of them, should be a felony rather than a simple offense. And the opinions of the members of the public regarding the official classification of 'bigamy' and 'personating' further support these standpoints of the lawyers, with three-fourths holding that bigamy should not even be a crime in Nigeria, let alone a felony.

Other findings are that about 68.7% of the lawyers describe the language of the law as too "technical" and "incomprehensible", while 86.7% of the police respondents hold that the language is not clear to the Nigerian populace. Similarly, the empirical data confirm this, with 52.4% of the public unable to understand the language at all. A close examination of the criminal and penal codes reveals that their language, particularly regarding the former, is largely convoluted and esoterically technical (e.g., SS 115, 252, 346 of the penal code, and 316, 383, 465 of the criminal code). A similar close examination of these codes reveals incoherent and/or hairsplitting manner in which the legal norms in the law are organized, e.g., lumping together of incompatible and separation of compatible offenses and 'acts', thereby substantiating the assertion that, structurally, the form of the Nigerian criminal law is "chaotic".

All the foregoing findings go to show that the linguistic and structural nature of Nigerian criminal law is a reflection of its English legal parentage.

It is further revealed that the pattern of criminalization in Nigeria is predominantly property-biased, thus confirming a socio-historical framework of analysis/explanation utilized by this study and revealing a close affinity between the content or orientation of the Nigerian criminal law and the enduring nineteenth century bourgeois socioeconomic formation in England.

It is also found that the general Nigerian populace seems to give less respect to the police (due to police brutality, undue detention, evidence-exaggeration, etc.) than the courts. But, with regard to respondents in direct contact with the courts, a good number of them are not satisfied with the way their cases have been handled in the past.

This study recommends a complete reconstruction of the Nigerian criminal law such that it will be a new body of laws, emanating largely from a sociological understanding of, and sympathy with, the norms, values, and social relations of the ordinary man in Nigeria, and not from the technical and foreign backgrounds of the lawyers. Thus, the existing law should be 'restated' and a massive legal educational program embarked upon by the government, with the sociology of law designed and operational within the tradition of 'critical sociology.'

## Sociology of Marriage and the Family

Sociology of Marriage and the Family studies marriage and the institution of the family. Both marriage and the family are intertwined. The family is universally acknowledged as the basic unit of society. It is the gateway through which every individual came into the world.

Empirical studies undertaken in the area of the Sociology of Marriage and the Family have come up with findings which are not only quite revealing, but are also of basic relevance to our existence. Even though the family is one of the primary groups concerned with face-to-face relationships, patterned interaction with the social and physical environments outside the family is focused upon as well. The import of this is that there is a number of the empirical studies that fall within other areas of sociology like Sociology of Education, Demography, Sociology of Mass Communications, etc.

The research into the influence of home background factors on school performance in Ughelli area of Bendel State (Oghifo, 1981) comes up with the finding that children staying with guardians tend to develop more confidence in themselves to pass examination than children living with their parents. Confidence should, therefore, be instilled by parents in their children to pass examination. The findings of the study on familial impact on educational attainment in Zaria (Awosan, 1980) reveal that there is a positive relationship between household heads' (i.e., fathers') education and their children's mean educational attainment. This study also focuses on children living with their kinsmen. And, based on the findings of this study, these children are not disadvantaged, educationally, vis-a-vis children who live with their own fathers rather than with their kin in loco parentis.

The study on child education and sociocultural change in the traditional and modern Nigeria (Ezeani, 1983) highlights the fact that human society is not static. This study, which uses the Igbo of Njikoka Local Government Authority of Anambra State as a case study, stresses that the achievements of Western education in the study area are represented by the extent of social change which has occurred at different levels of the structural framework of the community. Glaring change was readily noticeable in the manner of dressing; in the construction of shelter; in the type of medical services available; and in the type of familial setting.

Changes in marriage customs among the Kara Gwari community (Waminaje, 1971), as one of the research topics, relate specifically to premarital practices. This research study is aimed at evaluating the changes that occur in pre-marital behavior. Most young men do not have to accept choice of wives by their parents, girls can no longer be forced to marry non-lovers, and extra-territorial or inter-village marriages are now encouraged. All of these constitute the hallmarks of appreciable change in marital affairs.

Divorce—under the title "Marital Instability among the Kolokuma Ijos" (Koripamo, 1973)—has been well surveyed. The choice of this topic was originally prompted by the popular view that Ijo girls, in general, pride themselves on getting married to at least two husbands in their lifetime. In the Ijo traditional society, adultery was regarded as being unacceptable to society. And marriage was seen as an institution whose chastity was rarely broken. Girls could be espoused right from when they were babies or even still in the womb of their mothers. However, this and other customs are fast dying out in modern times.

Still on divorce, the research into divorce as a case study (Arungbemi, 1977), causes the empirical pendulum to swing to another ethnic group in Nigeria, namely, the Yoruba. This study considers and analyzes divorce in Isanlu in Kwara State—one of the numerous Yoruba towns in Nigeria—within the context of five forms of dissolution—separation, desertion, annulment, and death. Separation, desertion, and annulment are clearly indicative of lack of peaceful coexistence between the husbands and wives concerned.

The study on the impact of modernization on marriage custom among the Igala (Opaluwa, 1975) is typical of the marked change in a given social institution as a result of modernization.

Bridewealth among the Igala is traditionally paid in kind—mainly in farm labor. Essentially, there are three stages that validate Igala customary marriage, namely, the betrothal stage, the stage at which a girl's consent is sought and subsequent finalization of bridewealth and the *Eboji* ritual, culminating in the eventual formal transfer of the bride to the bridegroom.

Today, marriage scene among the Igala has changed considerably. This change is effected through modification, within the context of modernization, over time. This is a gradual change, however.

Sociology of Marriage and the Family is intimately connected with legal factors. This intimate connection has been amply demonstrated by some research studies. One of such studies is that concerning the laws of succession and inheritance among the Chamba of Gongola State, with the communities in Donga District and Kungana town of Muri Division as a case study (Saidu, 1976).

This study begins with the definition of the customary laws of succession and inheritance. It states that customary laws of succession and inheritance, like any other customary law, are the unwritten, indigenous law of societies. It goes further to explain that a given customary law is a reflection of the social attitudes and habits of various ethnic groups and that it derives its validity from the consent of the community which it governs.

The findings of this study show that the Chamba are double-descent, i.e., they trace descent from both the father and mother.

The Chamba have a centralized system of government, with the Gara at the head, surrounded by his counselors. The heads of the outlying villages owe allegiance to him. Succession to chiefship is found to be hereditary. Females are not totally excluded from office-holding. A good case in point is the *Mala,* who is one of the councilors of the *Gara* (i.e., the chief) and who happens to be the paternal aunt of the *Gara.*

Traditionally, women did not hold land, but were allotted a small piece by their husbands or fathers. Women can now hold land. This is a change in customary law in response to the growing importance of cash crop farming.

On the whole, cash cropping has led to a high individualization of landholding. Also, there are some slight changes in the roles of succession and inheritance, with the advent of the colonial rule.

This study claims to have contributed to the literature on Nigerian customary legal system on account of its having to do with smaller ethnic group, rather than larger ethnic groups like the Yoruba, Hausa, and lbo. Most of the literature on Nigerian customary laws, it argues, deals with the larger ethnic groups.

## Sociology of Mass Communications

Sociology of Mass Communications is concerned with Mass Communications as a social science. Hence, as the term implies, it is sociological.

Sociology of Mass Communications scientifically studies communication in society, focusing on its nature and function as well as on the relationship between it and the social process. It is also the mass production of pieces of information or message. And messages are disseminated, with deliberate immediacy, to the wide and heterogeneous public. These media of communication have a technological base. More important, they are different from face-to-face interactions/media which tend to hinder easy flow of information and limit the scope of geographical coverage in society.

The findings of empirical studies on sociology have proved that the modern media of communication are best considered on the basis of their contents, eventual usefulness, and societal, peculiar relevance. Their technological base and scope of geographical coverage should not, therefore, be viewed in the abstract.

The studies undertaken cover various aspects of mass media within the major context of electronic and print media. A good number of titles fall partly within the decolonization section of Political Sociology.

The research on the influence of the 'gatekeepers' in mass communication, using the *New Nigerian* as a case study (Lawal-Osula, 1978), is representative of an extremely clear insight into the print media. By the 'gatekeepers' are meant individuals who control the ultimate fate of news stories. This study, therefore, examines the behavior of those individuals—the reporters, the chief sub-editor, the sub-editors, the news editors, etc.

The researcher went on the 'beat' with some reporters, to be able to observe the process of 'gate-keeping' at close quarters. Observation of production process was also undertaken right in the newspaper house. The results of this study reveal that the news editor turns out to be the 'gate-keeper': he uses his discretion to select, modify, or even reject news gathered and prepared by reporters. He may reject certain news stories simply because the news concerned is, in his own words, "not interesting", "could put us in trouble", etc. The glaring structural and contextual difference between the handwritten news story submitted by a staff reporter and what ultimately appears on the front page of newspaper, which is the modified/edited version of the former, attests to the profound influence of the news editor as the 'gatekeeper' proper. (A photocopy of the raw handwritten news story submitted by the staff reporter is contained in the thesis as Appendix A.)

The news editor is, however, primarily concerned with handling news stories in such a way as to make successful attempt at gimmick, normally capable of attracting the attention of the public. The main aim here is profitability by way of increase in sales. Of more importance and, indeed, much lesser control on the part of the news editor are the enormous pressures put to bear on him by the government. These pressures are reflected in whether or not the news editor accepts, modifies, or rejects news stories from the reporters, depending on the perceived stand of the government on the issue(s) at stake.

In these circumstances, then, it is obvious that the newspaper house, itself, ceases to be the public watchdog which it is supposed to be. It is no more than the "megaphone" or mouthpiece of the ruling class.

Radio audience, too, has been focused upon (Atirbabiri, 1979). Emphasis is put on the fact that the extremely large number of radio stations and receiving sets should not be regarded as indices of development. What should be cherished is the role of enlightenment played by the media.

However, this noble role, the findings reveal, has not been effectively played in Nigeria. For programs which can generate feed-back from the audience are not in operation. This study, therefore, recommends that quality, rather than quantity, and concrete search for reliable and well organized 'feed-back' for the audience be accorded priority by the government.

Of great significance is the study by Ayam (1982) on T.V. viewers' program preference and the dependency of the T.V. industry. Nigeria Television Authority (N.T.A.) stations located in Kaduna and Minna are used as a case study in this connection. The result of this study shows that viewers do not really have preference for foreign programs. Nevertheless, it is found that viewers of less than thirty years of age prefer foreign programs as opposed to viewers between thirty and fifty years of age who prefer domestic programs. As in the case of the radio audience (Atirbabiri, 1979), referred to above, feed-back from the audience is hindered. Bureaucratic tendencies in the T.V. industry lead to unnecessary delay.

The T.V. industry is found to be dependent on foreign programs which reflect the sociocultural values of the producing country. Typical of such programs is *The Jeffersons*, an American comedy program.

The study by Abdullahi (1979) mainly on the dimension of cultural and economic dependency of T.V., using N.T.V., now known as N.T.A. (Nigeria Television Authority), Kaduna, as a case study is of relevance here. This study was motivated by the concept of 'free flow of information.' The concept of 'free flow of information' explains that the development of the Third World can only be achieved through the functioning of the world as a 'global village', where there is uncontrolled 'free flow of information'. But the findings of this study reveal an ugly situation in which there is no 'free flow of information' as such. It is also revealed that about 80% of the senior members of staff of N.T.V., Kaduna, are trained abroad. The problem in this connection is that, given the nature of their work, these people are subjected to different ideological values and form of training. Back home, their ideological values and training tend to be irrelevant to the Nigerian sociocultural setting.

The study, therefore, ends up, in recommendatory terms, by urging Nigeria to borrow a leaf from the Chinese government. For the Chinese government provides us with an admirably instructive example of how it has disengaged from the so-called international free flow of information. Moreover, it developed its own media facilities relevant to its own needs.

The imperialistic nature of television broadcasting in Nigeria, with N.T.A., Jos, as a case study (Joshua, 1985), has been highlighted. Historically, with the incorporation of Nigeria into the world capitalist system through colonialism was the advent of the mass media in Nigeria. The first newspaper was in the form of government gazette with a view to publishing and publicizing government policies and new market prices for goods. This was followed by the *Iwe Irohin* (literally meaning 'paper of news'), which was a vernacular (Yoruba) newspaper established in Abeokuta in 1859. The principal motive for establishing the media during the colonial era in the second half of the nineteenth century, according to this study, is summed up in the words of Ibrahim (1983), thus:

> ...to get raw materials and outlet for finished goods. They carried news regarding marketing board prices of commodity and commercial advertisement.

As is typical of the Marxian political economy approach it adopts, this study asserts that, being situated in a capitalist society, the television in Nigeria reflects the interest of the dominant class in the Nigerian society—the bourgeoisie. Also, the television has been used as a tool by the multinational corporation to manipulate people to buy their products. Nigeria is consequently turned into a consumer economy. Little wonder, then, that the media cannot be seen in the abstract, but in relation to the material base of the very society in which it is situated.

Cultural images in children television programs (Baba, 1985) are not out of empirical touch. The significance of such an empirical children-related study as this, particularly regarding their tender age, is evident in the assertion of Imam (1985). As she puts it:

> Many people, and in particular *children and adolescents* (i.e. those still in their *formative stages* and therefore most susceptible to media influence) tend not to be among news and current affairs audiences. (Emphasis added.)

The study by Baba referred to above comes up with a down-to-earth analysis of the contents of the various children's programs produced by N.T.A., Kaduna. It makes it quite clear that the programs are carried out in an effort to maintain the *status quo*—the maintenance of the establishment and existence of the system of private ownership and production and the maintenance of the promise of a greater future, while the possibilities of new departures for human development are concealed. This is exemplified by the concealment of reality by cooperation, emphasized in the 'Sesame Street' program, and by the portrayal of the relationship between Mr. Hare and Crocodile as natural and good in the 'puppet theatre' program.

The children's programs also tend to avoid social conflict by emphasizing cooperation and unilaterally blaming individuals mostly of poor family background. Individuals who disagree with those in authority are regarded as deviants—a tendency toward the culture of silence, which demands that violation of one's right is sacred, and so should not be challenged. Two programs—'Pot of Life' (a local program) and 'Sesame Street' (a foreign program)—tend to stress gender subordination and racial discrimination respectively.

This study comes up with a number of recommendations, with a view to disentangling our children from the transmission of the cultural traits of the ruling class in contradistinction to our own. The attendant downright mystification of social reality is also aimed at being exterminated.

The research into cinema in the western part of Nigeria, with emphasis on Western film as a medium of cultural imperialism and with lbadan city as a case study (Solanke, 1982), introduces a unique and engaging dimension into the mass media scene.

This study starts off with a definition of cinema as "a darkened room, a screen, a projector, a film being projected and an audience watching the film" (Bebey, 1977).

The findings of this study reveal that Western film was introduced by the British colonialists in order to destroy our culture, thereby laying foundation for their home products. This objective seems to have been achieved even to this day. For 75.83% of cinema viewers interviewed cherished Western type of marriage, 67% vowed never to consult traditional healers in their lifetime and 72.5% of the female respondents rated hair-perming as the best type of hair care for our society. Familial and socio-medical issues though these may sound *prima facie*, they constitute an unbridled drain on our foreign currency. For the finished products involved in this regard are imported from abroad. This is apart from the drain on our culture.

Additionally, from the observation of the researcher when *Jaiyesimi* (a Nigerian film by Herbert Ogunde) was screened at K.S. Cinema, lbadan, a sixty-two-year-old man remarked that "This is the type of film we want. All these stupid foreign films breed irresponsibility and rascality among our youth". So while T.V. tends to generate the culture of silence (Baba, 1985)—referred to above—cinema tends to indiscriminately breed irresponsibility and rascality. The latter tends to culminate in broad daylight brigandage and glaring moral decadence.

This study recommends, *inter alia*, that some foreign films like pornographic films be banned from our screens; that all foreign films be fully previewed and sections capable of damaging our culture deleted; and, borrowing a leaf from Germans, who dub most foreign films into German, that all foreign films must first be dubbed into Nigerian languages.

The possibility of restructuring the world system has been empirically explored, with a view to establishing a New International Information and Communication Order (NIICO). In this study by Abdullah (1984), it is amply demonstrated that there is enormous disparity in book and news production between the Third World and the technologically advanced countries of the world. The Third World, therefore, makes demand, articulated in different international fora. The reasons advanced for this demand include the fact that Western news items are disproportionately represented to the detriment of the Third World, whose views are either ignored or given very little space. Worse still, news concerning the Third World are not only distorted, but are also mostly those relating to wars, coups, etc.

It is worth recalling that global 'free flow of information' (p. 160) is nonexistent. The reasons advanced for the demand by the Third World in connection with NIICO, therefore, further underscore the unfoundedness of global 'free flow of information'.

The United Nations Educational, Scientific and Cultural Organization (UNESCO) have been dynamically instrumental in the frantic search for NIICO. However, the efforts being made from all quarters at the moment are exclusively at the secondary level rather than at the primary level. Not being an independent sphere of human existence, information is subjected to the vicissitudes of the class struggle at both the primary and secondary level. So the minority ruling class (the petty bourgeoisie) should be dealt with at the local level. Otherwise, the information and communication will continue to benefit their imperialist masters (i.e., the international bourgeoisie). In order for a NIICO to be translated into reality, this study recommends that "accounts be settled first with the local bourgeoisie".

The impact of agricultural broadcasting on farmers in Jos (Plateau State) and its environs (Orewere, 1984)[2] constitutes a study examining the relative effectiveness of two sources of farm information for the farming population, namely, mass communications and interpersonal communications.

Sampling-wise, it was ensured, in choosing the respondents (the Beroms), that the sample involved had nearly equal media reception, since Plateau State has a rocky and hilly topography which affects the reception and clarity of television messages.

This study reveals that of 119 farmers, 49.6% most frequently indicate that interpersonal sources are the most mentioned source of farm information, while, of 129 farmers, 53.7% indicate the same source as one considered most reliable. Results similarly in favor of interpersonal source were discernible in the study by Mirchaulum (1976) and also in that by Ogionwo (1978). Further, it is recognized from this study that farmers' exposure to the mass media has not contributed directly to the adoption of new farm techniques, and that the popularity of radio, expressed in terms of listenership, can be attributed to the fact that it is cheap and that it beats distance, and, to some extent, beats literacy barriers.

It is also revealed that since they are situated in a social network of interpersonal relationships and within patterns of sociocultural life, governed by the values and norms of the society, the farmers tend to favor corresponding interpersonal communications, thus enhancing their willingness to be receptive to change. And since they are to make their choice on cost-benefit grounds, however crude this may be, preference for interpersonal communications is, obviously, not out of the question. Moreover, adopters of farm innovations have different information networks than non-adopters, and this category of farmers indicate interpersonal sources as their sources on farm information.

This study comes up solely with a number of research-agenda-oriented recommendations—that research be conducted to ascertain whether the media may serve as a source of 'first information' for farmers; that research be conducted into the networks of communication within a rural community; and that research be conducted to ascertain whether the degree of a farmer's social participation score in a community is associated with his adoption score in that community.

### Endnotes
[1] This is a Master's thesis.
[2] This is a Master's thesis.

## DISCUSSION QUESTIONS/EXERCISES AND ESSAYS
### Sociology of Law

1. What are the meaning and significance of sociology of law?

2. Define legal pluralism.

3. Discuss the nature of the offense committed by adulterers.

4. Explain why it was the elders of the litigants that were responsible for payment of fines.

5. What were the far-reaching effects of the British expedition in 1905?

6. Explain the circumstances surrounding the *change from* issues involving misunderstandings *to* the prevalence of property offenses.

7. Critically examine and discuss the choice of law in a pluralist legal environment. How does the choice of law in a non-pluralist society compare to this? Is there any connection between a pluralist legal society and such a society as the United States where the operation of law may vary from one state to another?

8. Explain why the Marxist perspective is used in the "sociological examination of the form, content and operation" of the Nigerian criminal law. Can the same perspective be used in any other studies? Expatiate on your answer.

9. Discuss the linguistic and structural nature of criminal law and the predominantly property-biased pattern of criminalization in Nigeria.

10. Why does the general Nigerian populace seem to give less respect to the police than to the courts? Is the performance of the courts themselves not prone to criticism? Back up your answer with an explanation. What is the situation in America or any other country as far as these two questions are concerned?

## Sociology of Marriage and the Family

11. Examine the statement "The family is universally acknowledged as the basic unit of society."

12. What do you think might be the reason(s) why children staying with guardians tend to develop more confidence in themselves to pass examination than do children living with their parents? Relate this to the finding that children living with fathers are not disadvantaged, educationally, vis-a-vis children living with their kinsmen.

13. Enumerate the details of sociocultural change that has occurred at the levels of the structural framework of the community as a result of the achievements of Western education.

14. What are the changes that have occurred in marital behavior?

15. Considering such factors as adultery, marriage, chastity, and espousing of girls (which is fast dying out in modern society), discuss divorce in this part of Africa in relation to divorce in America or any other country. How about the status of women?

16. Explain what is meant by customary laws of succession and inheritance.

17. How does the Chamba's centralized system of government relate to any modern system of government in Africa or elsewhere in the developed societies?

### Sociology of Mass Communications

18. Define sociology of mass communications.

19. Discuss the role of the news editor as the 'gatekeeper'.

20. Explain why the newspaper house is no more than the 'megaphone' or mouthpiece of the ruling class.

21. What is the factor that should not be regarded as an embodiment of the indices of development, and why?

22. The TV industry is found to be dependent on foreign programs, which reflect the sociocultural values of the producing country. Why, in your opinion, are these programs preferred by young people? How about the role of globalization in this connection?

23. Discuss the concept of 'free flow of information.'

24. Critique the imperialistic nature of television broadcasting in Nigeria.

25. Critically examine the contents of the children's programs on television.

26. Discuss the role of Western films with respect to an unbridled drain on foreign currency and on culture, and the breeding of irresponsibility and rascality among youth.

27. Relate the possibility of restructuring the world system to the establishment of a New International Information and Communication Order (NIICO).

28. Evaluate the relative effectiveness of mass communications and interpersonal communications in a farming (and non-farming) community.

29. To what factors is the popularity of radio attributed?

# ·XI·

# SOCIOLOGY OF RELIGION

S ociology of Religion studies the social institution known as religion, which, according to Emile Durkheim, is "a unified system of beliefs and practices relative to sacred things, that is to say, things set apart and forbidden— beliefs and practices which unite into one single moral community..." (Bottomore, 1975). Like any other social institution, the institution of religion serves as a means of satisfying human basic needs. It is, therefore, clear that sociology of religion does not only study religion, but also studies the relationship between religion and other aspects of society.

On the question of sociology and religion, it is at times held that sociology emerged to supersede religion. For, Auguste Comte, who coined the word 'sociology' and *ipso facto* regarded as the first real sociologist, "treats theological thinking as intellectual error which is dispersed by the rise of modern science" (Bottomore, 1975). Similarly, it is at times held that, since the higher beings in the religious nexus are essentially supernatural, religion, in its entirety, necessarily lies outside the scope of science and is no more than a matter of belief. However, Murdock (1977) holds a different view on this score. As he argumentatively puts it:

> Because of this fact [that religion lies outside the scope of science] there has been, and still persists, a widespread notion that religion and science are inherently incompatible, or that the relation between them must be one of conflict. This notion tends to fade away as the truth becomes clear that science, as well as religion, has its limitations, and that the fields of the two are distinct, and not superposable.

Closely allied to this view of Murdock is the fact that Isaac Newton, whose great work on the physical world had laid bare all the secrets of physical nature and who consequently was the most admired scientist of the late seventeenth and the eighteenth centuries, remained religious to the end of his life and was also deeply interested in theological problems (Nisbet, 1982).

Regarding religion in African society, the Festac Colloquium (Amoda, 1978) has made it quite clear that it is only the traditional African religion that is indigenous to African society. The position is so tellingly put that it assumes the following tone:

> Inasmuch as every religion is always within a particular culture, the Christian, Muslim and Judaic religions are foreign to Africa because, historically, they are not, like traditional religion, moulded in African culture. But once they have been accepted by Africans, they cease to be foreign, just as certain writings imported from Europe are no longer thought to be foreign. This being so, in the struggle for the liberation of the continent, the relevant problem is not that of the origin or rightful place of religion, or the problem of the difference in its content. The problem that arises is in fact *how* religion *can be* wrested *by oppressive Group*, whose interests are opposed to the people's (the use to which religion is put by racists)... (Emphasis added.)

The Christian religion has been accorded an indigenous touch, since, as it will become crystal clear later in this chapter, the Christian religion, in the sphere of symbolically and literally acquiring an indigenous touch, turns out to have an upper hand on the brand of Christianity brought to the continent by European missionaries. The indigenous touch was given by those Christians, referred to on page 171 and collectively called the Aladura. As a matter of fact, the whole phenomenon of acquiring indigenous touch on the part of Christian religion can be convincingly said to be a *reindigenization,* since the earliest years of Christianity could not be divorced from Africa, as it is clearly evidenced by, for example, the prominence of Egypt—a country in North East Africa on the Mediterranean Sea—and Ethiopia in the horn of Africa. In this connection, there is no gainsaying the fact that Christianity is not a white-man religion. And, according to Bohannan and Curtin (1995), "Christianity has impinged on Africa for centuries. Ethiopia is largely Christian, and has long been so. The Coptic Church there and in Egypt is one of the basic forms of Christianity."

The research by Matankari (1970) into the *bori* spirit mediumship cult in Malumfashi (Kaduna State) focuses on a particular sort of traditional religion which exists to this day.

This study defines *bori* as both a spirit possession or a form of trance in which the behavior and actions of a person are interpreted as evidence of a control of his behavior by a spirit normally external to him, and constituting spirit mediumship, whereby the person is conceived as serving as an intermediary between spirits and men. Additionally, this study explains that people do distinguish between the world of human activity and the realm of spirits which are beyond the full control and understanding of human beings.

This study reveals that there are three situations making an individual become a member or undergo initiation—(1) if she has inherited *bori*, in which case she has to undergo a part of the initiation called *bincike,* meaning an investigation to determine which spirit possesses her; (2) if she has suffered from illness inflicted upon her by a certain spirit and wants to know the condition for curing her (and for the possibility of curing others by her in future); and (3) if she is attracted by the costumes and the income of the devotees.

It is also revealed that some of the activities of the cult other than possession include settlement of disagreements between members, healing (which, of course, is related to possession), and sorcery. This study further reveals a competition between *Bori* cult healing and Western medicine.

Although the outcome of the competition between *bori* cult healing and Western medicine, which so markedly characterized Malumfashi, was not yet known, there was evidence that the cult was in a state of crisis at the time of this research, both in terms of internal conflict and public opinion of it.

The Itapo festival, which takes place every seven years and which is the most widely observed in Ososo Community in Akoko-Edo area of Bendel State (Ladipo, 1974), constitutes a study on an importantly symbolic aspect of African traditional religion, characterized by pomp and pageantry. This study is based on oral tradition with, needless to say, elderly men as the respondents. However, the origin of the Itapo festival is not determined: oral traditions emphasize only its performance.

Using a descriptive analytical tool, this study demonstrates that the Itapo festival is an occasion on which young men are initiated into elderhood in Ososo community. The festival, in the absence of written history, serves to remind the Ososo people about their historical past both as a group and as individuals.

*Exhibition of basins of food (pounded yam), pots of melon soup with meat, melon "ball," and lumps of salt at the Itapo festival*

It is evinced that the festival tends to strengthen the matrilineal kinship ties that serve as a linkage among the four district wards in Ososo Community. It is also evinced, through sociological observation of actual celebration of the Itapo festival, that the functions of this festival can be seen not only from religio-political standpoint, but from economic, social, and cultural aspects of Ososo as well.

The research into the continuity of the *Sango* cult in Koso-Oyo (present-day Oyo) despite change (Bamidele, 1975) focuses on an aspect of traditional religion in Africa, namely, that of the Yoruba. This study, according to legends, describes *Sango* as the fourth *Alafin* (traditional ruler) of the Oyo Yoruba and as being deified after his death. Hence, we have, to this day, the Sango cult and his priests and worshipers.

The uniqueness of this study consists in its use of oral data and sources of information which include rare documents in the National Museum in Lagos and in the Institute of African Studies of the University of Ibadan.

This study reveals that taboos—which are things not to be done by the Sango priests and worshipers both as a consequence of their attachment to the divinity and for the sake of ritual performances—include non-abstinence from the kinds of food or drink which the divinity does not take and which, consequently, are forbidden to all his worshipers, sexual uncleanliness of a priest while entering his sacred office, and the presence of menstruating women in the shrine.

It is further revealed that the factors responsible for the persistence of the Sango cult in Koso-Oyo despite the incursion of Christianity and Islam include the role, on traditional demand, that Mogba—a Sango priest—has to play in the shrine on a visit by, and at the coronation of, a new Alafin (the visit, itself, by a new Alafin to Koso for divination is also in due allegiance to, and respect for, Sango, the deified Alafin of Oyo). The factors responsible for the persistence of Sango cult also include invitation from his priests to victims of fire-outbreak to become members of the cult, in order to avoid future reoccurrence; initiation of their male children by devout worshipers into the cult; and the cultural awakening in Nigeria, which makes possible some coverage of Sango festival by the mass media, as amply exemplified by that of 1973.

The study on the role of the Aladura Church, with Cherubim and Seraphim Church in Samaru, Zaria, as a case study (Ahimie, 1973), is one which extends beyond the scope of a single religious sect to that of the entire Aladura church, at least from historical and organizational perspectives, which, understandably, are intimately connected with Christianity as a whole.

This study involved interview with members and non-members of the Aladura Church in Lagos, Ile-Ife, Benin City, Samaru, and Kaduna. Also, it dug into the National Archives in Kaduna for source of rare data regarding the origin of Cherubim and Seraphim Church in Samaru, crowned with attendance— a sort of participant observation—by the investigator at the various services of the church in Samaru.

It is shown by this study that the Aladura as a religion consists of a number of denominations, the well-known ones being Cherubim and Seraphim Church, the Apostolic Church, and Church of the Lord, and that there exists a host of others, especially in Lagos area where many more are still springing up.

This study observes that Peel (1968) has asserted that the Aladura emerged in a situation against the background of industrialization, nation-building, and conversion of the African people from their traditional religion to the world religion, new beliefs, and practices, with a series of disasters, influenza, plagues, famine, and depression, following the rapid growth of a money economy, and that all of these demanded a new religious interpretation as the main cause of their emergence. On the contrary, the standpoint of this study is that the causes of the emergence of the Aladura were more fundamental than those which Peel has given and which were contributory factors, and that the Aladura origin antedated the era of development. Therefore, the origin of the Aladura cannot be divorced from the general move to found African Churches which started in the 1880s.

This study points to the founding of the first African Church—the African Native Baptist Church—in 1888 by a group of individuals who, due to the fervor of nationalism, had broken away from the original Baptist Church of the American missionary and that, following this precedent, a major action by a group of laymen of several churches including the long-discontented Anglican, Methodist, and Catholic culminated in the establishment of the United African Church, whose foundation meeting, according to Webster (1964), took place in 1891. However, this study makes it quite clear that most of these churches apparently developed more or less along the lines of the old established churches, thus constituting another 'denomination' of the latter, rather than an alternative to it.

This situation based more or less on the *status quo* contributed toward the emergence of the Aladura, with the Aladura serving as an alternative. For the Aladura, as noted by this study, did introduce new forms of worship, incorporating a lot of the aspects of the indigenous culture. Of course, the organizational structure, whereby the long-existing church was controlled solely by the clergy, imbued with constant harping on the old hymns, litanies, doctrines, and ceremonies, constituted huge problems. The rise of the Aladura movement was marked by the fact that it provided the solution to the problems of the African Church movement, making good these organizational anomalies and substituting them with, among other things, atmosphere-changing and unprecedented prayer, drumming (vehemently saturated with dance and doxology), hand-clapping, spiritual power, vision revelation, act of speaking in tongues, tearing down of the demonic strongholds of the devil, miracles, and healing—all in an echoing jubilation!

Concerning Cherubim and Seraphim Church, an integral part of which the church constituting the case study of this research is, the fact that the origin of the Aladura antedated the disasters following rapid growth of a money economy, as argued above, is best illustrated partly with the case of Baba Aladura (Spiritual

Father) Moses Orimolade Tunolase. Baba Aladura Orimolade had been doing his own praying for people in his hometown, Ikare, and later in Lagos, where, in spite of his not being literate, he was popular with his brilliant Biblical quotations. And Baba Aladura Orimolade did not until 1925 found the Eternal Sacred Order of Cherubim and Seraphim together with Miss Abiodun Akinsowon (now the Revd. Mother Captain (Dr.) Abiodun Emmanuel), for whom he prayed while she was for the first time ever in a trance. The incident of this trance, according to Captain Abiodun, occurred during the annual Roman Catholic Corpus Christi procession along Campus Square in Lagos and she saw an Angel above the Monstrance as the procession moved on, falling into a trance on reaching home for two days.

*Members of Cherubim and Seraphim Church worshiping during a service*

With respect to Cherubim and Seraphim Church in Samaru, Zaria—the church which is the case study—this study indicates that it was founded as an extension of another Cherubim and Seraphim Church, popularly known as K45 and situated in Benin street in downtown Sabongari, Zaria, for convenience sake, since all potential and substantive members were staff members of the defunct Nigerian College of Arts, Science and Technology (out of which the Ahmadu Bello University grew in 1962). Further, this study indicates that Cherubim and Seraphim Church has spread from the southern part of Nigeria to Kaduna and thence to other parts of the north and that the one in the north (distinctly known

as Cherubim and Seraphim Movement) is reputed to be the most centrally organized and well coordinated, with headquarters in Kaduna and a branch in the
United Kingdom.

In spite of the seeming separatist tendencies in the entire order of Cherubim
and Seraphim, this study takes note of a great desire for unification—for convenience and standardization sake—as is evident from the quality of leaders and
the composition of members.

However, it is noted that the Samaru Church and, indeed, the whole movement or even the whole order (embracing all the various Cherubim and Seraphim sects) are weak in terms of not having full-time leaders. Rather, most of the
leaders are 'part-timers' and the few 'workers' who are on full-time employment
are mostly illiterates.

On the question of authority in the church, things have changed a good deal:
the old situation in which authority was the prerogative of the lay-members, i.e.,
the congregation, have gradually given way to the rule by elders who in most
cases were rich and might have given the church grant of land or money to build
church. However, the trend now is that the young elements gain more power for
'governing' the church by occupying important organizational/administrative
status by virtue of their high level of educational attainment.

The hypothesis of this study that Cherubim and Seraphim Church (Samaru)
can help to develop modernizing attitudes amongst its members seems to be
confirmed, among other things, by (1) the greater numerical strength of the con-
verted members over the 'born Aladura', meaning those whose parents were
members before they were born, (2) reasons for becoming members (e.g., fear of
the devil and desire for jobs/further studies), (3) claim to non-visit to *Babalawo*
(i.e., traditional healer) since becoming Aladuras, and the relatively great role
played by the youth.

Students' voluntary activities, with the Fellowship of Christian Students
(FCS) at Ahmadu Bello University main campus as a case study (Chile, 1976) is
an evaluative study whose aim is to examine how members perceive the significance of the voluntary activities to themselves as well as to ABU main campus.

Being a participant in most of the students' voluntary activities, the investigator played a role partly as a participant observer, thus constituting a distinct
methodological basis for this study.

This study first focuses on three factors, namely, (1) group, since the FCS is
a group of students, (2) common goals shared by the members of the group and
(3) expansion of group membership through various activities.

The aim of the voluntary service is to be of service to local churches, requir-
ing the services of student volunteers. Such services include those of Sunday
School teachers, nursery teachers, youth group leaders, choir-masters, organists,
editors of church publications, etc., all of which are not intended for taking over
the existing leadership in the local churches concerned. Other voluntary services
include visits to hospitals and prisons, and organization of evangelical campaigns.
Closely allied to these voluntary services is that of the Students Aid Committee

which aims to give some financial assistance to students faced with financial constraints, irrespective of their religious affiliation. This committee is not originated by students, but, needless to say, is connected with them.

*Christians worshiping in a church*

On the perception by FCS members of the significance of the voluntary activities to themselves, this study reveals that, instead of interacting exclusively within the four walls of the "ivory tower," these activities make off-campus interaction with people in the local churches and surrounding rural areas a possibility. Moreover, volunteers, in the process of offering their services, are unwittingly groomed in organizational skills, mechanical skills, and editorial skills, which become professionally useful later in life, though these services accord them the opportunity to serve and worship God with their talents. This acquisition of skills is no doubt what in sociological terminology is known as the latent function (i.e., unintended effect) of their services.

Concerning the significance of the voluntary activities to the main campus, student volunteers are engaged in annual religious campaigns, rallies, initiation of new members, and Sunday School for children, all taking place on the main campus.

Much as church or church-going is accorded a distinct degree of recognition in the whole Christendom, it is widely held among many a Christian that this should not take precedence over, or even supersede, being a true believer. This viewpoint is conditioned by a related viewpoint that, in the strict sense of the word, Christianity is not a religion but a way of life, whereby one has experienced a new birth, that is, the Spirit-birth. The clear stand of Oyedepo (1986) on this issue, quoted below, is not only reflective of that of many a Christian, but is also illuminating:

> Let it first be understood that you are not a Christian merely because you go to church—no matter the kind of church involved... Rather it is by reason of the New BIRTH alone that one becomes a Christian... the Spirit-birth.

All followers of Jesus Christ are expected to comply with this, bearing in mind their commitment to lovingly represent Jesus Christ to other people both in word and in deed, not merely cherishing church-going. And the Spirit desires to use them in sharing the gospel, so that others can experience the New Birth.

Traditional vs. Contemporary Hadj (Sani, 1977) constitutes the focus of a study on the Islamic religion. This study observes that hadj is the fifth fundamental aspect of Islam, the remaining four being belief, prayers, Zakat (almsgiving) and fasting, all of which (together with Hadj) are obligatory. Those who can afford to go to the holy land should do so at least once in their lifetime. It is noted by this study that the acts of worship are performed in Mecca, Muna, Arafat, and Muzdalifa, and that pilgrims must also visit Prophet Mohammed's grave and offer prayers in his mosque in Medina. In the course of the performance, pilgrims dress alike, irrespective of their socioeconomic status. Thus, a situation, where people are reminded of human equality, is created.

This study explains that the word 'traditional' applies to the first means of transportation used by pilgrims from Nigeria to Mecca, that is, by road, either on foot, animal's back, truck, or lorry as well as by sea. This hazardous situation can be seen in contrast to the smooth operation of modern Hadj.

On the other hand, the modern means of transportation from Nigeria to the holy land relieves people of the hardship of the journey: pilgrims travel by air. And pilgrims are sure of meeting their people within hours from Saudi Arabia. This study further indicates that there is a Nigerian hospital organized annually in Jedda, with its branches in Mecca, Muna, Medina, and Arafat. There are also mobile clinics and ambulances in pilgrims' camping ground in Muna and Arafat for immediate attention, and, in case of sickness, for transfer to, and treatment in, the hospital.

This study comes up with the findings that 56.7% of the total of the survey sample consider traditional Hadj to be more expensive than modern Hadj and that 66.7% agree that pilgrims were more open to disease attack during traditional hadj than they were during modern Hadj. It is further found that wealth, commercialization, and educational achievement are primary factors in determining the increasing preference for modern hadj over the traditional.

Furthermore, the modern Hadj, according to this study, provides a flair for distance trade for an enterprising people like Nigerians. For they take advantage of the quick air passage sufficient to accommodate the vast quantity of goods they bring back to Nigeria. Hence, many local Alhaji traders make it a yearly trading outlet, especially as Saudi Arabia is a duty-free country. Contrarily, the inconvenient means of transport in traditional hadj tended to militate against the possibility of such a commercial venture.

It is also revealed by this study that the modern hadj does not give pilgrims opportunity to acquire any knowledge of African peoples and cultures. For it takes shorter time and also routes that do not allow for any reasonable degree of observation of peoples and cultures, but orients pilgrims toward becoming more aware of the commercial city of Saudi Arabia than of its people.

It is further revealed that most of the pilgrims have to resort to begging, to get feeding money, after having stayed for two to three weeks there. There is also the case of migrant pilgrims residing in Sudan and Saudi.

This study recommends that special agencies be set up to aid pilgrims in such matters as vaccination, acquisition of passports and sure transport arrangement.

Specifically for the findings in the penultimate paragraph above, this study recommends, respectively, that pilgrims should not be allowed to leave Nigeria until they have money enough to sustain them throughout their stay in Saudi, and that no pilgrims should be allowed to leave Nigeria, unless it is endorsed in their travel documents that they are definitely returning home.

The research into hadj as a *communitas* and an integrative process, with Nigerian pilgrims as a case study (Bakori, 1977), focuses on hadj as being characterized by group consciousness and unifying factor.

This study adopted participant observation method, whilst the investigator was in the process of killing two birds with one stone, simultaneously playing the role of a researcher as well as that of an Alhaji-in-the-making.

Concerning *communitas* (a Latin word, meaning an aggregate of individuals or groups bound together by virtue of common beliefs, values and attitudes towards a common goal), this study equates *communitas* with a Muslim community grouped together, following a common faith in Islam and a purpose, i.e., pilgrimage.

The findings of this research show that, during the pilgrimage, a common sense of belonging emerged. Also, interaction was not characterized by hierarchical arrangement: all pilgrims were regarded as being equal.

On the question of the hadj as an integrative process, it is revealed that, because the pilgrims commonly share norms and values, they tend to be geared toward unity, cooperation, and integration, as exemplified by inter-ethnic marriage many years after they have returned to Nigeria.

The importance of religion in a given society cannot be overemphasized. However, a question which would seem to be most crucial pertains not so much to what role is played by religion in a given society as to the extent to which religion is an instrument of class domination and oppression.

In this connection, the veteran sociologist, Ebow Mensah (1986), situates the whole issue within the context of class analysis, using Nigeria as a case study. Having highlighted how the North-South dichotomy[1] is another factor commonly employed to becloud and confuse the issue of national integration in Nigeria, with religion frequently seen as the actual force behind the division, Mensah un-covers the class character of religion. As he analytically puts it:

> ...religion and religious ideology (consciousness) may effectively be employed, most times consciously, to conceal what is in reality a class struggle, i.e., a com-petitive form of social relation. Consequently, rather than just enquire about the role of religion in national integration, the relevant question *would be the extent to which religion is employed as an instrument of class domination and oppression.* The signi-ficance of an answer to this question lies in how it succeeds in showing the ef-fectiveness of religion in promoting class struggle. (Emphasis added.)

The foregoing phenomenon, cunningly portrayed in a religious garb, demon-strates that the use of religion increasingly to further class interest is fast becom-ing the order of the day. Clearly, religion has continued to be turned into an ob-noxious mechanism for covering up what, in actual fact, is a class struggle. Echoing Mensah, we need to ask the relevant question, to which extent is reli-gion employed as an instrument of class domination and oppression? It is then, and then only, will we be able to uncover the reality at work.

## Endnote

[1] Typical of the North-South dichotomy was the disagreement in 1978 among members of the Constituent Assembly over the inclusion or non-inclusion of Sharia in the constitution. For the Sharia issue rapidly developed into a na-tional crisis, commonly perceived and interpreted as a general North-South confrontation (*ibid.*). However, most remarkable is the fact that "the *very same assembly men* who were so resolutely and irrevocably divided over the Sharia question *regrouped themselves* shortly afterwards, on the basis of shared interests, *in a number of political parties* with no religious or North-South differentiation" (*ibid.*). (Emphasis added.)

## DISCUSSION QUESTIONS/EXERCISES AND ESSAYS

1. With particular reference to the position of Comte, Bottomore, and Mur-dock, explain the statement that "science as well as religion has its limita-tions, and that the fields of the two are distinguished, and not superposa-ble".

2. Break into small groups, with each discussing a possible critique (or vindi-cation) of the idea that Christianity is a foreign religion to Africa or that it is a white-man religion. Then all the groups will come together and discuss the views of each group.

3. Suppose you perceive that there is nothing like bori (defined as both a spi-rit possession and a form of trance) in your country. Do you think there is what is called a spirit world together with its demons in your country that constitutes evil forces out there, directing human affairs? If you do, what

are the consequences, real and potential, for modern society? This exercise may take the form of a group discussion.

4. What are the factors that constitute the main cause of the emergence of the Aladura?

5. Discuss the new forms of worship introduced by the Aladura, especially the factors that serve as substitutes for the organizational anomalies of the African church movement.

6. Explain how the study on FCS exhibits a distinct methodological basis.

7. Recalling how *ivory-tower* is used in chapter eight (sociology of education), explain why *ivory-tower* is put in quotation marks when off-campus interaction by members of FCS with people in the local churches and surrounding rural areas is referred to.

8. How would you explain the figurative expression that FCS members' activities are best described as "killing two birds with one stone"?

9. Compare and contrast traditional Hadj with modern Hadj.

10. Discuss the five fundamental aspects of Islam.

11. What is meant by *communitas*? Relate this to inter-ethnic marriage.

12. How important is the statement: "However, a question which would seem to be most crucial pertains not so much to what role is played by religion in a given society as to the extent to which religion is an instrument of class domination and oppression"?

# ·XII·

# Urban Sociology and Women in Society/Women's Studies

## Urban Sociology

Urban Sociology is the study of city life, i.e., the study of people and their values in an urban setting. A basic thread of critical significance that runs through urban sociology is epitomized by rural-urban relations, which find practical expression in rural-urban linkages.

Arising from the way urban sociology studies city life are the differences and similarities of city life and village life, thus providing one with an insight into the consequences of human action.

Inextricably tied in with urban sociology is urbanization, which is a movement of people and a spread of ideas and culture. And the process of urbanization is universally known to be studied in a historical perspective. This is of great analytical relevance to Africa, where the process of urbanization is best examined within the framework of periodization, namely, within the context of precolonial, colonial, and postcolonial periods.

The study on Idoma ethnic union and association in Kaduna (Ogbe, 1970) is an analysis of ethnic unions in an urban setting. This study shows that Idoma unions in Kaduna are segmentally arranged—a reflection of the political and social setting in the home area. For instance, 'family' unions are an equivalent of *ipooma* (i.e., sub-lineage), which constitutes a village back home. So the word 'family' does not mean conjugal/nuclear family or even extended family. A 'family union' is, indeed, a union of Idoma people from the same village or, in some cases, a union of Idoma people from the same lineage or clan.

This study reveals that the activities of the unions include regulation of the behavior of members, mutual cooperation, financial assistance to members (with monthly membership fees as a basic source), burial of deceased members, and settlement of disputes between quarreling members.

Ethnic (or voluntary) associations in an urban setting are what the research study on continuity and change of Ishan life in Kaduna (Orukpe, 1971) is all about.

This study deals mainly with the ethnic association called the Ishan Progressive Union (IPU).

This study comes up with the findings that apart from IPU, there are church associations and family/class meetings, which serve as a good alternative to the ethnic association. For members of the church concerned (Cherubim and Seraphim Church) have their prayer requests granted by the Lord and, hence, are blessed with jobs, while other prayers of theirs continue to be answered. Some of the members of family meetings are also members of IPU. It is worth noting that the use of the word 'family' here is different from how it is used among the members of the Idoma union discussed above.

The goals of IPU are to keep peace and harmony among the Ishan in Kaduna (this is in keeping with its motto *"Kobe bi Four"*, meaning Unity and Peace), to provide mutual benefits for all members, to further progress, both educationally and culturally, and to educate children of the Ishan. I.P.U. has achieved appreciable success as far as these goals are concerned, except that it has not been able to award scholarship even to a single Ishan child.

The research into urban dominance in metropolitan Kano (Ahmed, 1976) is a typical study on rural-urban relations with urban Kano both as a parasite and, to echo the investigator just as he echoes Galtung (1971), as "a 'bridge head' to exploit the village people for the benefit of the imperialist countries."

This study focuses on two villages, Dorayi Babba and Dorayi Karama, which are close to each other, and also on metropolitan Kano. The findings revealed are that weekly visits between people in the two villages to each other are much less frequent than visits to urban Kano. If anything, it is social events/ceremonies that primarily constitute the purposes of visits. For instance, no villager from Dorayi Babba sells anything in Dorayi Karama and only three villagers from the latter go to the former for economic transaction.

Housing problems in Kaduna within the context of Kaduna State Housing Authority is the focus of the study by Ogbena (1979). In particular, this study examines the operation of housing authority as well as its impact on the populace.

This study observes that, in spite of the fact that the New Nigerian Development Company (NNDC) built low-cost housing units in 1963, the Federal Housing Authority was established in 1973 (specifically to avoid shortage of accommodation during Festac scheduled to take place in Lagos and Kaduna in January 1975 but later postponed to January 1977) and that in spite of the fact that Kaduna State Housing Authority was established in 1976, serving as an agent for the Federal Housing Authority, housing problems in Kaduna continued to exist.

This study reveals that the rents paid by occupants of the housing units are based on the principle of a rent/income ratio, i.e., 20% of an individual's income equals rent. Therefore, tenants with low incomes feel the brunt of this rent formula harder than those with high incomes. It is also revealed that the quality of the materials used for building the houses is questionable.

This study recommends that, in order to achieve national housing objectives, there should be a renewed effort to coordinate housing policies and plans. It further recommends the use of cheaper, relatively long-lasting concrete blocks instead of burnt bricks now in use, and that allocation on the principle of need be preferred to allocation by the ballot system.

The study on the class structure and housing problems in Zaria (Adamu, 1979) undertakes to ascertain whether class relations are reflected in housing arrangements and housing policies of government. The areas where the houses are located are Sabongari, Tudunwada, Zaria City, Samaru, and Government Reservation Area (GRA).

This study comes up with the findings that about 75% of the respondents, particularly businessmen constituting the upper class, own houses on the GRA or in Tudunwada or Zaria City. Some members of this class (25%) who are salaried workers and for whom accommodation cannot be provided are given rent subsidies by the employers. It is the same entire members of this class who own houses that charge very high rents, payable by the members of the lower class with low incomes. The middle class, too, fall prey to these shylock landlords and are worse off than the members of the upper class.

This study concludes that, obviously, housing problems of our society (with Zaria as a typical example) can be associated with class, since these problems are related to conditions arising from the class structure of society. It, therefore, recommends that our policy makers get their priorities right, not only regarding housing needs, but also regarding all others.

The study on urban relationships with particular reference to socioeconomic characteristics and participation in voluntary associations (Yunusa, 1979) focuses on the determinants of degrees of participation by individual members of voluntary associations in Dekina, Benue State, rather than on structures, goals, and objectives of the associations themselves.

This study comes up with the findings that 65.4% of the respondents hold memberships of various associations, and that those with the highest level of education tend to participate more than those with low or no level of education. 78.3% of all the respondents are also members of their ethnic or religious associations for material and spiritual support.

Other findings are that while businessmen tend to belong to more associations and frequently attend meetings and pay subscription rates, civil servants and professionals tend to hold more positions and are more involved in the organizational aspect of the associations, most probably due to their education and competence, apparently acknowledged by the rest of the members. Apart from surplus resources and money at the disposal of the businessmen *vis-a-vis* the civil servants and professionals, the possibility of discussing business among members is another factor that tends to motivate them to participate more than the latter. This pattern of participation does not agree with Little's (1965) statement that the associations are dominated by those in need, the poor migrants, including the unemployed, who need mutual aids, social security and care from other urban dwellers, if they are to survive.

The first implication of this study is the implicit division of society into various socioeconomic groups, whereby the high socioeconomic group dominates the other groups, and participation in the associations tends to relate to participants' life careers. The second implication is that, consequent upon the first implication, the high-status individuals will tend to use the various associations to achieve an end in their career. The third implication is that what views are expressed by these associations are bound to be those of their dominating high-status members.

This study suggests that voluntary associations be encouraged by the welfare departments of the governments, and that they embark on humanitarian and philanthropic ventures; that their members who are politically-minded and wish to join political parties be encouraged to do so; and that cooperation between the associations and the government (in terms of assistance) be encouraged.

## Women in Society/Women's Studies

Women in Society, popularly known as Women's Studies, is mainly concerned with the plight of women with respect to their position both in the home and in the wider society. This concern is a global phenomenon. For example, the sex discrimination act is being enforced in Britain. The propelling forces behind this are, on the part of women themselves, effective organization and dynamic action, without which women's liberation is most likely to be no more than chasing the mirage. Hence, the point has been pungently made by Pittin (1982) that:

> Through collective action, understanding, and strength, we can prevail against the deeply-rooted, millennia-old and systematic oppression which all women have endured.

The family, which is the basic unit of the society, has been criticized as being exploitative and oppressive, with women at the receiving end *vis-a-vis* men, who have been socialized as a most domineering potentate in the home. In the public sphere of life, too, women are exploited and oppressed. This situation—whose basis is the dual productive relation of women (both in domestic and public affairs)—has been elucidated by Perchonock (1982), when she says:

> Women are, along with men, oppressed by particular types of class structures and forms of exploitation. In addition, there are often certain forms of oppression in society which are applied to women as a group, as distinct from those institutions which also oppress women. This phenomenon is usually referred to as the "double oppression" of women, i.e., women suffer oppression by virtue of their class position in society, and also by virtue of their sex.

Any meaningful concern with women's liberation must be concretized within the context of the examination of both class relations and sexual asymmetry. This, according to Pittin (1982), will make for an adequate comprehension of the nature of women's oppression. The nature of the plight of black women in America readily captures the essence of this statement, even in such a way that it transcends dual, relational factor. For these black American women, according to Bell Hooks (1995), are discriminated against not generally by men, but specifically by white racist patriarchs, their white female counterparts, and sexist black men.

On the question of employment for working mothers, Kisekka (1981) has, without mincing words, asserted that gainful employment for mothers is a right rather than a privilege.

What is needed in Nigeria, particularly with the inauguration of *Women in Nigeria (WIN)*—a women's Organization—is that women's movement should transcend exclusive gender inequality. As Imam (1982) has succinctly opined:

> I suggest what is required is a women's movement prepared to tackle the specificities of gender inequality but imbued with a historically concrete understanding of class relations, working to develop theoretical and practical links with other oppressed groups.

Technically prominent among the studies undertaken in the area of women's study is that on the dual career syndrome, focusing on Ahmadu Bello University students as a case study (Abubakar, 1981). The dual career syndrome refers to the lifestyle of women who are mothers and, at the same time, university students.

It is observed in this study that women find it difficult to get married on graduation. Hence, they get married before or during the duration of their university education.

This study is not only a case study, but a time allocation study as well. That is, it undertakes a case study of students as well as the time, which is allocated to, or at the disposal of, each student and which covers both daily academic and baby-care activities. Using that methodology, this study reveals that the student mothers are faced with very tight schedule as a result of their dual career. During the 1,440 minutes making up a day, role conflict sets in at times.

This study recommends that the university and the government take cognizance of the inevitability of dual career and thus provide hostel and day-care center for student mothers, in order to afford both men and women equal opportunity to acquire knowledge. The government is expected to do this for the whole country.

The study by Abdurrahman (1979) on friendship patterns amongst Amina Hall women at ABU demonstrates that friendship is a form of informal social relationship, largely influenced by the socioeconomic status of the individual involved in it. These women prefer to choose friends with whom they are in similar status.

The position, place, and situation of women in the police force, their general state affairs and factors affecting their participation in the force constitute the main thrust of the study by Nimyel (1978) on women in the Nigeria Police Force (NPF) in Kaduna.

The findings of this study show that from the perspective of the public, women should be treated in the same manner as men. However, policemen should perform different types of duties from those performed by their female counterparts, e.g., handling of female accused persons, juvenile delinquents, lost and found children, and office routine. The public respondents emphasize specialization based on sex-role differentiation, since this makes for efficiency and effectiveness.

The findings of this study reveal, from the perspective of the police, that policemen lay claim to better remuneration than that enjoyed by their female counterparts on account of differential work-performance. This, however, is through no fault of the policewomen: differential training is undergone by them. Hence, they are not allowed to use arms and batons and to do night duties.

Factors that constitute a barrier to the employment of women in industries have been uncovered by the research into the scope of women's employment in Nigerian industries, with Kaduna Textiles Limited and Nigerian Breweries Limited (NBL), Kaduna, as a case study (Agboola, 1981).

Although modern industries are, theoretically, supposed to be sex-blind, the domination of high technology by men constitutes a barrier on this score. This discrimination has been revealed to be discernible in manufacturing industries in Nigeria.

The findings regarding the nature of work show that 68% of the women workers at NBL are in the administrative department, while only four work in the department of technology and twelve in the mechanical department, making up 32% of the entire sample. 76% of them exhibit a 'self-fulfilling prophecy', i.e., that, being women, they cannot do most of the factory jobs.

On trade unionism, women are less interested in NBL union meetings and only a few of them are members, there is no woman on the executive.

The study by Vihishima (1983) on the portrayal of women in daily newspapers and magazines provides one with a most illuminating, empirical mirror by which how men perceive women and how women perceive themselves are readily discernible.

This research study undertakes a content analysis of six publications—*New Nigerian, The Punch, Lagos Weekend, Sunday Standard, Women's Own,* and *Women Magazine*—covering January to December 1982. Textbooks and discussions with respondents over matters concerning women also constitute sources of data collection.

Of the total sample of 316 women portrayed by the various papers and magazines, 75.9% were by women and 24.1% by men. Women writers portrayed women favorably, while male writers (including cartoonists) portrayed women unfavorably. More fundamentally, a newspaper or magazine dominated by men tended to portray women in an unfavorable light. A newspaper, the *Lagos Weekend,* whose editorialship is predominantly male, portrayed women most unfavorably. Women portrayed their fellow women in the economic and political life of the society. Men portrayed women merely within the context of the latter's place in the family—no doubt a stereotyped portrayal.

The study the on economic roles of women in an expanding market town, with Mangu, Benue-Plateau State (now Plateau State), as a case study (Drew, 1975)[1], focuses on the ways in which women earn money and on how they spend their money, comparing and contrasting their economic roles from familial, religious, and social perspectives.

This study utilizes verbally-administered questionnaire with heavy reliance upon informal discussions, e.g., upon the history of Mangu, the traditional role of women, the social composition of mangu, etc.

The major thrust of this study is that religion is a very important factor accounting for the variation in female economic roles in Mangu. However, religion does not offer a full explanation, since there is variation in these roles within the Christian and Muslim groups taken separately.

It is revealed that mat-makers tend to be Muslim women, while beer brewers and traders tend to be Christian women. Women of both religions engage in food processing and preparation. Christians are just as likely to be food processors as Muslims. Food processing is, therefore, an exception to the general rule of division of female labor by religion. However, the only differences found are in terms of the type of food produced and the mode of marketing, while the scale of production and profits earned appear to be similar.

Other findings are that Christian women are in a position to become increasingly involved in the market economy, whereas the Muslim women have far more limited opportunities. It is unlikely that they will be able to engage in relatively large-scale trading. However, Muslim women, found to be earning lesser income than Christian women, have far fewer financial obligations within their families. On the other hand, Christian women support the family with most, if not all, of their earnings.

Concerning Christian women, they are engaged in farming, mat-making, and trading. Those of them earning low profits are engaged in farming, whereas those earning high profits do not, participating only in mat-making and trading, since only men, as husbands, have right over the farmland.

Regarding Muslim women, the Suras (members of an ethnic group) among them are engaged in both mat-making and food processing as their primary occupations. Certain occupations are associated with certain ethnic groups, because they originally brought these occupations to Mangu. Participation by young women is, on the whole, low, since they, unlike old women, have no children to help with the out-of-home sales of products. Consequently, so many young Muslim women are engaged in mat-making rather than in food processing.

It is further revealed by the findings of this study that wives of high status Muslims do mat-making, while those of low status Muslims do food processing.

It is also revealed that, as in most traditional African societies, women in Sura and Pyem societies did play a very active role in providing for the needs of the family, mainly in agricultural activities. However, the role of Muslim Sura and Pyem women in Mangu have significantly changed *vis-à-vis* those of the traditional past: they are no longer involved in agricultural production and are only marginally involved in any form of trading. The economic roles of Christian women are also different from those of the traditional past, with the difference being predominantly in the form and content of their roles.

Interestingly, this study provides a successful empirical test of 'role cluster' model within the wider context of role theory. The model has enabled us to see, *inter alia,* that no one single system of stratification applies to all women in Mangu. Fundamental to this are differential female financial obligation and differential dependency on husband. Furthermore, the findings of this study reveal that the status of women *vis-à-vis* that of men is a dependent one, as far as their participation in social and public production is concerned. Overall, in light of its findings, this study takes the position of Engels (1880) as its frame of reference, as indicated below:

> Engels presents a historical dynamic by which women are transformed from free and equal productive members of society to subordinate and dependent wives and wards. The growth of male-owned private property, with the family as the institution that appropriates and perpetuates it, is the cause of this transformation.

It, therefore, goes without saying that the dependent status of both Muslim and Christian women in the study area (Mangu) is attributable to the growth of male-owned private property.

## Endnote

[1] This is a Master's thesis.

## DISCUSSION QUESTIONS/EXERCISES AND ESSAYS

### Urban Sociology

1. What is urban sociology?

2. What is meant by urbanization?

3. Explain how the term "family" does not mean conjugal/nuclear family or even extended family within the context of Idoma ethnic union.

4. What other associations serve as a good alternative to IPU? Explain.

5. Discuss the importance of the goals of IPU to any given society.

6. Explain how the fact that the villagers of Dorayi Babba and Dorayi Karama make less frequent visits to each other's village can be attributed to their dependent relations to the urban area.

## Women in Society/Women's Studies

7. With what is the subdiscipline of women's studies concerned?

8. To what extent is it true that the family is exploitative and oppressive?

9. Discuss how African women in Africa differ from African American women in terms of discrimination experienced by them.

10. What do you think is the relevance of using time allocation strategy to the study on dual career syndrome and the relevance of content analysis to the study on the portrayal of women in daily newspapers and magazines?

11. Discuss the dependency of women on men in Mangu. Is there any connection between their roles and those of their Western counterparts?

# ·XIII·

## OBSERVATIONS AND CONCLUSIONS

Casting a retrospective look on the trajectory of sociological knowledge, both at the macro- and micro-levels, one is inclined to be under the impression that sociological perspectives are of paramount significance, but that they nonetheless require much more to be done. This is particularly so regarding currents of thought in African sociology and the global community, and all the more so in the face of unique, stark African realities.

Theories and methodologies should meet the test of relevance or else they lose their applicability. A good number of research studies conducted and whose findings are articulated in this book take cognizance of the applicability of theories and methodologies to the African situation. The research on agro-industrialism in rural areas is of classical significance in this connection. In a bid to keep track of the applicability of research (specifically, the theoretical and methodological orientations), this study recommends that a study primarily on the effectiveness or efficiency and on the actual productivity of various forms of organization in an agro-industrial project be undertaken (p. 97).

The difficulties of applying research methodology in the African context constitute an engaging factor. Some techniques of surmounting these difficulties have been resourcefully devised. Take, for instance, the case of income per annum in the African context (p. 80). Income per annum is calculated on the basis of guinea-corn sold per bag by rural dwellers who, needless to say, are predominantly farmers. The usual practice of asking the respondents (farmers) to tell the researcher their annual income has, from experience, not elicited enough responses. For, understandably, a typical farmer loses no time in either refusing to declare his actual income or distorting it, for fear of its being used as a basis for personal income tax assessment which, historically, was the brainchild of colonial authorities. Even in post-colonial period, taxes paid are not recouped into the socioeconomic conditions and, therefore, the wellbeing of taxpayers. But income tax is well worth paying. Indeed, the crux of the matter is that the issue of income per annum is a crucial one, since the research under reference has to do specifically with the health status of the rural dwellers. Hence, some techniques of surmounting the difficulties of inadequate information from the farmers were so resourcefully devised by the researcher.

Tax evasion seems to assume a unique dimension, as typified by the case of returning migrants to villages in Igala land of Nigeria (p. 46) from the western area of the country. The fact that the rationale for this return was to evade income tax payment in the western area and that similar tax payment in their town district is a must is eloquent testimony to the corollary that, once entangled in the snare of the system, an escape is difficult to come by. There is seemingly a parallel between this tax evasion and that which obtains in America and which is called whitecollar crime. However, the prevailing socioeconomic environments in both countries are different: in the former it is practiced by people in low socioeconomic status, while in the latter by those in the middle/upper class. And the latter are able to do this by virtue of their accompanying professional skills.

Social inequality is no doubt ubiquitous. The solution proposed by Huxley (1937) cited on page 108 is still of relevance within the context of what he called "income tax and duties," emphasizing that such taxation can be used for the purpose of reducing economic inequalities between individuals and classes. The solutions offered by African governments, as evidenced by the Nigerian case, was sabotaged by the very people charged with the responsibility for effecting them. The Nigerian Enterprises Promotion Decree 1972, otherwise known as the Indigenization Decree, was prevented by this class of people from 'indigenizing' foreign business enterprises in Nigeria. Contrary to the solution proposed by Huxley, taxation is not used to reduce economic inequalities. Indeed, taxation can be used in a detrimental manner, as is the case in America, where tax cut, whenever it is being activated or effected, benefits only the rich business tycoons to the chagrin of the poor, reverberating in budget cuts for education, health care services, etc.

One of the studies on deviance (p. 39) lays the basis for unique insights into how the conventional understanding of the relativistic nature of deviance can be further dichotomized. For just as deviance is regarded as an antisocial conduct in Africa, so it is in America, but assumes a different dimension in the latter. Indeed, the nature of deviance in the latter—which stems from indiscriminate claim to freedom and rights—further turns out to be one that assumes terrifyingly staggering and dichotomous proportions. For example, the Columbine school shooting on April 20, 1999, at Columbine High School in the suburban town of Littleton, Colorado, was once regarded as America's deadliest school shooting and the most overwhelmingly shocking. And, unprecedentedly, the Virginia Tech shooting on April 16, 2007, that claimed the lives of a good number of people, with its nature currently superseding the hitherto deadliest nature of the Columbine school shooting, unequivocally lends credence to this indiscriminate claim to freedom and rights in America.

It has been found in one of the studies on juvenile delinquency (p. 41) that the average inmate is non-recidivist and that delinquency is *not yet gang-oriented*, nor is the juvenile offender as hardened and sophisticated as he is often thought to be. This is attributable to the fact that the average juvenile offender is a victim of circumstances: a child of parents of unfortunate socioeconomic circumstances who runs into trouble with official agencies in the process of trying to make ends meet. The uniqueness of delinquency on this score lies in its very nature of *not being gang-oriented* in contradistinction to what obtains in such other countries as America, Canada, Britain, and France.

Subjected to test by the study on motivation among industrial workers (p. 144), Herzberg's theory of motivation turns out to be out of context with the experience of the workers, since Herzberg's classification of variables like salary and supervision as 'dissatisfiers' does not fit into Nigerian situation. Indeed, salary and supervision feature prominently as satisfiers/motivators. Monetary incentive, as a great motivator, accounts for this. And the whole phenomenon is better explanatorily captured by the low standard of living of workers in such a neo-colonial society as Nigeria with relatively low salary.

The psychology of taste could be seen in practice when eggs, garden eggs, butter, and gruel are hawked in beautifully decorated calabashes made by craftsmen, whose use of tools is said to go hand-in-hand with their imagination (p. 149). The purchasers or consumers hold that the decorated calabashes remind them of their cultural past and present. This, indeed, mirrors the sociological imagination of C. Wright Mills (1959) that makes grasping of history and biography and the relation between the two a possibility. And this is crucial nowadays when people, particularly Africans and people of African descent, cherish their rich cultural heritage like never before or would like to circle back to their roots. It is further revealed by this study that several individuals are lured into buying decorated cultural items because of their taste for decorated works. Theodore Levitt's (1986) marketing imagination—a perspective which is an outgrowth of the sociological imagination—aptly underscores this taste-driven propensity to buy products. The marketing imagination takes the marketing researcher beyond the nature and characteristics of the specific product to the meaning this product might have for its potential purchasers and consumers (Korsching and Wilson, 1996). Hence, Levitt's assertion that people do not just buy things, but what they buy are solutions to problems. He also asserts that the marketing imagination makes an inspired leap from the obvious to the meaningful.

The marketing imagination as a perspective could be seen as being strategically useful in the realm of the styles of supervision adopted in a given industry. For example, one of the studies (p. 152) comes up with the finding that a 'soft supervisory style' is adopted in the sales department unlike a 'hard supervisory style' in the production department. Complaints are more tolerated in the sales department than in the production department, because there is more interaction in the sales department with people, mostly customers, whom they cannot afford to lose to other competing companies due to customers' dissatisfaction. This is a unique application of the marketing imagination in that it goes beyond the conventional, exclusive focus on production and marketing *per se* to the styles of supervision adopted in the big picture.

The use of a metaphor in projecting a theory is so illuminating as to paint a vivid picture in a real-world situation. Clearly, this is exemplified by Erving Goffman's dramaturgical perspective (p. 79). Hence, the research findings in this connection reveal that the patients devise a drama-like strategy for getting themselves prepared behind the scene, and then publicly present themselves in a manner that is intended to be acceptable to others—all in a frantic effort to cover up their medical condition. The whole "drama" finds practical expression within the context of material culture in terms of clothing, one resourcefully used as a means of concealment, just as the catheter, an artificial aid to their medical condition, is itself a material culture. Hence, the stage is so readily set for the dramatic!

One of the dilemmas triggered by polygamous marriage featured in the study on traditional birth attendants (TBAs) and their clients, leading to a sudden change in the research design while the researcher was already in the field. It was originally planned to interview one woman only in every household. But the first few interviews were interrupted by co-wives who were left out of the interviews, thereby showing their displeasure at being excluded. Hence, contrary to what was originally envisaged, they were included (p. 77).

Of great significance to sociological knowledge in the African context are the findings of the study on children television programs (p. 163). For the emerging knowledge clearly demonstrates that television programs, traditionally regarded merely as a medium of entertainment, have turned out to be potent ideological weapons at the hands of the producing (Western) countries to the chagrin of the consuming countries. As is usual with all class struggles, the former are bent on protecting their class interests. They are bent on doing so through television programs designed and produced by them specifically for their selfish end and aggrandizement. So just as, for example, structural-functionalist perspective and positivist or empiricist methodology are used to mystify realities, so television programs, too, are consciously oriented to conceal realities.

The same situation obtains in the case of literature and, indeed, the mass communications/mass media in general. Obviously, they are not ideologically neutral. In this connection, the reliability of positivist or empiricist methodology is in question. For positivist sociology (with its built-in emphasis on sensory experience) is incapable of unfolding underlying structures which shape surface phenomena. A focus exclusively on the television programs merely as a medium of entertainment would tantamount to hoodwinking people from the possibility of unfolding the logic and dynamics of the *status quo,* the exclusive preserve of the producing countries. Phenomenology offers an alternative way of understanding this in that it focuses on the state of human consciousness which tends to reverberate in a real-world situation, even though it is a subjective factor rather than an objective factor (characterized by quantitative methods), which is a dominant hallmark of positivism. Hence, for instance, a focus exclusively on the television programs would tantamount to downright deception. Needless to say, the content analysis approach used by the study under reference is methodologically instrumental regarding the results which have turned out to be capable of shaping our sociological knowledge as it relates to the mass communications/mass media in Africa and, indeed, in all developing countries.

There is another area in which our African sociological knowledge can be said to have become particularly glaring. This is with regard to the observation that not only history, but also topography/geography, is useful in revealing social realities. The study on the impact of agricultural broadcasting on farmers in Jos and its environs (p. 165) uniquely typifies this observation.

Yet another area of African, methodological significance has to do with the use of a praise song in tracing the origin, the political status, and the founder of Satiru (a study area), which has been rendered absolutely desolate (p. 89). Fundamental to the choice of its use is the fact that, in addition to the assertion that praise compositions are delivered much faster, and in a higher tone than ordinary prose utterances, songs themselves have the potential to serve a useful purpose in a given sociocultural grouping (p. 58). The usefulness of songs is readily underscored by the celebration of Live 8 on July 6, 2005, coinciding with the G8 summit in Scotland. A cursory examination of the objectives of the G8 summit, bringing together leaders of 8 industrialized nations (United States of America, Japan, Germany, Britain, France, Russia, Italy, and Canada) would throw more light on this. Those objectives were, among others, to drop the debt and make the trade laws binding on African countries a set of fair laws. The major purpose of Live 8, organized as a musical forum or a concert by artists from Africa and other parts of the world, was to make the attendees of G8 summit (namely, the leaders of the 8 industrialized countries) feel the impact of the presence of these artists performing in Scotland, thereby judiciously using song-based forum as a vociferous mouthpiece, capable of appealing to their sensibilities.

Indeed, music has come to be acknowledged as a universal culture. Its potential to influence children has come to be accentuated also. For instance, children from the age of four in Venezuela are taught music twelve hours a day throughout the week, except Sunday, because, remarkably, profound spiritual influence from music does help them by making them responsible citizens. While traveling and leading the children to play in countries across the globe, their music director has emphasized that such an endeavor as this can help any child, regardless of culture, race, gender, etc., in this lofty ideal of responsible citizenry. Little wonder, then, that, as contained on page 58, "songs can serve functions of social control, as well as educational and historiographical functions" (Marriam, 1968).

Music serves as part of oral tradition, as is evident from the case of Satiru, referred to in the penultimate paragraph. Oral tradition assumes a distinguished, enviable characteristic in the African cultural heritage. It was originally a substitute for written history. The idea of telling the history of a people is so indispensable that the performance of the Itapo festival (pp. 171-172) is illuminated by oral tradition. For the study on the festival employed oral tradition as well as non-oral tradition, demonstrating that the festival is an occasion on which young men are initiated into adulthood in Ososo community—a phenomenon known as the *rite of passage*. Interestingly enough, it is the same oral tradition that serves as a key factor to the understanding of the inner workings of the Sango cult in Koso-Oyo (p. 172). There is, indeed, no gainsaying the fact that oral tradition is an illustrious, identifying characteristic as far as African cultural heritage is concerned.

From the study on stigmatized diseases (p. 70) has emerged an insight into an important function of oral tradition. In addition to the case history of each patient, the guides or village heads, who led the investigator to the patients, furnished him with some information. This was later used to corroborate the responses from the patients themselves. Here emerges the insight into an important functional aspect of oral tradition: it serves as a corroborative and double-check technique.

One of the research studies focuses, *inter alia*, on the use of the term "family" to denote sublineage by the migrant members of Idoma ethnic unions in urban Kaduna in sharp contrast to the conventional use of the term "family" as the basic unit of all known societies. This research study comes up with the finding that a "family" union is, indeed, a union of Idoma people from the same village or a union of Idoma people from the same lineage or clan. The unions are segmentally arranged in line with the segmental arrangement of the political and social setting in their home area (p. 183). Interestingly enough, the uniqueness of this finding lies in the fact that an attempt to understand the rationale underlying "family", as it is used here, obviously transcends our conventional understanding of the meaning that the term "family" conveys to us. For, clearly, what matters is not only the much-talked-about variability of the "family", but also the *variability of the use* of this all-important term from one society to the other.

As revealed by the findings of one of the research studies undertaken, farmers from two villages—Dorayi Babba and Dorayi Karama—do not sell commodities in each other's village (p. 184). A cursory examination of Gunder Frank's (1966) satellite-metropolis relation would throw more light on this finding: visits between people in both villages are less frequent than visits to metropolitan Kano. And non-sales between them mean loss for both of their villages, but gain for metropolitan/urban Kano. A juxtaposition of this transactional phenomenon with what goes on globally would illuminate the justification for the formation of regional economic integration in Africa, as typified by the Economic Community of West African States (ECOWAS), East African Community (EAC), and Economic Community of Central African States (ECCAS), all of whose objectives are, among others, to achieve collective autonomy, reciprocity, and economic stability. These objectives are formulated in order to obviate the necessity for having to interact economically exclusively with countries outside the soil of Africa. For upholding such a necessity is imbued with the far-reaching consequences of rendering Africa's dependency even tighter and more pauperizing.

The justification for the formation of regional economic integration materializes in terms of the volume of goods and money that flows across the borders of all member states—a situation that has the mutual potential to make for regional, and so continental, socioeconomic, and political development. Indeed, the basis of dependency will tend to crumble, since the basis of dependency on the West, the metropolis, is expected to crumble, just as will that of the dependency on urban Kano by these two villages in the surrounding rural areas. Typically, urban Kano is representative of the purveyor belt through which resources are siphoned from Africa and, indeed, from other Third World societies to the West. One's understanding of the parasitical, dualist nature of the dependency paradigm is further deepened by the findings (p. 95) of the research on the relation between rural areas in the lake region of Mali and urban Bamako, which is the country's capital city, especially as the findings are corroborated by those of the study on the two villages and urban Kano in Nigeria.

Concerning the formation of regional economic communities in Africa discussed in the penultimate paragraph, reciprocal exchange is foundational to this. For example, the finding of one of the studies (p. 61) indicates that, following the monetization of the economy, reciprocal exchange superseded trade by barter, emphasizing that exchange integrates the social network within a given community. Besides, exchange theory itself is characteristically anchored on the principle of reciprocity.

As pointed out in one of the studies (p. 61), the Anglo-French Imperial Treaty of 1898, gave two-thirds of the old Kebbi Empire to Niger. Clearly, this illustrates how boundaries were unilaterally artificially created by Western colonial powers alongside the partition of Africa, with consequent border disputes among Africans (even to this day), long after all colonial powers—not only France—left the continent. Dependency theory is, of course, still at work as an explanatory tool within the context of the protean form of colonialism, namely, neo-colonialism since independence. It was by dint of dependency that, to use the expression of Walter Rodney (1973), Europe underdeveloped Africa.

Moreover, the whole strategies of exploitation, marginalization, and pauperization have changed to ones utilized and maintained by the multinational corporations, which, with the demise of the Cold War, the present author (Awosan, 1999) collectively dubbed *the sole superpower.* It is worth noting that local collaborators tend to facilitate the strategies within the context of globalization or global capitalism. These collaborators are the petty bourgeoisie, who constitute a stratum within a class and are puppets at the hand of the international bourgeoisie. Within this class (which is not homogeneous), however, is another stratum made up of intellectuals who are known as revolutionary bourgeoisie and who have committed "class suicide" (Wilmot, 1985). As a corollary, they truly deserve to be accorded a distinguishing degree of commendation and respectability. According to Wilmot, those African leaders who have committed "class suicide" are Amilcar Cabral (an agronomist, whose liberation theory focuses on mobilization, culture, and identity), Frantz Fanon (a psychiatrist), Eduardo Mondlane and Antonio Neto (physicians), and Nelson Mandela and Oliva Tambo (lawyers). If the petty bourgeoisie class were homogeneous, it would have been impossible to transform the lives of their fellow Africans.

At this juncture, the sociological imagination—the brainchild of C. Wright Mills (1959)—comes in handy. The sociological imagination, referred to by Mills as the quality of mind, highlights and cherishes biography and the history of a given society, emphasizing the organic connection between individuals and the history of their society. For instance, the character of the history of their society will determine the social conditions or even the destiny of those individuals. In the case of these African leaders who have committed "class suicide" (just referred to), the stance of the sociological imagination of Mills is less than being adequate, though it sounds impressive. For they went the extra mile by not merely focusing passively on the character of the history of their societies, but, much more than that, by selflessly providing the spark that ignited the revolutionary power that transformed the character of the history of their countries. And the changed historical character reverberated in their individual social conditions in terms of engaging in a revolutionary action. Consequently, they were able to bring about a realistic, social change—one capable of releasing their countries from the shackles of colonial domination or Western hegemony. Their unimpeachable integrity that distinguishes them from the vast majority of other African leaders has nothing in common with the obnoxious, callous leadership role, lacking in transparency and accountability, on the part of those other leaders—military and civilian—on the continent.

The findings of the study on oil exploration in the Ogoni area of Rivers State in 1981 by Shell Company (p. 50) turns out to be amazingly prophetic in terms of analytically, albeit implicitly, identifying, beforehand, possible basis for dissatisfaction on the part of the people who were bombarded with horrendous oil spillages in the process of oil exploration. For, over a decade down the road (specifically in 1995), there erupted a vociferous agitation, spearheaded by Ken Saro-Wiwa, a minority rights activist, who was consequently executed together with eight minority rights leaders of the area by the military government of the day headed by Sani Abacha. This no doubt is a clear demonstration of the blatant collaboration of the heartless military government with the multinational corporation exploring the oil. And this occurred in spite of mind-moving appeals from, among others, such a world dignitary as Nelson Mandela. Deaf ears were accorded the appeals.

Given the findings of the study (p. 164) that explores the possibility of reconstructing the world system—a reconstruction aimed at establishing a New International Information and Communication Order (NIICO)—the Western news are represented to the detriment of the Third World. Hence, the study recommends that accounts be settled first with the petty bourgeoisie. Clearly, this underscores a sharp contrast between them and the leaders who have committed "class suicide" and are referred to in the penultimate paragraph.

Gunder Frank (1966), Dos Santos (1970), Immanuel Wallerstein (1974), and Samir Amin (1978)—theorists of the world systems—have highlighted the predatory role of Western society in relation to the underdeveloped societies of the world. This role has been made possible by the integration of these societies, prominent among them African countries, into the world capitalist system. And sociological understanding is illuminating for this approach known as the world systems theory.

It is easily discernible from the studies in the subdiscipline of sociology of education that it is not only African material culture, but also African nonmaterial culture, that has become colonized. The nonmaterial culture is represented by knowledge and language. Hence, for instance, looking to the future of the sociological enterprise on the African continent, Akiwowo (p. 128) anticipates the time when great and significant works in Africa will be published in such African languages as Zulu, Xhosa, Hausa, Igbo, Yoruba, Luo, Fulfulde, etc. The time when inaugural lectures will be delivered in the language of the area in which a university is located is also anticipatorily in view. If these are translated into reality, then a unique landmark would have been genuinely accentuated in terms of not paving the way for ivory-towerism. For a forum in which gown and town truly meet would have been created. Closely allied to this paradigm of gown-town relation is the legal language in use (p. 157), one which is largely convoluted and esoterically technical. Quintessentially, the paradigm itself has the potential to innovatively pave the way for reliable information gathering, authentic service learning, and dynamic community partnership—no doubt a genuine negation of ivory-towerism.

The gown-town paradigm fits in with the African perception of the concept of education. For instance, utilitarian values of the academic citadel are expected to be creatively brought to bear on the utilitarian values of the community. Herein lies the meeting-point embracing these two values within the context of gown-town relation. Of paramount importance is the aphorism "knowledge is power". Cognizance must, however, be taken of the fact that, in the African sociological context, education is not confined exclusively to a formal system of learning (Awosan, 1992). Hence, education can take place in the home, on the farm, and even during the celebration of a particular festival. The fishing festival and the Itapo festival (pp. 123, 171, and 172) are eloquent testimonies to this. The importance of non-traditional/unconventional education has even come to be realized in America. This is corroborated by the finding of a study by Jenkins, Awosan, and Barnes (1995) on drugs, alcohol, and crime among teenagers in Massachusetts that "traditional education is not working for many young people." As a strategy for intervention, it has been recommended by them that such an unconventional education should be inclusive of material that is relevant to the community and that violence, prevention, the law, racism, and understanding of drugs should be part of the material.

The whole matter of gown-town paradigm eminently captures the very essence of sociology of knowledge, which is a key sociological perspective that attempts to locate all knowledge in its social context. Indeed, a knowledge located in its social context would be of inestimable value not only to the academic citadel, but also to the community, an integral part of which that academic citadel is. For, to use a language of statistics, it is a subset of the universe! Simply put, this gown-town paradigm does not envision *laissez faire* attitude, characteristic of a loaner. Rather, it focuses on being endogenously empowering in its obligatory, exigent involvement with the community. Its utility consists in its sound epistemological foundation in that it inherently lends itself to a realistic appreciation of how the inner dynamics of the academic milieu exogenously find practical, rather than abstract, expression.

It, therefore, behooves members of the academic community to cherish and celebrate gown-town paradigm or, alternatively, what the present author calls **deivory-towerism** at the expense of negativism. **Deivory-towerism** is a situation where the academic citadel is stripped of its ivory-towerish integument or characteristic. In this way, the constructiveness and usefulness of the academic community will loom large on the horizon for the benefit of mankind. The academic community needs to be a strong, endogenously functional citadel rather than being mired in claustrophobia. One of the ways to this end is for its members to engage in collaborative efforts within its four walls. For instance, in order to move with technological innovation, it should embrace being turned into a virtual community in certain spheres of its existence, creating a listserv—an electronic conversation among a group of individuals who share a common interest—that can be internally operational. Although it applies at the global level, the virtual community listserv created by Earl Babbie (1996) and his colleague, Art St. George, eminently serves as a model of great significance. Research methods, procedures, and any complicated issues can be tackled in an atmosphere of stimulating cross-fertilization of ideas, having been thrown across the board internally. Thus, the question of being endogenously empowering in its involvement with the community will be facilitated. And, what is more, the definition and maintenance of all that is best in local (community) traditions and cultures (p. 129) will be translated into reality. Of course, the academic members of the community, their students, and the community are poised to benefit maximally in this endeavor.

The internal grooming-ground for deivory-towerism can be facilitated or enhanced by engaging in cross-fertilization of ideas, since the flavors of the diverse theoretical, methodological, and other backgrounds of interacting individuals within the "internal virtual community" can complement each other. George Herbert Mead's (1934) game stage, which has to do with the development of the self (a continuous, lifelong process) perfectly falls in line with this, especially as he illustrated this with sportsmanship, using the game of baseball. In a frantic effort to get poised for community involvement, the academic, interacting individuals need to be interdependent in a spirit of sportsmanship, like that involving baseball. For example, according to Mead, though the pitcher, the batter, and others play distinctly different roles, each of them plays the roles of others simultaneously. And, on an interesting note, much as each of them plays his own role physically, he, at the same time, plays the role of others mentally. This makes sense as each of them has the responsibility for keeping track of the performances of others on the team, thereby contributing to the success of the team in its totality.

The whole question of gown-town paradigm/deivory-towerism fittingly resonates in an analogy from the internet terrain. Let us suppose the e-mail address of the academic citadel is scholars@academy.edu at a given point in time. The desirable and veritable e-mail address that transcends this and connects with the community should be scholars@academycumcommunity.edu, thereby celebrating deivory-towerism or gown-town paradigm! This is particularly so since deivory-towerism is organically related to pragmatism. Thus, it is capable of making its mark in the community, creatively changing lives. Appreciable efforts have been frantically made by universities and higher institutions, living up to the mission-based factors that constitute, as indicated in the preface to this book, one leg of the tripod on which a university or an academy stands, namely, research, teaching, and dialogue (which include community engagement). A lot of things nonetheless still remain to be done. Much as this is true for universities worldwide, it is particularly true for African universities and higher institutions as well as those of other developing societies. Efforts being made are predicated on scholarly networking. For example, Kenya Education Network (KENET) constitutes a mechanism for interconnectivity among educational institutions in Kenya. The National Research and Educational Networks (NRENS) in Nigeria, the Cameroon Interuniversity Network (CIN), the Malawi Academic and Research Network (MAREN), and the China Education and Research Network (CERNET) are established to foster interaction among various institutions within each of these countries. The beauty of it all is that the way is paved for forming an innovative basis for collaborative engagement with the community rather than each institution individually expanding beyond its vibrant frontier to the community. A sort of consortium among the institutions may even result.

The importance of gown-town paradigm/deivory-towerism cannot be overemphasized. The characteristically indefatigable efforts made by the Carnegie Foundation for the Advancement of Teaching vividly captures this in terms of coming up with a community engagement classification of U.S. colleges and universities on the basis of "the nature and extent of their engagement with the community, be it local or beyond" (Gilbee, 2006).

To this end, the Carnegie Foundation has classified the institutions in one of three categories, *viz.*, Community Engagement category that "describes the collaboration between institutions of higher education and their larger communities (local, regional/state, national, global) for the mutually beneficial exchange of knowledge and resources in a context of partnership and reciprocity"; Curricular Engagement category that "includes institutions where teaching, learning, and scholarship engage faculty, students, and community in mutually beneficial needs, deepen students' civic and academic learning, enhance community well-being, and enrich the scholarship of the institution"; Outreach and Partnerships category that "includes institutions that provided compelling evidence of one or both of the two approaches to community engagement. Outreach focuses on the application and provision of institutional resources for community use with benefits for both campus and community. Partnerships focuses on collaborative interactions with community and related scholarship for the mutually beneficial exchange, exploration, and application of knowledge, information, and resources (research, capacity building, economic development, etc.)" (Carnegie Foundation, 2009).

Interestingly enough, 72 institutions were classified in 2006 and 119 in 2008, and successfully at that. This classificatory approach is no doubt admirably productive. And the success story connected with it is a sure index of getting one's priority right. Indeed, it mirrors a word-picture, which is in timely consonance with the assertion of Lee S. Shulman, president of the Carnegie Foundation. As is evident from the report by Gilbee (2006), Lee S. Shulman's assertion, indicated below, is as much crystal clear as the success story that mirrors it:

> Finding new and better ways to connect with their communities should be *a high priority* for higher education institutions today. The campuses participating in this elective classification provide useful models of engagement around teaching and learning and around research agendas that benefit from collaborative relationships. (Emphasis added.)

The Carnegie Foundation and another foundation held in a high esteem—the Ford Foundation—have made their marks on the soils of African universities and those of other Third World societies, especially in the area of academic staff development and the enhancement of the missions of those universities as they relate to research endeavors. Both of these foundations' roles are glaring worldwide, not only in the academic arena, but also in other spheres of life. For example, as a resource for innovative people and institutions around the world, the unique, grant strategies of the Ford Foundation seek to advance human welfare, strengthen democratic values, reduce poverty and injustice, promote international cooperation, and advance human achievement (Ford Foundation, 2009). Clearly, research projects undertaken under the auspices of these foundations, among others, serve as a potent bridge that strategically links the academic citadel to the community.

Indeed, universities and other institutions of higher learning all over the world have come to the realization that deivory-towerism must be embraced. The geographic locations of these academic citadels include the United States of America, Britain, African countries, France, Canada, Japan, China, Germany, Australia, Israel, Italy, and India. The appreciable efforts they have been making in the sphere of community engagement are eloquent testimony to this realization on their part.

Academic/university autonomy (p. 132) is inevitably central to the performance of intellectuals. Society itself must give the leeway to the academic community to take imaginative, innovative, and creative perspectives and discoveries to the larger community, in order for it to prove its vibrancy by crossing the traditional academic boundaries and by bringing learning to life in the larger community. Indeed, much as academic/university autonomy (in other words, academic freedom) does not connote being caught up in the web of ivory-towerism, the society, too, must not stand in the way of the academic community through political, legal, or fiscal rigidities and aridities. In a nutshell, harmonious encouragement must pervade the atmosphere of the entire reciprocal, dual entity.

Still on the question of nonmaterial culture, sociological knowledge does analytically make it clear that Africa was integrated into the world capitalist system, not only in terms of its raw materials, but also in terms of its nonmaterial culture, namely, knowledge. In other words, that world capitalist system is a system of knowledge as well. Hence, education is sociologically situated in a whole new light, one capable of translating it into an instrument of emancipation. Little wonder, then, that Patrick Wilmot (1980) focused on apartheid South Africa, critiquing the obnoxious educational system established exclusively for Africans by whites in that part of Africa.

Sociological knowledge in Africa and the diaspora, i.e., such countries as the Americas, the West Indies, Australasia, and other parts of Europe to which Africans were dispersed during the era of slave trade and migration (Ogunyemi, 2004), has no doubt richly augmented the body of human scientific knowledge. This is clearly exemplified by the fact that, as pointed out earlier on by Akiwowo (1983), sociological knowledge has exerted "a liberating impact" (p. 15) and also by the fact that the liberation theory of Amilcar Cabral of Cape Verde, focusing on mobilization, culture, and identity (as contained in chapter eight) is a clear pointer to an appreciable sociological contribution. That Amilcar Cabral came up with this theory in spite of being an agronomist tends to underscore the encyclopedic nature of sociology, referred to in the preface to this book.

Sociological knowledge in Africa was originally regarded as being useful only in the area of social work until around the mid-1970s. Today, an appreciation of the varied and indispensable uses of sociology has led to the appointment of sociologists to positions outside of social work (Awosan, 2000). Sociologists, to mention but a few, have been directors and/or research fellows of social and economic institutes/centers. Typical examples of these are the Nigerian Social and Economic Research Institute in Ibadan, Nigeria, the Council for the Development of Economic and Social Research in Africa located in Dakar, Senegal, and the UNO Institute for Crime Control and Prevention in Kampala, Uganda. This appreciation is eminently well deserved. Just an example will suffice: the founding director of the UNO Institute for Crime Control and Prevention (who is a sociologist and a pioneer Nigerian criminologist) was appointed amid extremely tough competition with magistrates, judges, and other legal luminaries. Indisputably, authentic knowledge produced by sociologists underpins this well-deserved appreciation.

Perhaps there are a few entities where religion is used as an instrument of class domination and oppression. The analytical statement by Mensah (1986) readily captures this assertion. As contained in his scholarly work, there was a disagreement in 1978 among members of the Constituent Assembly from different religious backgrounds over the inclusion or non-inclusion of the *Sharia* in the Nigerian constitution. But, most remarkably, "the very same assembly men who were so resolutely and irrevocably divided over the *Sharia* question regrouped themselves shortly afterwards, on the basis of shared interests, in a number of political parties..." (p.179). Even in the area of the prevailing three types of law—general law, customary law, and Islamic law—the research on "problem of choice of law in a pluralistic legal environment" (p. 156) comes up with the finding that the socioeconomic status of individuals from various ethnic groups influences their choice of law. Both of these findings underscore the fact that not only is religion used as an instrument of class domination and oppression, but also as a façade. Religion and ethnicity are, in actual fact, a mere smokescreen, while the underpinning culprit is class or economic factor.

It has been found that women (indeed, African women) are not opposed to the utilization of obstetric services, but rather that their indigenous childbirth practices and beliefs run counter to the organization of, and practice in, the hospital, particularly regarding childbirth (p. 78). The fact that the study under reference here recommends that traditional birth attendants (TBAs) be trained in order to minimize congestion in the hospital and harms sometimes caused to both mother and child in error eloquently attests to the desirability of the integration of traditional African medicine into Western medical system. That traditional doctors typically specialize in treating certain diseases in which they are more competent than Western medical doctors further reinforces this lofty ideal. Prominent among such diseases are malaria and mental disorder (p. 69).

Further reinforcement also obtains in the case of the recommendations on page 76 regarding interdisciplinary research into the chemical constituents of African medicinal plants, which have been widely acknowledged as having superb, efficacious strength. Additionally, one of the studies (p. 71) comes up with the remarkable finding that experientially highlights the indispensability of African traditional medicine. For the majority of patients who have sought help from either African indigenous system or Western medical system signify that they believe more in the efficacy of indigenous medical system than in the efficacy of Western medical system. Phenomenology serves as a clear, explanatory and interpretive tool in this connection. For phenomenological focus on the profession of healing is based on rigorous emphasis on patients' subjective experience (Benner, 1995). After all, the perspective from which the patients make their statement is clearly an experiential one, in which case their personal beliefs, feelings, conceptions, and emotions constitute an unmistakable bedrock.

The development of sociology, as an academic discipline in Africa, was characterized by structural-functional theory. This was done in the interest of colonial authorities, in order to produce docile and obedient civil servants. The conceptual *affinity* of structural-functionalism *with* the existing structural and institutional arrangements fostered and enhanced the *status quo*. There was, however, a shift in academic programs, with newer, mainly indigenous, academic staff most open to Marxism in the 1970's, followed by neo-Marxism (p. 18). As a result, structural-functional paradigm gave way to conflict paradigm. This consequential phenomenon occurred in order to challenge the monopolistic utilization of survey method. And, as pointed out in chapter one, it has marked a watershed in the intellectual development of African graduates.

The importance of structural framework as a concept cannot be overemphasized. This fact analytically resonates in the study on the Njikoka Local Government Authority (p. 158), since achievements of Western education are indicative of the extent of social change that has occurred at different levels of the structural framework of the community. In other words, Western educational attainments are a function of the prevailing structural framework.

The multiplier effect of structural change is enormous. A good case in point is that in which, following the British expedition, community-based, judicial procedures were displaced, since property was no longer communally-owned (p. 156). Moreover, *property offenses* superseded issues involving *misunderstandings* due to encouraged individual competition and capital accumulation. This infectious phenomenon is best articulated within the perspective of the sociological imagination. For, focusing on the linkage between history and biography, we will understand that not only was the communal setting of society replaced with capitalist structure, but that individuals' interaction, having being so infected by the new historical trajectory, changed dramatically from one kind to another. That is, from one rooted in mere *misunderstandings* to another rooted in *property offenses*— from *civil* offenses to *criminal* offenses! This is further corroborated by the fact (as contained on page 157) that even in modern time criminalization in the country is predominantly property-biased, thereby revealing the affinity between the content of criminal law and the enduring nineteenth century bourgeois socioeconomic formation in England. In general, the replacement of the communal setting of society with capitalist structure (p. 99) was not without a tactical and inconsiderate modality, with far-reaching consequences: the change in labor and property relations, to the chagrin of labor, led to the fragmentation of landholding and destruction of free communal or cooperative labor. Worse still, not only did labor become drudgery and time-consuming, it was also individualistic, isolated, and subjected to being purchased and sold.

The exploitation, oppression, and denigration with which women are confronted in society come to the fore. This is vividly exemplified by the finding of the study that, of the workers in the department of technology and mechanical department of Nigerian Breweries Limited, Kaduna, only 32% are females (p. 188). This domination of high technology by men aside, the research that undertakes a content analysis of six publications (newspapers and magazines) with the finding that male writers (including cartoonists) portray women unfavorably (p. 189) is a classic illustration of a stereotyped portrayal. Similarly, sex-role differentiation in the training of people as police men and women (p. 188) is the order of the day.

Worse still, the exploitative role of the institution of the family surfaces in the study (p. 189) that reveals that women who are engaged in farming earn low profits, since only men, as husbands, have right over the farmland. The ideological aspect of capitalist orientation together with its blatant, oppressive social relations lends itself to be critiqued at the hands of feminist scholars and women's liberation activists. The material conditions of a people, of course, reflect in their thoughts. And the thoughts tend to proactively culminate in meaningful reconstruction in a world that, by its very nature, is not static. As far as feminism is concerned, a critique of this double oppression, whereby women suffer oppression by virtue of their social class position and sexual asymmetry, is quite in order.

On a positive note, one begins to see the emergence of women's political freedom on the horizon, as typified by the case of Ellen Johnson-Sirleaf of Liberia, emerging as the first female president on the African continent. Similarly, Luisa Diogo has emerged as the first prime minister of Mozambique. Both mythologically and historically, African women were a power to be reckoned with, even in some instances on the battlefield. The legendary example of Moremi of Ile-Ife and the example in the 14th century of Queen Amina of Zazzau (present-day Zaria) both of whom were successful, gallant warriors in Nigeria, the example of Aba market women in Nigeria who rioted in 1929 (an event known as the Aba women's riots) against a rumored extension of taxation to them by the British colonial authorities, since they were dependent on their husbands, on whom taxation had already been imposed, the examples of Candace, Queen of Ethiopians, in the 1st century, and Queen Nzinga of Matamba of Angola, who was not only a monarch, but also a warrior in the 17th century, to mention but a few, easily lend these African women to the admirable and indomitable status of being a power to be reckoned with.

Women in other parts of the world beautifully model this status as well. For example, Mary McAleese was the elected president of Ireland in 1997, Sirivamo Bandaranaike of Sri Lanka was the world's female premiere minister in 1960, Mireya Moscoso Rodrigez became the female president of Panama in 1999, Gloria Macapagal-Arroyo was elected president of the Philippines in 2001, Ertha Pascal-Trouillot was acting president of Haiti in 1990-91, and Ruth Dreifuss was elected president of Switzerland in 1999, to mention but a few on their long list. All of these strategically mirror an audacious change in the landscape of feminist struggle.

A parallel phenomenon is identifiable among African American women in the United States of America. For instance, Rosa Parks fuelled a chain of revolutionary event when she bluntly refused to give up her seat on a public bus in Montgomery to a white man in 1955. The aftermath of this turned out to be a 381-day boycott of the bus system, organized by Martin Luther King, Jr., thereby marking the dawn of civil rights movement. Indeed, little did anyone imagine that the refusal by Rosa Parks "could be galvanized into such an event of historic significance and bring about a radical change in the legal system of America" (Awosan, 2005). For, henceforth, *de jure* segregation (i.e., segregation by law) in the use of such public utilities as buses, water fountains, etc., ceased.

Justice and equality, however, continued to be pursued. The dream of Martin Luther King, Jr., which he optimistically disclosed at the Lincoln Memorial in Washington, D.C. on August 28, 1963 that he had a dream that one day his children might not be judged by the color of their skin, but by the content of their character, once seemed to be a non-comer into truthfulness or fruition. Gratefully, it has come into reality after a long period of forty five years. A new dawn has amazingly come into a most captivating play: Barack Obama, an African American young man, has been elected the first black president of the United States of America. His landslide victory

*Rosa Parks*

*Martin Luther King, Jr., delivering his "I have a dream" speech*

in the presidential election on November 4, 2008 is vehemently supported, regardless of racial differences, throughout the length and breadth of the country and across the globe. For a good number of African Americans, it is a situation that has intuitively ushered them into uncontrollable tears of heartfelt joy. Indeed, the concept of change resoundingly permeated the course of his campaign, but little did observers know that the change would be in the form of a revolution that triggers the whole political terrain and, of course, the nation into a brand new dawn of gargantuan proportions! There is, therefore, no gainsaying the fact—to echo Martin Luther King, Jr.—that justice has rolled down like water and righteousness like a mighty stream *in this specific connection*, whereby an African American is not judged by the color of his skin, but by the content his character. On a general plane, however, it would be less than appropriate, and even misleading, to rush to the conclusion that racism, injustice, and inequality are over.

An analytical focus on the whole episode would reveal a *continuum* of historic significance. The remarkably audacious *step* by Rosa Parks and the nonviolent *step* by Martin Luther King, Jr. became experienced in a developmental *stage*—no longer characterized by *de jure* element—and later established in a phenomenal *dimension*, ultimately culminating in triumph. Amazingly, the triumph has literally thrown a young African American man into a unique, presidential limelight. That young man, as indicated above, is Barack Obama, the 44th president of the United States of America.

Ethnomethodology fascinatingly sheds light on the findings of the research that reveal the seeming satisfaction of farmers with the exploitative role of their rulers and the change-agents (p. 96). For, at first sight, one is prone to regard these farmers as just being fatalistic, but viewing their situation within the context of ethnomethodology, one would uncover what is it that is at work, namely, existence of a given phenomenon that has to do with how the people actually see and describe the world around them and how they actually see themselves, as opposed to how an independent, third party does see them. For them, the rulers are just at the helm of their political culture, whilst the change-agents are external, modernizing individuals, both of whose actions are intimately connected with their domestic circumstances.

On the whole, some of the research studies are not without their inadequacies in terms of methodological perspective. The preponderance of positivist or empiricist approach is glaring. Non-survey methods are given comparatively scanty attention. For instance, informal interviews are rarely used. Life histories of other individual sociologists or non-sociologists do not feature in the methodological aspect of the studies.

Much as a good number of the research studies are empiricist or positivist in orientation, an attempt at striking a balance has been made in terms of a fairly consistent combination of this orientation with other non-survey methods. Such non-survey methods are archival source and library source, predominantly Marxist-Leninist in orientation. Thus, the inadequacy of empiricist or positivist

*Barack Obama*

methodology—in terms of its resulting in superficiality and exclusive reliance on data collection, analysis, and interpretation—would tend to be eliminated or improved upon. Better still, since logico-deductive and archival or historical methods are used, phenomena get easily concretized rather than being merely trivialized!

A cursory examination of the research studies would reveal that a few of them—see, for example, page 42 (sociostructural arrangement), page 49 (capitalist socioeconomic formation), page 85 (split of the kingdom), page 89 (the struggle continues), page 98 (perspective that differs fundamentally), page 99 (maximization of the exploitation of the peasants), page 100 (institutional transformations), and page 102 (fundamental re-organization)—are imbued with the possibilities of departures for social engineering, since they sound as if they are committed to changing the structure of society. The various sociological perspectives, as pointed out in chapter one, form the basis for a balanced curriculum, spanning, as they do, the gamut of social nuances.

So far, one seems to have been treated to a stimulating taste of significant theoretical grasp of social realities in this book. It is relevantly interesting that Thomas Kuhn's (1962) landmark work, *The Structure of Scientific Revolutions*, throws more light on this. He refers to what he calls normal science, that is, paradigm-based research, whose main concerns are the "determination of significant facts, matching facts with theory and articulation of theory." To Kuhn, there could be no normal science without a paradigm. Hence, it is normal science that most scientists practice at any given moment. And normal science is established once a given scientific theory becomes accepted by the scientific community, as exemplified by Copernican astronomy, Newtonian mechanics, or Einstein's theory of relativity. Far from being subtle, the title of this book vividly captures and seeks to illuminate the concerns of normal science, that is, the concerns of paradigm-based research. Indeed, the title says it all.

It is instructive to know that the various theoretical and methodological approaches do not cancel out, but rather add up to, one another in a suitable combinatorial manner. A particularly magnificent benefit accruable in this connection is the possibility of fostering a team-based approach to scholarship, even multi-disciplinarily. And there is something magnificent about such a combination: the dearth of a wide scope of analysis and discovery is avoidable.

Moreover, the entire pioneering efforts on the part of the author of this book and the research studies themselves are a stimulating guide to further thought, research, and discovery. Readers might use this work as a springboard for their own reflections on contemporary issues. In this way, their reflections can blaze a trail for them into new realities. This is particularly so as one is most likely to be exposed to the intricacy of research in its various ramifications. The learning of sociological perspectives and African sociology, imbued with contextual cognizance of peculiar, continental, and global circumstances, will thus become increasingly meaningful and rewarding.

## DISCUSSION QUESTIONS/EXERCISES AND ESSAYS

1. With particular reference to the study on oil exploration, explain how the findings of a given research project can turn out to be prophetic.

2. Write a critique of the use of television programs merely as a medium of entertainment.

3. Regarding the mass media, explain why the reliability of positivist or empiricist methodology is in question. Also, reinforce your explanation with a possible alternative.

4. Examine the usefulness of songs as exemplified by the celebration of Live 8 musical forum coinciding with the G8 summit in Scotland.

5. Given the nature of oral tradition, how would you explain the statement: "Music serves as part of oral tradition?"

6. "Oral tradition constitutes a key factor as far as African cultural heritage is concerned." Do you agree?

7. Discuss the justification for the formation of such regional economic communities in Africa as ECOWAS, EAC, and ECCAS.

8. Compare and contrast petty bourgeoisie who did commit class suicide and their colleagues who did not.

9. With particular reference to petty bourgeoisie, explain the sociological imagination of C. Wright Mills.

10. With specific illustrations, discuss the significance of gown-town paradigm/deivory-towerism.

11. How does the assertion of the Committee of Vice-Chancellors of Nigerian Universities (contained in chapter eight) tally with the efforts being made by the Carnegie Foundation regarding community engagement? How about the efforts being made by the Ford Foundation? And how about the efforts being made by African universities and universities in other parts of the world?

12. Discuss the importance of structural framework in relation to social change, and the multiplier effect of structural change in relation to community-based, judicial procedures.

13. How does phenomenology enhance our understanding of patients' preference for African traditional medicine?

14. "From the 1st century to the present, women across the globe are a power to be reckoned with." Would you regard this as an apt portrayal of women? If yes, discuss; if no, explain.

15. Discuss the connection between the dream of Martin Luther King, Jr. and the landslide victory of Barack Obama in the presidential election as the first black president of the United States of America. How about the future of the nation, particularly in relation to racism, injustice, and inequality?

16. Examine sociological knowledge and its contribution in Africa.

17. What is the difference between empiricist/positivist methodology and non-survey method?

18. How could we come up with a balanced curriculum both in terms of methodological orientation and sociological perspectives?

# APPENDIX

## Selected research projects whose findings are, among others, articulated in this book

Abba, Baba Gana (1980)
Towards the mechanization of agriculture in Nigeria and the role of the peasantry: Some aspects of the Chad Basin Development Authority.

Abdullahi, Yahaya Abubakar (1983)
Social relations of production in peasant agriculture: A case study of simple commodity production in Kaura Namoda area of Sokoto State.

Abdul-Qadir, Ahmadu B. (1978)
Problem of choice of Law in a pluralistic legal Enviroment.

Abduraham, Bilkisu (1979)
Friendship pattern amongst amina hall women: A case study of the Ahmadu Bello University main campus female students.

Aboderin, Adefolakemi Modupeolu (1981)
Doctor-patient relationship in a Nigerian hospital: A case study of the University College Hospital, Ibadan.

Abubakar, Fatima I. (1981)
The dual career syndrome: a case study of Ahmadu Bello University students.

Adaji, Samuel (1971)
Labor migration without economic change: A study of seasonal labor migration from Igalaland to the Western State of Nigeria.

Adamu, Humairi Ahmed (1979)
The class structure and housing problem in Zaria.

Adamu, Sanusi Abubakar (1980)
Rural health care provision in Kano state: A case study of Ringim Rural Health Center.

Adebola, Richard I. (1978)
Nigerian tobacco company limited, Zaria: Rank and file apathy among Nigerian trade union (a case study).

Adekunle, Lawal Majeed (1981)
The socioeconomic impact of the Oyo State Cocoa Development unit's Cocoa project on the participating farmers in Ejigbo local government area of this state.

Adewale, Ayodele Harry (1984)
The victims of crime: A comparative case study of Ajegunle and Victoria Island in Lagos.

Ado, Abdul-Rahman (1980)
The theory and practice of national liberation in Africa: A comparative analysis of the decolonisation process in Nigeria and Mozambique.

Agbonifo, Peter (1974)
Agro-Industrialism in the greater Zaria area.

Agbontaen Idueko E. (1973)
Juvenile Delinquency in Benin City: A case study.

Agboola, Sherifat Lami I. (1981)
Scope of women's employment in Nigerian Industries (Factors that constitute barrier to their participation): A case study of Kaduna textiles limited and Nigerian breweries limited, Kaduna.

Agum, Judith M. Mnguechia (1977)
Achievement, motivation and education in the development of sex-role differentiation in Zaria.

Ahimie, F. Abosede (1973)
The role of the Aladura church: A case study of Cherubim and Seraphim church in Samaru, Zaria.

Ahire, Philip Terdoo (1977)
Delinquents and non-delinquents compared: A study of juvenile deviance in Gboko.

Ahire, Philip Terdoo (1981)
Juvenile justice and correction in Nigeria.

Ahmed, K.T. (1976)
Urban dominance in metropolitan kano.

Ahmed, Younus D. (1977)
Attitudes towards abortion.

Akoshile, Ameen Adedoyin (1977)
Pottery in Abuja: A case study of convergence in traditionalism and modernity.

Akubor, Vincent Y. (1981)
Wage differentiation between the public and private sectors: A case study of Kaduna industrial area.

Alade, Busari Ajani (1973)
The effect of Kwara State local government reform on Ilorin division.

Alh., Hassan Zakariyawu Adeyemo (1980)
Development, organization and functions of taxi and taxi-drivers union: A case study of Bida.

Alkali, Rabiu (1977)
A comparison of urban and rural primary schools' performance in NCEE and the migration of the school leaver in Fika L.G.A.

Alti-Mu'azu, Mairo (1985)
Traditional birth attendants in Zaria: A case study of Jama'a and Koraye villages.

Alubo, Sylvester Ogoh (1977)
Criminal law of substance and procedure among Idoma: A case study of Oglewu community.

Are, Helen Yemi (1980)
Socioeconomic status and fertility differentials among married women: The case of Ilorin, Kwara state, Nigeria.

Arungbemi, Kehinde Moses (1977)
Kinship: Divorce and divorcee—a case study of Isanlu.

Atirbabiri, Alfred B. (1979)
Radio audience: A study based on Yola and its suburbs (Gongola State).

Awosan, Joshua Adekunle (1980)
Familial impact on Educational Attainment: A socioeconomic analysis.

Awosan, Joshua Adekunle (1984)
The impact of health education on the personal and environmental health status of rural dwellers: A case study of rural communities around Zaria.

Ayam, Janet (1982)
T.V. viewers' program preference and the dependence of the T.V. industry: A case study of N.T.A., Kaduna and Minna.

Ayinla, Joshua D. (1975)
The re-adjustment of Nigerian returnees from Ghana: A case study from Igbeti.

Baba, Mercy M. (1985)
Cultural images in children television programs: A case study of N.T.A., Kaduna.

Bah, Hauwa (1979)
A sociological and comparative study among the acceptors and non-Acceptors of family planning methods: A case study of Maiduguri, Borno state of Nigeria.

Bakori, Garba Ismaila (1977)
The hadj as a *communita* and an integrative process.

Bamidele, Moses O. (1975)
The continuity of the sango cult in Koso-Oyo despite social change.

Balobo, Issa Maiga (1981)
Rural proletarianization: A case study of Lake Region in Mali.

Bogunjoko, Sally N. (1978)
Evaluating Nigeria Police Force performance: A case study of Okene.

Braimah, W.A. (1973)
Continuity and change in Igala political system.

Dandien, Donatus Peter (1976)
The social organization of crafts: A case study of the pottery craft among the attakar of Jema'a Federation.

Dansoho, Christopher Tyowase (1980)
Social interaction in a psychiatric setting: A case study of Makurdi General Hospital, Psychiatric Unit.

Daodu, James Ayokunle (1977)
Job-seeking experiences amongst school-leavers in Sabongari, Kaduna.

Drew, Catherine Frances (1975)
Economic roles of women in an expanding market town: A case study in Mangu, Benue State, Nigeria.

Essang, E. E. (1974)
The sociology of calabash carving.

Ezeani, Maureen Bandele (1983)
Child education and sociocultural change in traditional and modern Nigeria society: The case of the Igbos of Njikoka L.G.A. of Anambra State.

Folorunsho, Yunusa Ayinla (1977)
The social aspects of production and marketing of traditional cloth weaving in Ilorin town.

Fulata, Abubakar Hassan (1985)
The genesis of the Nigerian economic crisis.

Gefu, Jerome Oni (1977)
Title succession—structure and functions: A case study of Kabba District (Owe).

Goshen, Carolyn J. (1976)
Textile workers and trade unions in Kaduna.

Gyams, Henry Shehu (1976)
The presence of *Yan Iska* in Zaria town.

Hellandendu, Joseph M. (1981)
The study on Kilba conception and treatment of stigmatized diseases.

Ibrahim, Sarki (1971)
Traditional gift exchange in wudil, Kano State.

Igbiankyaa, Stella Sarah (1977)
The Nigerian worker motivation: A case of N.T.C., Zaria.

Igoil, Iyortange (1985)
The cultural aspects of Tiv music: A perspective of the musical activity as ritual behavior.

Iliyasu, Mohammed Lawal (1978)
The Kadawa irrigation scheme: An evaluation of the problems and prospects of a settlement scheme.

Isa, Adam Amimi (1977)
Productivity and industrial worker: A case study of Nospin industry.

John, Moses Chiwake (1980)
A study of the relationship between family size and land utilization for agricultural purpose in a rural area (The case of Kamuru station in Kachia local government area of Kaduna state).

Kabiru, Aminu (1980)
The sociological study of the development, organization and current status of the Islamiyya school in Kano city, the social origins of the pupils and the teachers, and occupational opportunities of the products.

Koripamo, Patience A. (1973)
Marital instability among the Kolokuma Ijos.

Koripamo, Patience A. (1979)
Some problems of industrial labor: A case study of labor turnover in the Nigerian Tobacco Company, northern states of Nigeria.

Kungwai, Ntiem (1983)
The political economy of rural development: A case study of the Funtua Agricultural Development Project in Bakori District.

Kyom, Matthew Yaji (1988)
The psychosocial consequences of urological diseases: A case study of urethra stricture in Ahmadu Bello University Teaching Hospital, Zaria.

La'ah, D.Y. (1976)
A preliminary survey of Kagoro criminal law of substance and procedure.

Labesa, Yohanna (1977)
The extended family and economic change in farman village.

Ladipo, Clement Ekundayo (1974)
The Itapo festival in Ososo community.

Lawal-Osula, Edna U.M. (1978)
The "Gatekeepers" influence in mass communication: A case study of the *New Nigerian* newspaper.

Mamman, Musa Dikko (1977)
Police-public relations in Funtua: Its effects on the efficiency of police on duties.

Masapara, Isaac A. (1970)
Recruitment, training and self-employment in the photographic trade in Kaduna.

Matankari, Edith (1970)
The bori spirit mediumship cult in Malumfashi, North Central State, Nigeria.

Matanmi, Babatunde Michael (1981)
The employment process of the junior workers on A.B.U. main campus, Samaru, Zaria.

Mohammed, Abubakar Sokoto (1983)
A social interpretation of the satiru revolt of C. 1894-1906 in Sokoto Province.

Mohammed, Isa (1974)
The argungu fishing and cultural festival: An aspect of social integration.

Nimyel, Mary Dinchi (1978)
Women in the Nigeria Police Force (N.P.F.): A case study of Kaduna.

Nkom, Steven Adamu (1983)
The political economy of farmers' cooperatives in Jemaa area of Kaduna state.

Noma, Rebecca Asabe E. (1984)
River Basin development projects as a strategy for national development: A case study of the impacts of Goronyo Dam Project on surrounding communities (resettlements).

Obafemi, Seidu Dada (1977)
Social stigma of imprisonment and its socioeconomic effects on exconvicts.

Ogbe, Emmanuel Omale (1973)
Idoma tribal unions and association in Kaduna.

Ogbogu, Patricia (1973)
Ibo integration in Kano after the war.

Oghifo, Patrick Richard O. (1981)
The influence of home background factors on school performance in Ughelli area of Bendel State.

Ogunkoya, Esther Adeyosola (1984)
The opticom farm system in Ogun state: A case study of a strategy for solving the problem of food shortage.

Oko, Innocent Agada (1982)
Supervisory style and worker productivity: A case study of Nigerian bottling company, Kano.

Okoli, Victoria Ndalaku (1981)
The impact of the oil industry on Nigerian agriculture: A case study of Ogoni area of Rivers State.

Omaji, Paul Omojo (1980)
Socioeconomic correlates of malnutrition among pre-school children: A case study of Idah community.

Omaji, Paul Omojo (1985)
The Nigeria criminal law: A sociological examination of the form, content, and operation.

Omokore, Yemisi Ibiwumi (1980)
An evaluation of the health care services: A case study of the Physiotherapy Department, Ahmadu Bello University Teaching Hospital, Zaria.

Opaluwa, Augustine A. (1975)
The impact of modernization on marriage custom among the Igala.

Opaluwa, Gabriel Uwada (1979)
Motivation among Nigerian Industrial Workers: An empirical verification of Herzberg's theory of motivation (A case study of Nigerian Fertilizer Company Limited, Kaduna).

Orewere, Benjamin Aduonata (1984)
Impact of Agricultural broadcasting on farmers in Jos and its environs.

Orukpe, Maria Constance Ebehireme (1971)
Continuity and change of Ishan Life in Kaduna.

Osatuyi, Cynthia Olufunmilayo (1980)
The influence of age at marriage, type of marriage, education and socioeconomic status on fertility: A case study of Gyellesu, a residential area in Zaria.

Otesanya, Bernadette Ekwutosi (1984)
Survey of traditional healers in Zaria.

Othman, Aminu Mohammed (1981)
Socioeconomic impact of the green revolution: A case study of Dawdawa under Funtua Agricultural Development Project (FADP)

Otowo, Rosaline Alache (1974)
The Zaria children's home as a social institution.

Owomero, Basil Othuke (1980)
Sentencing patterns of Nigeria lower courts

Saidu, Flibus Mushiya (1976)
The laws of succession and inheritance among the chamba.

Salawu, Kareem (1979)
Property criminal victimization and public attitudes towards crime and crime-prevention: A victim survey of resident household in Kaduna township.

Sani, Mohammed Aishatu (1977)
Traditional vs. contemporary hadj.

Sanyu, Margaret Susan (1983)
Maternal education as factors in infant and child mortality.

Saror, Stella F. (1978)
Delinquents and Non-delinqents compared: A study of juvenile delinquency in Zaria and Kaduna.

Solanke, Dehinde Oluwole (1982)
Cinema in Western Nigeria: The Western film as a medium of cultural imperialism: A case study in Ibadan city.

Tuggarlergo, John Michael (1977)
Mental disorder: An examination of admissions.

Tuggarlergo, Michael John (1981)
Social correlates of mental illness: A case study of Kaduna state.

Tukura, David Wodi (1985)
The political economy of food dependency in Nigeria: A case study of Lafia Agricultural Development Project in Plateau State.

Ujiri, Michael O. (1985)
Nutritional status and socioeconomic background: A case study of the under five children attending health clinics in Zaria Local Government.

Usman, Binta Fati (1977)
Civilian-military relation: The solder's perspective.

Verenyol, James D. (1978)
The socioeconomic determinants of interpersonal interaction among rural-urban migrants.

Vihishima, Msur Comfort (1983)
The portrayal of women in daily newspaper: A content analysis.

Waminaje, David (1971)
Change in marriage customs among the Karu Gwari community.

APPENDIX

Yahaya, Mairo (1979)
Primary health care delivery services: A comparative approach.

Yakowa, Patrick E. (1972)
Functional literacy as a factor for development: A case study of Kagoma farmers.

Yunusa, Mohammed Bello (1979)
Primary health care delivery service: A comparative approach.

Zamani, Joshua E. (1975)
A study of the factors underlying concern or indifference to medical care among the Hausa in Zaria.

Zasha, James Achin (1977)
Migration to Gboko Rice Mills Settlement: A socioeconomic perspective.

Zhizhi, Joseph Audu (1981)
A study on labor circulation among the Bassas in Bassa district of Benue State.

Zubair, Mutiu Idris (1977)
Class consciousness among the elites (A case study of Minna, capital of Niger state, Nigeria).

# GLOSSARY

**Abortion.** Premature and deliberate termination of pregnancy.

**Anthropology.** A comprehensive study of man the animal and of man the social being through time and space. The study of human, cultures, or ways of life.

**Apartheid.** An inhuman system of a white minority over a black majority, with the former living, as a consequence, in affluence and the latter wallowing in abject poverty.

***Bori.*** A word meaning spirit possession or a form of trance in which the actions of a person are interpreted as an evidence of a control of his behavior by a spirit, normally external to him. Bori is also a spirit mediumship, whereby the person possessed is regarded as an intermediary between spirits and men.

**Catheter.** An artificial tube into which urine flows and is then emptied by patients.

**Cesarean section/cesarean.** The delivery of a baby by making an incision through the abdomen walls and uterus.

**Cinema.** "A darkened room, a screen, a projector, a film being projected, and an audience watching the film" (Bebey, 1977).

**Class struggle.** A competitive form of social relation.

**Class suicide.** Voluntary quitting of one's social class. And this is made possible since social class is not homogenous.

***Communitas.*** A Latin word meaning an aggregate of individuals or groups bound together by virtue of common beliefs, values, and attitudes toward a common goal.

**Customary law of succession and inheritance.** The unwritten, indigenous law of society.

**Deivory-towerism.** A situation where the academic citadel is stripped of its ivory-towerish integument or characteristic.

***De jure* segregation.** Segregation by law.

**Diaspora.** Such countries as the Americas, the West Indies, Australasia, and other parts of Europe to which Africans were dispersed during the era of slave trade and migration.

**Diversion.** Ordinarily, this always conveys the notion of a change in direction or course. Legally, it is a structured informal interaction making possible the handling of the individual offender outside of the conventional criminal justice system.

**Double oppression.** Oppression suffered by women by virtue of their class position in society and also by virtue of their sex.

**Dual career syndrome.** An expression referring to the life-style of women who are mothers and, simultaneously, university/college students.

**Educational system.** A structural aggregate of the interests and activities of formal education in phases as well as in an orderly arrangement.

**Ethnocentrism.** Evaluation of one's culture as being superior to other people's culture.

**Ethnomusicology.** 1. The crosscultural study of music. 2. The study of music in its cultural context.

**Ex-convicts.** People convicted in the past and are actually out of prison.

**Free Flow of Information.** A concept explaining that the development of the Third World can only be achieved through the functioning of the world as a 'global village', wherein exists uncontrolled 'free flow of information'.

**'Gatekeepers'.** Individuals who control the ultimate fate of news stories.

**Heterophilous and homophilous.** The adjectives of nouns heterophily and homophily respectively.

**Heterophily.** The degree to which individuals who interact differ in certain attributes.

**Homophily.** The degree to which pairs of individuals interacting are similar in certain attributes.

**Ivory tower.** 1. Place of retreat or seclusion from the realities of life. 2. A word commonly used as an indictment of the seclusion of universities from the rest of the society.

**Latent function.** The unintended effect of an action.

**Legal pluralism.** Multiple legal systems.

**Medical sociology.** A subdiscipline of sociology concerned with the problems associated with physical and mental health from the social perspective, in which case the main sociological theories relating to health and illness behavior come in handy and are put into practical test.

**'Opticom'.** This word is coined from two words: *optimum* and *community*.

**'Opticom' farm system.** A farm, where members of a community are cooperatively engaged in productive activities for the optimum well-being of the populace.

**Political economy approach.** An approach which studies the continuous struggle of man to transform natural resources into usable and consumable forms and the intricate relationship emerging between men in the process of meeting their material needs, thereby focusing basically on the socioeconomic formations of society.

**Psychologism.** An attempt to explain social phenomena in terms of facts and theories about the make-up of individuals.

**Recidivists.** 1. People imprisoned more than once and are currently serving a prison term. 2. Persistent or habitual offenders/criminals.

**Rite of passage.** An event involving a passage of individuals from one stage of life to another, as in the case of initiation of young men into adulthood.

**Sango.** The fourth *Alafin* (traditional ruler) of Oyo in the Yorubaland, deified after his death, thereby making possible, even to this day, the existence of *Sango* cult and his priests and worshipers.

**Social economy.** The study of the structural system of the mobilization, conservation, and utilization of the social resources in a given society.

**Social inequality.** Difference in social prestige based chiefly on differences in social class, family backgrounds, wealth, income, political influence, education, manners, and morals.

**Social psychology.** The scientific study of the mental processes of man, regarded as a social being.

**Social welfare.** The organized effort of a society to improve people's well-being by tackling and solving social and economic problems.

**Sociology of education.** A subdiscipline of sociology concerned with the analysis of educational institution or organization, studying the functional relationships between educational institution and the rest of the social institutions.

**Sociology of knowledge.** A sociological perspective which attempts to locate all knowledge in its social context.

**Sociology of religion.** A subdiscipline of sociology that studies the social institution known as religion, which is "a unified system of beliefs and practice relative to sacred things."

**Stigmatized Diseases.** Diseases which conspicuously project their sufferers, who, physically, are disabled and so are glaringly different from non-sufferers in society, thereby stigmatizing them.

**Talaka.** A Yoruba word, having the same meaning as *mẹkunnu*, meaning the poor or the masses. It is known as *talakawa* in Hausa and *umu ogbenye* in Igbo.

**The *Aladura*.** A Yoruba word literally meaning 'praying people'; it is an indigenous denomination of the Christian religion. It consists of a number of sects, the well-known ones being the Cherubim and Seraphim Church, the Christ Apostolic Church, the Apostolic Church, Church of the Lord, Celestial Church of Christ, and a host of others springing up.

**Turnover.** 1.The total amount of sales made during a given period by a company or an industry. 2.The termination of the period a worker is employed. (This refers specifically to labor turnover.)

**Urethera stricture.** A universal urological condition which involves inability to  pass urine due to a blockade in the urethra, the channel that  conveys  urine  from  the  bladder  to the penis for  discharge.

*Yan iska.* A Hausa word meaning undesirable elements or deviants.

**Women in society.** A field of study mainly concerned with the plight of women, the exploitation, oppression, and denigration they suffer in the home and in the wider society. It is popularly known as **Women's Studies.**

# REFERENCES

Adamu, H.R. (1974) *The North and the Nigerian unity: Some reflection on the political, social and educational problems of Northern Nigeria.* Gaskiya corporation, Zaria.

Adebo, Ademola (1985) "The state and underdevelopment in Nigeria." *Clarion,* Vol. 1, No. 1, January-March, 1985.

Adeleye, R.A. (1972) "Mahdist triumph and British revenue in Northern Nigeria: Satiru 1906," *Journal of the Historical Society of Nigeria,* Vol. VI, No. 2, June.

Adesuyi, S.L. (1970) "Priorities in health care" in Akinkugbe,O.O. et al., *Priorities in national health planning,* The Caxton Press (West Africa), Ibadan, 14.

Adeyanju, Thomas K. (1986) "Language policy across educational levels since independence: Problems and prospects." Unpublished Ahmadu Bello University Public Lecture, 20th February, 1986, 126, 27, 44.

Adeyemi, A.A. (1972) "Scientific approach to sentencing." In Elias, T.O. (1972) (Ed.), *The Nigerian Magistrate and the offender,* Ethiope Publishing Co., Benin City, 49, 68.

Ahmadu Bello University, Zaria (1969) *News Bulletin,* 31st January, 1969.

Ake, Claude (1979) *Social Sciences as imperialism: The theory of political development,* Ibadan University Press, Ibadan, 70.

Akinde, Charles O. and Omolewa, Michael (1982) "Background issues relating to the proposed mass literacy campaign in Nigeria." *International Review of Education,* Vol. XXVII, 1982, quoted in Adeyanju (*op. cit.*), 7, 93.

Akiwowo, Akinsola (1983) "Sociology: The state of the art in Nigeria today." Paper presented at the departmental seminar, Department of Sociology, Ahmadu Bello University, Zaria, 9, 21-22.

Al-hajj, M. A. (1973) The Mahdist Tradition in Northern Nigeria, unpublished Ph.D. thesis, Department of History, Ahmadu Bello University, Zaria.

Amin, Samir (1978) *Accumulation on a world scale: Critique of the theory of underdevelopment,* Harvester Press, London.

Amoda, Moyibi (1978) *Festac colloquium and black world development,* Nigeria Magazine, Federal Ministry of information, Lagos, and Third Press International Division of Okpaku Communications Corporation, New York, 216.

Armstrong, David (1989) *Outline of sociology as applied to medicine,* Arnold Publication, London.

Awosan, Joshua A. (1992) *Starlab: The African model,* African-American Institute of Northeastern University, Boston, and Learning Technologies, Inc., Cambridge.

————(1999) "Racism, ethnicity, and violence in America and other nations: A Comparative, critical analysis." Paper presented at the 1999 Fall Conference of the New England Sociological Association on "The Sociology of Hate," Saturday, November 6, 1999, Northeastern University, Boston.

———— (2000) "Sociological knowledge in Africa and the diaspora: Retrospects and prospects." Paper presented at the 2000 Spring Conference of the New England Sociological Association on "21st Century Sociology: Retrospective/Prospective," Saturday, April 29, 2000, Albertus Magnus College, New Haven, Connecticut.

———— (2005) "Changing lives: Rosa Parks, racism, deviance, integration, and beyond." Paper presented at the Fall 2005 conference of the New England Sociological Association at Bryant University, Smithfield, Rhode Island, on Saturday, November 5th, 2005.

Babalola, A. (1977) "Care of destitutes," *Nigerian Herald,* Ilorin, February 2, 1977.

Babbie, Earl (1996) "We am a virtual community," *The American Sociologist,* Spring 1996.

Badgley, Robin *et al.* (1973) "Behavioural Sciences and medical education: the case of sociology," *Social Science and Medicine,* Vol. 7.

Barber, W.J. (1975) British economic thought and India, 1600-1858: A study in the history of development economics, Oxford University Press, London.

Bebey, Francis (1977) *The awakening African cinema courier,* Unesco, 30.

Benner, Patricia (1995) *Interpretive phenomenology: Embodiment, caring and ethics in health and illness,* Thousand Oaks, Ca., Sage.

Berger, Peter L. (1963) *Invitation to sociology,* Anchor Books/Doubleday & Company, Inc.

Bisno, Herbert (1970) "A theoretical framework for teaching social work methods and skills," *Journal of social work education,* Winter 1970.

Bohannan, P. and Curtin, P. (1995) *Africa and Africans,* Waveland Press, Inc., Grove, Illinois.

Bottomore, T.B. (1975) *Sociology: A guide to problems and literature,* George Allen and Unwin Limited, London, pp. 237, 238.

Bown, Lalage (1977) "Live-long learning – prescription for progress." Inaugural Lecture delivered at the University of Lagos, 20th December, 1977, Ibadan University Press, Ibadan, 15, 17.

Chabal, Patrick (1983) *Amilcar Cabral: Revolutionary leadership and people's war,* Cambridge University Press, Cambridge.

Caldwell, J.C. (1979) "Education as a factor in mortality decline: An examination of Nigeria data," *Population Studies,* Vol. 33, No. 3, 395.

Carnegie Foundation (2009) "Community Engagement Elective Classification," http//www.carnegiefoundation.org/classifications/index.asp.

Chukwudum, A.M. (1981) *Nigeria: the country in a hurry,* John West publications Ltd., Ikeja, Lagos, 2.

Committee of Vice-Chancellors (1975) *The Nigerian Universities and the Udoji Commission,* Committee of Vice-Chancellors of Nigerian Universities, 8, 18, 19, 180.

Cooley, Charles Horton (1964) *Human nature and the social order,* Schocken Books, Inc., New York.

Cowon, J.M. (1961) *A dictionary of modern written Arabic,* Otto Harrassowitz, Wiesbaden.

Cuff, E.C. *et al.* (1979) *Perspectives in Sociology,* George Allen & Unwill, London, 2.

de Tocqueville, Alexis (1968) "On war, society, and the military" in *War,* Bramson, Leon and Goethal (Eds.), Basic Books, New York, 331.

Dudley, B.J. (1975) "Scepticism and political virtue." Inaugural lecture delivered at the University of Ibadan, University of Ibadan Press, Ibadan, 11, 21.

Easton, David (1965) *A framework of political analysis,* Prentice-Hall, Englewood Ciffs, 124.

Eisenstadt, S.N. *et. al.* (1985) *Macrosociological theory: Perspectives on Sociological theory,* Vol. 1, SAGE Studies in International Sociology 33, International Sociological Association/ISA, London.

Engels, Friedrich (1880) *The origin of the family, private property and the state,* Progress Publishers, 1977.

Erinosho, O.A. (1982) "Health planning in Nigeria," *The Nigeria Journal of Sociology and Anthropology,* Vol. 8, September 1982, 34.

Essien, E.S. (1981) "The incidence of Gastroenteritis among children (0-10 years) in Malumfashi" in Kisekka, M.N (1981) (Ed.), *Children in Kaduna State, Nigeria: Problems and needs,* Kaduna Childwelfare Committee and Department of Sociology, Ahmadu Bello University, Zaria, 117.

Evan-Pritchard, E.E. and Fortes, Mayer (1940) *African political systems,* Oxford University Press, London, 1, 7.

Fadahunsi, Akin (1977) "External Aid and National Development Plans," the Nigerian Institute of International Affairs seminar series No. 3, the Nigerian Institute of International Affairs, Lagos, 17.

Fajana, A. (1982) "Educational policy in Nigeria: a century of experiment." Inaugural Lecture delivered at the University of Ife, January 6, 1982, University of Ife Press, Ile-Ife, 1, 2.

Fasina, 'Dipo (1985) "The Nigerian economic crisis and the working people: Whither the Nigerian intellectuals," *New Dimension,* August 1985, 2.

Ford Foundation (2009) http://www.fordfoundation.org/regions.

Forsberg, Mats (1984) *The solution of social welfare policy in Sweden,* The Swedish Institute, 1984.

Frank, Gunder (1966) "The development of underdevelopment," in *Monthly Review,* Vol. XVIII, No. 4.

Fulton, Lord (1972) "The expanding world of the universities." Foundation Day Lecture delivered at the School of Oriental and African Studies, University of London, 10.

Gilbee, Aaron M. (2006) "[Civic-engagement] Carnegie Foundation for the Advancement of Teaching selected 76 U.S. colleges and universities for its new Community Engagement Classification," https://lists.uwrf.edu/archives/civic-engagement/2006-December.

Galtung, J.P. (1971) "A structural theory of imperialism" in the *Journal of Peace and Research,* No. 2.

Garbarino, M.S. (1977) *Sociocultural theory in anthropology: A short history,* Holt, Rinchart and Winston, New York, 27.

Garvin, R.J. and Oyemakinde, J.O. (1970) "Economic development in Nigeria since 1880," Department of History, Ahmadu Bello University, Zaria (mimeographed), 30.

Goffman, Erving (1963) *Stigma: Notes on the management of spoiled identity,* Prentice Hall, England.

Gough, Kathleen (1968) "Anthropology: child of imperialism" *Monthly Review,* 12, 27.

Grebenik, E. (1977) 'Demography' in Michell, G.D. (Ed.) (1977), *A dictionary of Sociology,* Routledge and Kegan Paul, London, 52, 53.

Gutkin, P.C.W. (I 974) "The social organization of the unemployed in Lagos and Nairobi" in Gutkin, P.C.W. (Ed.) (1974) *African Social Studies,* Briddles Ltd., Guildford, Surrey, 251, 262.

Hasenfeld, Y., *et al.* (Ed.) (1974) *Human social organization,* University of Michigan Press, Ann Arbor, 2.

Headrick, W.C. (1972) "Social inequality" in Fair-child, H.P. (Ed.) (1977), Dictionary of Sociology and related sciences, Littlefield, Adams and Co., New Jersey, 284.

Herber, B.P. (1975) *Modern public finance: The study of public sector economics,* Richard D. Irwin, Inc. Homewood, Illinois, 11.

Herzberg, Frederick (1965) *The motivation to work,* John Wiley & Sons, Inc., Hoboken, New Jersey.

Hooks, Bell (1995) *Killing Rage: Ending racism,* South End Press, New York.

Huxley, Aldous (1937) *Ends and means: An inquiry into the nature of ideals,* Harper and Brothers, New York.

Ibrahim, J. (1980) "Towards the Political economy of mass communications in Nigeria." Paper presented at the Annual Conference of the Nigerian Political Science Association, Port Harcourt, 22.

Igbozurike, Martin (1983) *The social and cultural factors involved in the Nigerian production and marketing of food crops: The case of the small farmer of Hanwa village,* Zaria, Unesco Report, Paris, March, 1983, 80, 127.

## REFERENCES

I.L.O. (1977) *Meeting basic needs: Strategies for eradicating mass poverty and unemployment*, Geneva.

Imam, Ayesha (1982) "Towards an adequate analysis of the position of women in society." Paper presented at Women in Nigeria seminar, Ahmadu Bello University, Zaria, 27th-28th May, 1982, 6.

_____ (1986) "Ideology, hegemony, mass media and women." Paper presented at the departmental seminar of the Department of Sociology, Ahmadu Bello University, Zaria, January 29th, 1986, 50.

Ishola, S.A. (1985) "Cash management in a period of economic crisis" in the *New Dimension*, Zaria, August, 1985, 6.

Jenkins, M., Awosan, J., Barnes, D. (1995) *G.U.T.S., Drugs, Alcohol, and Crime: Evaluation of Governor's Urban Teens Service Corp*, Massachusetts Governor's Alliance Against Drugs, Boston.

Kano, M. Zakari (1982) "Culture and the views on corruption in Nigeria: A theoretical perspective." Paper presented at the Nigerian Anthropological and Sociological Association conference held at Ahmadu Bello University, Zaria, May 1982, 13.

Kazah, T.D. (1981) "Social welfare services in Nigeria with special reference to Kaduna State." Lecture delivered on 25th February, 1981, at the Department of Sociology, Ahmadu Bello University, Zaria, 2.

Keil, F.C. (1967) *Psychologism*, Plenum Publishing Corporation, New York.

King, Jr., Martin Luther (1963) "I have a dream." Speech delivered on the steps of Lincoln Memorial in Washington, D.C. on August 28, 1963.

Kisekka, M.N. (1981) "Social-cultural eradication and the child," in Kisekka, M.N. (Ed.) (1981), *Children in Kaduna State, Nigeria: Problems and needs*, Kaduna Childwelfare Committee and Department of sociology, ABU, Zaria, 171.

Korsching, Peter F., and Wilson, Jannette J. (1996) "An application of the sociological imagination" in *Social Insight*.

Kuhn, Thomas S. (1962), *The structure of scientific revolutions*, The University of Chicago Press, Chicago.

Lang, Oscar (1963) *Political Economy*, Pergamon Press, Oxford.

Lateef, Y.A. (1983.) "Instrumental music as non-verbal language." Paper presented at the staff seminar of the Centre for Nigerian Cultural Studies, Ahmadu Bello University, Zaria, 6.

Lenin, Vladimir Ilyich (1964) *Collected works*, Vol. 25, Progress Publishers, Moscow.

Levitt, Theodore M. (1986) *The marketing imagination*, The Free Press, New York.

Lewis, S. (1983) Sociology of health and illness, Routledge, New York.

Little, Kenneth (1965) *West African Urbanisation: A study of voluntary associations in social change*, Cambridge University Press.

Machel, Samora (1977) "Knowledge and science should be for the total liberation of man in our Ahmadu Bello University." Speech delivered at the convocation ceremony of Ahmadu Bello University, Zaria, on 10th December, 1977, having been conferred an honorary degree of Doctor of Laws of the university.

Magubane B. (1976) "The evaluation of class structure in Africa" in Wallerstain, I. (1976) (Ed.), *The political economy of contemporary Africa*, Beverly Hills.

Makinwa, P.K. (1981) *Internal migration and rural development in Nigeria: Lessons from Bendel State*, Heinemann Educational Books (Nigeria) Ltd., lbadan, 173.

Mani, Abdulmalik (1970) *Zuwan Turawa Nijeriya ta Arewa*, Gaskiya Corporation, Zaria.

Mann, L. (1969) *Social Psychology*, John Wiley and Sons Australia PTY Ltd., Sydney, VII.

Marriam, Alan P. (1968) Ethnomusicology" in Sills, D.L. (1972) (Ed.), *International Encyclopedia of the Social Sciences*, The Macmillan Co., and The Free Press, New York, 562, 565.

Maslow, A.H. (1954) *Motivation and personality*, Harper and Row, New York.

McDougatt, W. (1908) *Introduction to Social Psychology*, Methuen and Co., London.

McVeagh, John and Young, Peter (1969) *Ibadan Studies in English*, Vol. 1, Number 2, December 1969.

Mead, George Herbert (1934) *Mind, self, and society from the standpoint of a social*
*Behaviorists,* Charles Morris (Ed.), University of Chicago Press.

Mensah, Ebow (1986) "Religion and national integration in Nigeria," Department of Sociology, ABU, Zaria (mimeographed), 37, 43.

Mills, C. Wright (1959) *The Sociological imagination*, Oxford University Press.

Mirchaulum, P.T. (1976) "The diffusion of the ox-plough innovation in Longuda District of Gongola State, Nigeria," Department of Geography, Ahmadu Bello University, Zaria, *Occasional paper,* No. 6.

Murdock, G.P. (1977) "Religion" in Fairchild, H.P. (1977) (Ed.), *Dictionary of Sociology and Related Sciences,* Littlefield, Adams and Co., New Jersey, 256.

Naletov, Igor (1984) *Alternative to positivism*, Progress Publishers, Moscow, 256.

National Policy on Education (1977) Federal Ministry of Education, Lagos.

Nisbet, Robert (1982) *The social philosopher: Community and conflict in Western thought,* Washington Square Press, New York, 127

Norman, D.W. (1972) "An economic survey of three villages in Zaria Province: An input-output study." *Samaru Miscellaneous Paper* 1991, Zaria.

Nzimiro, Ikenna (1985) *The green revolution in Nigeria or modernisation of hunger,* Zim Pan-African Publisher, Oguta, xviii.

Obianwu, H.O. (1984) "Traditional medicine and drug development in Nigeria," Ahmadu Bello University public lecture, 30th May, 1984, 3.

Oculi, Okelle (1982) "The political economy of the planning of the Bakolori Irrigation Project: 1974-80" in Usman, Y.B. (1982) (Ed.) *Political repression in Nigeria,* Bala Mohammed Memorial Committee, 97.

Odekunle, 'Femi (1985) "Laying the foundations for crime control in Nigeria," Ahmadu Bello University public lecture, 13th February, 1985, 22.

Ogionwo, W. (1978) *Innovative behavior and personal attitudes: A case study of social change in Nigeria. Schenkman Publishing Company, Cambridge, Mass.*

Ogunyemi, Yemi D. (2004) *Literatures of the African Diaspora*, Gival Press, Arlington, VA.

Ojanuga, D.N. (1979) "Health problems and their effects on health services," Ph.D dissertation of the University of Wisconsin.

Olatunbosun, 'Dupe (1975) *The Nigeria's neglected rural majority*, Oxford University Press, Ibadan, 1.

Olayide, S.O. (1976) "The food problem: Tractable or the mere chase of the mirage?" Inaugural lecture delivered at the University of Ibadan, University of Ibadan Press, Ibadan, 14.

Oloko O. and Oloko A. (1980) "Towards a general theory of integrated rural development and planning." Paper presented at the national conference on integrated rural development, University of Benin, 22-26 September, 1980.

Oloko, O. (1982), "Employment and national development: An analysis of Nigerian labor employment statistics (1960-80)," the *Nigerian Journal of Sociology and Anthropology,* Vol. 8, September 1982.

Omaji, P.O. (1985) "Law and social change: A survey of some major thoughts on their relationship." Paper presented at the national seminar on "Sharia and the problem of indiscipline in Nigeria" at the University of Sokoto, July 8-10, 1985, 16.

Omojuwa, R.A. (1982) "The new educational system" (editorial), the *Nigeria Educational Forum*, Vol. 5, No. 1, 1.

Onoge, Omafume (1983) *New Dimension*, February, 1983.

Onwubu, Chukwuemeka (1976) "West African education and the challenge of a lingua franca," *West African Journal of Modern Languages*, No. 1, January 1976, 43.

Orley, J. (1970) *Culture and Mental Illness*, East Africa Publishing House.

Osoba, Segun (1970) "The Nigerian 'power' elite, 1952-65: A Study on some Problems of modernization." Paper presented at the Historical Society of Nigeria 16th annual congress, December 1970, 1, 17.

Otite, Onigu (1971) "Anthropological responsibility in Nigeria" in Wilmot, P.F. (1973) (Ed.), *Sociology in Africa*, Vol. 1, Gaskiya Corporation, Zaria, and Ahmadu Bello University, Zaria.

Oyebola, Areoye (1976) *Black man's dilemma*, Academy Press, Ltd., Lagos, 122.

Oyedepo, D.O. (1986) "A peculiar people," *Faith Bulletin*, January/February 1986, Faith Liberation Hour Ministries, Kaduna, 1.

Peel, J.D.Y. (1968) *A religious movement among the Yoruba*, Oxford University Press, London.

Perchonock, Norma (1982) "Double oppression: Women and land matters in Kaduna State." Paper presented to the Women in Nigeria seminar, Ahmadu Bello University, Zaria, 27-28 May 1982, 56.

Phelps, H.A. (1977) "Social Psychology" in Fairchild, H.P. *et al.* (Ed.) (1977), A *dictionary of sociology and related sciences*, Littlefield, Adams and Co., Totowa, New Jersey, 290.

Pittin, Renee (1982) "Organizing for the future." Paper presented to the Women in Nigeria seminar, Ahmadu Bello University, Zaria, 27-28 May, 1982, 1.

Reading, L. (1977) 'Ethno' in Michell, G.D. (Ed.) (1977), *A dictionary of sociology*, Routledge and Kegan Paul, London, 79.

Rodney, Walter (1972) *How Europe underdeveloped Africa*, Bogle-L'Ouverture Publications, London, 10, 21, 22.

Santos, Dos (1970) Quoted in Chilcote, T.H. and Edelstein, J.C. (Ed.) (1974), *Latin America: The struggle with dependency and beyond*, Schenkman Publishing Company, Cambridge.

Sargent, C. (1982) "The implications of role expectations (or birth assistance) among Bariba women" in *Social Science and Medicine*, Vol. 16, 483.

Second National Development plan (1970-75), Federal Ministry of Information, Lagos.

Sherif, M. (1963) Social Psychology: "Interdisciplinary problems and trends." in S. Koch (Ed.), *Psychology: A study of a science*, Vol. 6, McGraw-Hill Book Company, New York. Quoted in Mann, L. (1969) *Social Psychology*, John Wiley and Sons, Australia PTY Limited, Sydney.

Smith, Adam (1776) *The wealth of nations*, Vol. One, Everyman's Library, Dutton, New York.

Sofowora, A. (1982) *Medical plants and traditional medicine in Africa*, John Wiley, Chichester, cited in Obianwu (1984), "Traditional medicine and drug development in Nigeria." Ahmadu Bello University public lecture, 30th May, 1984.

Solarin, Tai (1974) "The beginning of the end." Unpublished but signed and widely circulated paper, Mayflower School, Ikenne, October 4th, 1974.

Surakat, Y.T. (1986) "Translating aspect of Yoruba orature into English: Problems and prospects." Paper presented at English Department Seminar, Ahmadu Bello University, Zaria, May 1986, 7.

Tahir, I.A. (1975) "Scholars, sufts, saints and capitalist in Kano, 1974: The pattern of bourgeois revolution in an Islamic society." Unpublished Ph.D. thesis of the University of Cambridge.

Tawiah, B.O. (1984) "Determinants of cumulative fertility in Ghana," *Demography*, Vol. 21, Number 1, February, 1984, 2.

Teriba, Owodunni (1978) "Illusions and social behavior." Inaugural lecture delivered at the University of Ibadan, University of Ibadan Press, Ibadan, 27.

Therborn, Goran (1985) "The rise of social scientific Marxism and the problems of the class analysis" in Eisenstadt, S.N. *et al.*, (Eds.) 1985, *Macro Sociological theory: Perspectives on sociological theory* Vol. 1, SAGE Studies in International Sociology 33, International Sociological Association/ISA, London, 140.

Tomanyshyn, M. John (1971) *Social welfare: Charity to justice*, Random House, New York, 55, 56.

Transler, G.B. (1977) "Criminology" in Michell, G.D. (1977) (Ed.), *A dictionary of Sociology*, Routledge and Kegan Paul, London, 45.

Tugbiyele, E.A. (1965) The place of chiefs in local and national government, Ibadan, 23rd January, 1965, University of Ibadan (mimeographed).

Ukpabi, S.O. (1974) "Northern Nigeria, Lugard and the Satiru war" (Unpublished photocopy seen in the Sokoto History Bureau Library, Sokoto).

United Nations (1958) *Multilingual Demographic Dictionary*. Quoted by Brebenik, E. in Michell, G.D. (Ed.) (1977), *A dictionary of Sociology*, Routledge and Kegan Paul, London.

Usman, Y.B. (Ed.) (1982) *Political repression in Nigeria*, Bala Mohammed Memorial Committee, xv.

Utomi, Pat (1978) "Implications of political gift," *Newbreed*, Mid-March, 1978, 4.

Webster, J.B. (1964) *The African Churches among the Yoruba, 1888-1922*, Oxford University Press, London.

Wallerstein, Immanuel (1974), *The modern world-system*, Academic Press, New York.

Wamba-dia-wamba, K. (1982) "Economic Dependency and Imperialism," *Ikwezi, A Black Liberation Journal of South African and Southern African Political Analysis*, No. 20, July, 1982, 29, 32.

Weber, Max (1918) *Essays in sociology*, Oxford University Press, London.

WHO (1985) "International Nonproprietary Names for Pharmaceutical Substances" *Supplement to WHO Chronicle*, 1985, Vol. 39, No. 41.

Wilmot, Patrick F. (1980) *Aparthied and African liberation: The grief and the hope*, University of Ife Press Ltd., Ile-Ife, 2, 34.

———— (1983) "The West and Nigeria's economy." Paper presented at the Nigerian Union of Journalists Press Week, Jos, 26th April, 1983.

————(1985) "Beyond the sociological imagination: A brief note to C. Wright Mills." Paper presented at the Faculty Seminar Series, Faculty of Arts and Social Sciences, Ahmadu Bello University, Zaria, Saturday, 4th May, 1985.

Yahaya, A.D. (1975) "The Native Authority System in Northern Nigeria, 1950-70: A study in political relations with particular reference to the Zaria Native Authority," Unpublished Ph.D. thesis of Ahmadu Bello University, Zaria.

Zasha, James (1985) "The state and trade unions," *The Nigerian Journal of political Science*, Vol. 4, Numbers I and II, 120.

# NAME INDEX

# SUBJECT INDEX

abortion, 114, 119, 212
academic citadel, XII, 197-199, 219
academic outpost, 18
academy, 199
adult education, 132, 135
African heritage, 31, 129
African Native Baptist Church, 171
African politics, militarization of, 90, 103
African sociological knowledge, 193
African sociology, XI, 19, 32-33, 208
agribusiness, 99
Ahmadu Bello University, XI, XV, 17, 25,
    71, 79, 108, 117, 128-129, 131, 172-173,
    183, 211, 215-216, 223-229
Aladura church, 170, 212
Alafin, 30, 170, 220
alien cultural domination, 124
American comedy program, 160
American Sociological Association, 65
anthropology, XIII, 19, 57, 62, 102, 225
anthropometric measurements, 76
applied sociology, 19
Arafat, 175
archival source, 30-31, 206
Argungu fishing festival, 61, 121
aristocracy, 88-89, 97
Ashby Commission, 128
Asquith Commission, 127, 135
Attakar, 27, 138-139
Australasia, 201, 219
ayurvedic, 69
Babalawo, 173
Bakolori, 51, 109, 227
balance of payments, 144
balanced curriculum, 32, 209
Basic Needs Approach to Development,
    143
Bori, 169, 219
bourgeois ideology, 89
bourgeoisie, 23, 29, 56, 62, 98-101, 160-
    162, 195-196, 209
bridewealth, 157
Britain, 42, 122, 134, 182, 191, 193
Cameroon, 199
Cameroon Interuniversity Network, 199

Cape Verde, 131, 201
catheter, 79-80, 192
causally-related variables, 116
Chamba, 157-158, 164
Cherubim and Seraphim Church, 170-
    173, 180, 221
child mortality, 25, 72-73, 80-81, 217
child of imperialism, 57, 62, 225
children, 22, 25, 29-30, 39-41, 46-48, 67,
    72-77, 105, 108, 114, 117, 121, 133, 156,
    160-165, 170, 174, 180, 184-185, 192-
    193, 213, 216-217, 224
China, 67, 81, 102, 130, 138, 199
China Education and Research Network,
    199
civil offense, 203
class, 23-31, 40, 46, 49, 52, 68, 85, 88, 92,
    96-97, 101-102, 105-109, 119, 127, 133-
    134, 149, 159-165, 176-183, 190, 192,
    195-196, 201, 209-211, 219-220, 226,
    229
class consciousness, 27, 31, 109, 119
class struggle, 162, 177, 192
class suicide, 195-196, 209
cocoa, 23, 47-52
Cold War, 195
colonial administrative officers, 57
colonial authority, 24, 59
colonial rule, 57, 88, 158
colonialism, 32, 57, 88-89, 160
Committee of Vice-Chancellors of
    Nigerian Universities, 118, 129-131
community partnership, 197
compensation, 49-51, 93
compradors, 49, 52
concurrent list, 130
congenital malfunction, 79
content analysis, 29, 184, 187, 193, 203,
    217
contract illusion, 129
cooperative thrift, 62
Copernican astronomy, 208
corruption, 22, 37, 106, 226
cotton culture, 98, 104
craft, 27, 138-144, 151

# ABOUT THE AUTHOR

Professor Joshua Adekunle Awosan has had a checkered career in and outside the academic environment. He was Personal Assistant to the Vice-Chancellor (President) of Ahmadu Bello University, Zaria, Nigeria, where he subsequently taught for ten years, and has taught at a number of universities in the United States of America. A distinguished, prolific author, he has authored or co-authored scholarly works, including *The Concerned Black Men of Massachusetts, Incorporated Paul Robeson Institute for Positive Self-*
*Development: A Dream Come True and an Inspiring Model* (1992), *G.U.T.S., Drugs, Alcohol, and Crime: Evaluation of Massachusetts Governor's Alliance Against Drugs* (1995), and *Understanding Sociology* (2008, Horizon Textbook Publishing). He has undertaken research studies under the auspices of the World Health Organization and the Ford Foundation. Professor Awosan has been teaching at the University of Massachusetts Dartmouth for quite a number of years.

# PRAISES FOR

# *CURRENTS OF THOUGHT IN AFRICAN SOCIOLOGY AND THE GLOBAL COMMUNITY*

"This book focuses on the transition of sociology. An attempt is made by Professor Joshua Awosan to link this change with the development of an indigenous African sociology. This book is, indeed, an important resource for further sociological scholarship, fostering the formation of an indigenous sociology in Africa within a global context."

—Robert J. Durel, Professor Emeritus
Department of Sociology, Anthropology, and Social Work
Christopher Newport University, Newport News, Virginia

"Joshua Adekunle Awosan's thoughtful and comprehensive book provides needed information about African sociology. The comprehensiveness of its survey and the variety of studies on some of the general directions the development of an African sociology has taken in the past thirty years are admirable. The relevance of the book to policy is evident in Professor Awosan's conclusions. Among the most important is the suggestion that has to do with the need, defined in contrast with the typical use of positivist methods of gathering and analyzing information, for a flexible and context-sensitive approach to the technical features of research. This would involve, according to Professor Awosan, a methodology that systematically takes account of and is organized by 'African realities,' including patterns of domestic life, consumption, economy, and community."

—Michael E. Brown, Professor
Department of Sociology and Anthropology
Northeastern University, Boston

CPSIA information can be obtained
at www.ICGtesting.com
Printed in the USA
LVHW011206260921
698748LV00010B/999